CHAPPELLI
SPEAKS OUT

CHAPPELLI
SPEAKS OUT

ASHLEY MALLETT WITH **IAN CHAPPELL**

ALLEN&UNWIN

First published in Australia in 2005

Allen & Unwin
83 Alexander Street
Crows Nest NSW 2065
Australia
Phone: (61 2) 8425 0100
Fax: (61 2) 9906 2218
Email: info@allenandunwin.com
Web: www.allenandunwin.com

National Library of Australia
Cataloguing-in-Publication entry:

Mallett, Ashley, 1945-
Chappelli speaks out: Ashley Mallett with Ian Chappell.

Bibliography.
ISBN 1 74114 456 6.

1. Chappell, Ian 1943- . 2. Cricket players - Australia -
Biography. 3. Cricket captains - Australia - Biography. 4.
Cricket - Australia - History - 20th century. I. Title.

796.358092

Typeset in 11.5/16 pt Joanna by Midland Typesetters, Maryborough
Printed by Griffin Press, Adelaide

Contents

Preface

Talking to Ian Chappell about cricket is easy for here he is in his element. He loves the game with a burning passion and when he talks cricket he wears his heart on his sleeve. Chappelli is honest and tells it as it is: he doesn't mince words or frame his answers in a considered manner.

I set out to write a traditional biography. After biographies of two legends of the game, Victor Trumper and Clarrie Grimmett, I thought this book would be a breeze. But with Ian it was different. A journalist friend of mine, Trevor Gill, suggested I needed to 'get inside Ian's head' to make this book work. To achieve that metaphorical possibility meant Ian talking and talking big time. He did not shirk any issues, even the 'can't bowl, can't field' jibe which Queensland and Australian fast bowler Scott Muller attributed to Shane Warne. I would regularly fly to Sydney where I would sit with him and talk cricket. I have some twelve hours of Chappelli on tape and when he read a transcript of one particular story, he said, 'Hey, hang on Rowd, I don't think I swear that much.' I was astounded. The bloke surely has mellowed.

Chappelli has always sworn a lot. His swearing has caused him and his wife, Barbara-Ann, some angst on at least two separate occasions, threatening his television career as a cricket commentator and probably strengthening the public perception that Chappelli was a bit of a sledger. The public seems to hold the view that Ian Chappell was the Test captain who led the cricket world into the sledging era. Chappelli did not start sledging in cricket, in fact, he only ever swore in retaliation. If someone had a go at him, he gave his opponent both barrels, but he never instigated a war of words.

There were two reasons I believed I was the person best placed to write a biography on Ian Chappell. Firstly, I had played with and against him in club cricket and alongside him in state and Test cricket, and we had toured England, India, South Africa and New Zealand together. We had experienced the highs and lows of senior level cricket and often enjoyed a beer and talk about the game and the players. Secondly, there was a mutual respect of our skills as cricketers and a shared passion for the game.

Ian spoke so candidly about cricket, people and events. His drive to acknowledge the 1868 Aboriginal cricket team, the first major Australian sporting team to tour abroad, will amaze some, but never those who are close to him. Ian also hits out at the Howard Government over the Tampa affair and the treatment of asylum seekers. And, he does not hold back his strong opinions on Sir Donald Bradman, Steve Waugh, Ian Botham and Tony Greig.

Chappelli provides a fascinating insight into the business nous and surprising fairness of Kerry Packer, perhaps a man, like Chappelli, who has never been particularly well understood by the Australian public. He speaks fondly of cricketers of years past such as Neil Harvey and Keith Miller. He praises some from his own era, players such as Dennis Lillee, Graeme Pollock, the great Garry Sobers. And, unlike many old cricketers, Chappelli speaks admiringly of the moderns, men such as Shane Warne, Glenn McGrath, Sachin Tendulkar, Brian Lara and Adam Gilchrist.

The widespread belief that Chappelli was a sledger annoyed me nearly as much as the general conviction that he led a bunch of blokes akin to the Dirty Dozen; a gang of flannelled hoodlums who ran roughshod over the game in the 1970s, and were disrespectful of both opponents and authority. Certainly Chappelli and his team were peeved over the Australian Cricket Board's treatment of the players. What Chappelli and others did in 1977 was to pave the way for professional cricket and Packer's television cricket revolution. From that evolved better pay and better playing conditions for players today. It is thanks to Chappell that Ricky Ponting's Australian team does not have to play State cricket for $30 a match or a Test game for $200 or that players have to somehow eke out a living outside cricket to survive. Warne may have stuck to a baked beans diet had he played thirty years ago.

As upset by the Board as players had become during Chappelli's reign, Australia always played hard, but fair. Ian Chappell led a very good side, one that ex-greats Neil Harvey and Alan Davidson consider to be superior to the Australian team of today led by Ricky Ponting. Chappelli is one of the great Australian Test captains. Former England captain Ray Illingworth reckons 'Ian Chappell is as good a captain as Richie Benaud. I cannot give higher praise than that.'

The Ian Chappell story is a hard-hitting account, but it also dispels a few myths. My motive was in many respects to put the record straight. If I got inside Chappelli's head I have achieved what I set out to do.

I knew him pretty well way back then.

Now, I know him even better.

Ashley Mallett

One

A piece
of paper

At the time I wasn't too fussed about the idea, but a couple of days
later I thought, 'Why not?' So I took a piece of paper and wrote,
'My ambition is to captain Australia'.

Ian Chappell, the man they call Chappelli, became the Australian
Test cricket captain on Thursday, 4 February 1971. As was his
habit at lunchtime, away from duties as a sales representative
with WD & HO Wills, Ian had ducked into Adelaide's Overway
Hotel for a schnitzel and beer when the barman called him to
the phone.

'Congratulations Chappelli, well done,' The News reporter Allan
Shiell called down the line. 'You are now the Australian Test
captain.'

Ian reached for his wallet and took out a crumpled piece of
paper. He looked at the words: 'My ambition is to captain
Australia'.

It was in 1959 that Ian Chappell, aged 16, was picked to play in the South Australian State Schoolboys' Team of the Year after he showed good form in a match between metropolitan juniors and country schoolboys. The reward for his selection was two days' coaching at the Adelaide Oval from then state coach Geff Noblet. 'We had the coaching,' Chappell says, 'but I remember being very disappointed that we didn't get the chance to bat against some of the state squad bowlers. That would have given us all a good indication of how much we needed to improve, how much work we needed to do to get to district level.'

During a break in training, Noblet took all the boys out onto the main ground, Adelaide Number Two Ground, to have a look at the wicket. There he stood, with the others, on the lush green of magnificent Adelaide Oval within divine reach of St Peter's Cathedral, which stands majestically beyond the Moreton Bay fig trees to the north-east of the ground. This place was an inspiration, a young cricketer's dream.

Noblet then led us up the stairs to the inner sanctum of the South Australian dressing-room. We had another good look around, then he said, 'Now boys, as you are walking down these stairs, make a little mental note to yourself that you want to be back here walking out to play for South Australia one day.'

When we got to the bottom of the steps, he spoke again: 'In fact, the best thing for you all to do is to write down your cricket ambitions on a piece of paper, then stick the piece of paper in your wallet and carry it with you always as a constant reminder of what you wish to achieve in this game.'

At the time I wasn't too fussed about the idea, but a couple of days later, I thought, 'Why not?' So I took a piece of paper and wrote, 'My ambition is to captain Australia'.

Frankly, to this day I don't know why I wrote down those words, because I don't think I really had any great ambition to be captain of Australia. I think what happened was that I thought: 'What was the highest thing you could achieve in Australian cricket?' The answer was, logically, to captain Australia. So that's what I wrote on my piece of paper. I still had that little piece of paper in my wallet the very day I learnt that I was picked to be Test captain in 1971. It had done its job, so after some time I tossed it away.

Ian Chappell went on to play 75 Tests for Australia. He scored 5345 runs at an average of 42.42, with 14 centuries and 26 50s. He led Australia 30 times—winning 15, losing five and drawing ten—and is regarded alongside Mark Taylor and Richie Benaud as one of Australia's most outstanding captains. As a batsman, he hit out with belligerent joy, taking the attack to all opposition bowlers. And he hits out still, as a commentator on the game of cricket and, more recently, as a crusader for worthy causes such as heading the drive to have Cricket Australia officially recognise the Australian Aboriginal cricket team which toured England in 1868, and lobbying for fair treatment of asylum seekers. Ian Chappell is totally honest—in fact brutally so, for he doesn't hold back. Like his father, Martin Chappell, he pulls no punches and will not curry favour with anyone.

Chappell's mother, Jeanne, says, 'Mart would say absolutely what he was thinking and sometimes it was pretty rude. Sometimes people didn't take it the right way, which made it rather embarrassing. It wasn't my style. I wouldn't say things to hurt people, but he didn't care whether he did or he didn't.'

Ian Chappell is not an easy man to describe, for he is a lot of things to a lot of people. He could be rude when refusing to sign his autograph in a crowded bar, but as a batsman and a captain he was smart. He learnt from his mistakes and he had the knack of empowering his players. He never bawled anyone out on the field.

When relaxed Chappell is articulate, with interesting and provocative ideas about the game and the direction in which it is heading. Unlike many former cricketers, he doesn't think that all the players from his era were better than the players of today. He lauds the likes of oldies such as Garry Sobers, Keith Miller, Richie Benaud and Graeme Pollock, the spin of Indian maestro Erapally Prasanna and the pace of Dennis Lillee, Andy Roberts and John Snow, but equally he marvels at the skill of the moderns, among them Ricky Ponting, Adam Gilchrist, Shane Warne, Glenn McGrath, Sachin Tendulkar and Brian Lara. Alan Knott is his choice as the best wicket-keeper he has seen, just ahead of Rodney Marsh.

Loving nothing better than a debate on sport, Chappell is in his element with someone similarly passionate. But what Chappell calls a debate, others might call a heated argument; his discussions with Allan Border are legendary on the cricket circuit, invariably ending in a blazing row, yet there has never been any animosity between the pair. Whether playing cricket, tennis or backgammon, it is 'game on' with Ian Chappell. The fighting spirit fairly exudes from his being; a smack-in-the-face combativeness that can be compelling to watch, but intimidating to face.

He is perceived by many as being the tough, uncompromising cricketer who led the 'ugly Australians' in the 1970s and thumbed his nose at authority. In reality, Ian Chappell led a highly committed bunch of cricketers, possessing a collective desire to become the best cricket team in the world. His men were not 'ugly' in the sense that they verbally abused opponents on the field. The talk was mostly gamesmanship. It could be brutal, but it was usually clever and funny. In England in 1972, after repeatedly playing and missing, the captain of Combined Universities found he had a bootlace undone and gestured at Chappell with a request to tie it. The Australian captain's response was: 'You're not doing anything else out here pal; do it up yourself!'

In his book *Innings of My Life*, English cricket writer Jack Bannister wrote, 'If I wanted someone to bat for my life, it's Ian over Greg.

Just. That is if I am convinced he thinks my life is worth saving'.

Former Test team-mate on the 1972 tour John Inverarity said:

> Ian Chappell was the embodiment of the warrior. He is a man with a strong and compelling personality, a man who is drawn to contests—pitting his will, his physical prowess and his psychological assertiveness against opponents—like a moth to a flame. As a player and a captain he used his very considerable cricket skills and his team-mates to seek and engage in battle. He loved it all and inspired others to 'go there' with him. There are many reasonably good captains, and a very few outstanding ones. Ian Chappell was most certainly an outstanding captain.
>
> Ian was always Ian: forthright, fearless and with no time for deference. It was a happy coincidence for Ian and for Australian cricket that he won the captaincy of South Australia and then Australia in 1970/71 at a time of significantly changing social attitudes; the 1960s and all that came with it. There was a harmony from which a powerful force arose. He was the central figure in the development of one of Australia's finest and most talented teams: the team of the 1970s.

Ian Chappell was destined for greatness in sport. Weaned on a potent mix of cricket and baseball, sport was in the blood.

The eldest of three boys born to Jeanne and Martin Chappell, Ian took his first stance in this world on 26 September 1943, 12 months to the day after his parents married. Throughout his childhood, Ian's father taught him lessons that would not only help him cope in sport, but in life generally. When Ian was about nine or ten he used to score for the Glenelg third-grade team. Martin was captain and young Ian was ever the optimist—not many scorers wear whites to matches, but Ian was hoping that he might get a game if someone failed to turn up. He was fitted out in his cricket gear, just in case.

Well, one day one of the players didn't turn up and I ended up getting a game to make up the numbers. I was in seventh heaven. I batted about number nine. The fast bowler for the other team was a fiery redhead called 'Blue' Ballantyne. When I was thirteen Blue seemed like an enormously big bloke and I thought he was frighteningly quick. However, I was able to stay in for about 45 minutes. I didn't make many runs, but I was delighted that I had been able to stay in so long.

In the car on the way home I kept expecting Dad to say something like, 'Well done,' or to give me a pat on the back. But there was nothing. We sat down to dinner later. Still no word from Dad. I was mulling this over when Dad finished his dinner, pushed his plate away and spoke for the first time. 'That's it son, you're not playing C grade any more.'

I was stunned and just managed to mutter, 'Why? I batted for 45 minutes and I reckon I did all right.'

He said, 'No, you are not playing because you are scared. Until you learn not to be scared you're not playing with the men any more.' I questioned him, asking what he meant about being 'scared'.

He replied sharply, 'Well, you backed away from one delivery from Blue Ballantyne and until you get behind everything you are not playing in C grade again.'

It would be a pretty fair guess that Ian Chappell never again backed away from any fast bowler in his whole career. To the contrary, he loved the thrill of the battle against the quick bowlers and he was always looking to cut or pull or hook the short stuff. The quicker the better, it seemed. His body language was ever an open invitation to any bowler: 'Bring it on, the faster the better.'

Martin came up with a novel way to help his sons catch a ball. Years later he explained: 'I worked out that if you stand in front of your son trying to get him to catch a ball his eyes follow yours and therefore he doesn't watch the ball at all. So I decided to experiment. First try worked. I showed Ian the ball, then tossed it gently underhand against a brick wall. Ian's eyes followed the ball and he easily caught it. I taught Greg the same way. Both of the boys could catch a cricket ball long before they had reached the age of three.'

Martin never used a soft ball. It was always the hard cricket ball, and Ian revelled in the play.

Cricket was in the blood. Jeanne was the daughter of Vic Richardson, a great all-round sportsman and captain of both the South Australian and Test cricket teams. Martin played district cricket as an opening batsman and off-spin bowler for some 22 years. He was in the South Australian state squad one season and had a reputation for being a tough character on the sports field. Martin represented South Australia as a baseball catcher as well. There was never a hint of having been pushed into cricket. I just loved it.

Martin sensed the need to have Ian coached, but he was wise enough to seek someone else to do the job. In Lynn Fuller, a former AIF player and a good country cricketer, he reckoned he found the perfect coach for his lad.

Lynn had a good reputation as a coach. He was a retired farmer and came to live in the city, and through his two sons he became involved with the Glenelg Cricket Club as curator and coach. It all started one day at Unley Oval when Dad and one of Lynn's sons were playing B grade for Glenelg. I was sitting in the stand with Mum and Dad, and Lynn was there too.

Dad introduced me to Lynn and said to him, 'I'd like to have Ian coached . . . When do you think would be the right age for him to start?'

Lynn asked how old I was and Mum told him I was five. Lynn said, 'You might as well start him now.'

So every Sunday of every summer from the time I was five until I had reached the age of 17 I went around to his home for coaching.

Lynn Fuller worked hard with Ian on correct technique—elbow up, front and backward defence—but, whenever Martin was throwing a few balls to him in the backyard, Ian would play correctly for a while then lose patience and hit the ball over the fence.

Dad used to get annoyed with me when I whacked one over the fence and, after the blast from Dad, I'd play correctly for a while then I'd let fly again. Because Lynn told me not to hit the ball in the air, I never did while I was with him. If I did accidentally, he would say in his calm manner that it was the wrong way to go and eventually I just didn't want to hit the ball in the air when I was with Lynn at his coaching sessions. He was very patient with me and spent hours working on perfecting my forward and back defence. He would say, 'Son, you can't make runs sitting in the pavilion . . . You've got to be able to keep the good ones out.' He also explained that if I could get the forward and back defence right, all the other strokes would develop from those two basic shots.

Lynn would bowl to me for long periods. Despite his age he was an accurate medium-pacer and would send them down to me for an hour or so, sometimes for even longer spells.

Ian's brothers Greg and Trevor were also coached by Lynn Fuller. Greg remembers Lynn as a real student of the game, particularly on batting technique: 'There we would be at Lynn's place with three or four other kids and Lynn would be working on our batting technique, especially in the area of defence. Afterwards Dad would throw the ball to us for half an hour or so to give us practice at hitting the bad ball.'

Martin's baseball years had given him a strong throwing arm—a necessity for all those hours chucking the ball at the boys in the backyard net. When the boys were still very young, around 1960, Greg reckoned it was time to upgrade the net. The worn patches in the lawn were covered with a bag of black soil the lads had secured from the club ground down the road. However, a few scattered bits of soil was hardly satisfactory for a decent net so, with help from Lynn Fuller, they brought in a few trailer loads of rich, black soil—enough to make a proper wicket about half the normal length and twice the normal width of a pitch. The extra width gave the boys lots of room in which to move the stumps, limiting the wear in one particular spot. The boys all chipped in and helped, taking turns to prepare the track with the aid of an old tennis court roller, also from Lynn Fuller.

Those backyard 'Tests' were fiercely competitive and, at times, tempers became frayed. Jeanne Chappell was forever coming out to intervene. According to Ian, 'Most of the time, it seemed to me, Mum would settle any argument in Greg's favour, probably because he was younger. She'd say, "Let him bat and get on with it . . . and keep the noise down."' However, Greg reckons he invariably paid for his mother's intervention in his favour: 'We never used pads or gloves in those days and whenever Mum gave me the benefit of the doubt and I batted on, I'd pay with whacks to the legs and the hands. I remember that when the track got too slow we wet the wicket a bit to liven it up. One particular day Ian gave it a bit too much water and the ball leapt all over the place. Inevitably he hit me on the fingers and I went down in a heap. Ian stood over me: "Don't worry about the fingers, mate," he said. "Next time it'll be your head." '

By the time Trevor was old enough to face his brothers in the backyard he found the same competitive edge. Greg had learned the hard way playing against Ian, and he, in turn, gave Trevor the 'treatment'. Knocks to the fingers and too much water on a good length contributed to Trevor also developing a thick hide. There was a time when Trevor became so incensed with Greg's antics that he chased him around the backyard brandishing a tomahawk. Luckily for Greg, Trevor and Australian cricket, Greg proved too elusive to get the chop. Trevor says of his brothers Ian and Greg: 'Ian always stood up for me against Greg, or so Ian tells me anyway. Because of the nine-year age difference between Ian and I, we didn't battle each other directly that often in the backyard. I can remember facing some short-pitched bowling off the Leak Avenue ridge from Ian and losing a few fingernails in the process. I wasn't wearing any batting gloves and after the first whack I said to Ian that I wanted to put on some gloves. Ian said that wouldn't be necessary as it was an accident and that he wouldn't bowl short again. Stupidly, I believed him.'

The backyard net was used for most of the year—an estimated 300 days. When it rained and the wicket was too wet to bat on, the boys would get out the baseball gloves and have a throw. If it was too wet to venture outdoors Martin might take the opportunity to give the boys a blackboard lesson on rules and strategy, the importance of concentration, or tactics in batting, bowling and fielding.

Over the years the pitch at Lynn Fuller's place became a good deal higher than the surrounding grass, through constant top dressing.

Where the roller rode up from the lower level onto the pitch, part of the wicket was nicely rounded and made it a perfect spot to bang them down and get them up. One day Dad said to me, 'Right, now, you've got to learn to defend yourself.' He proceeded to ping the ball at me off the rise. That's how I learnt to hook. I don't remember being taught to duck or get out of the way. It was just a matter of hooking the ball or pulling it.

As Ian Brayshaw writes in *The Chappell Era*, those early years for Ian, Greg and Trevor were invaluable.

> If you sat down to write a script for the creation of boys who would in time go on to become champion cricketers, you surely couldn't do a better job than describing the development of the Chappell boys. They were born with the right pedigree, were fed and trained right, given all the encouragement and opportunity they could have wished for . . . and they ended up winning the blue ribbons!

Ian was chosen for the South Australian State Schoolboys (under 14) team during his last year at St Leonard's Primary School. The team travelled to Perth and there he played against Graham McKenzie, even then a huge, muscular lad. Chappell recalls, 'I think Graham McKenzie got me lbw in one of the matches we played against one another. The ball hit me just below the kneecap and as well as being out they had to cart me off the field because I couldn't walk.'

When Ian played his first Test match, McKenzie was already the mainstay of the Australian attack—a lion-hearted fast bowler who ultimately ended his career with 246 wickets. The following year young Ian went on to Prince Alfred College. As a result he played only one year for the South Australian State Schoolboys' team, as that honour could only go to students attending state-run schools.

Ian Chappell is understandably grateful for what his parents did for him, and for Greg and Trevor. They were devoted parents in every sense and travelled thousands of miles back and forth through the suburbs of Adelaide to watch their boys play cricket. And later they travelled interstate and overseas to watch their sons as Test cricketers. 'Mum and Dad gave up a lot to give us a chance to play international cricket,' Chappell says. 'After I retired I recall saying to Mum, "I know you gave up a lot for us and I hope you feel it was worthwhile." She said, "We would not have changed a thing."'

Recently, Ian read an article by Sydney-based cricket writer Phil Derriman, who claimed that Steve and Mark Waugh had the best cricket education of all time.

I felt like ringing Greg and saying 'Phil Derriman doesn't know much.' The Waugh twins had parents who were tennis players. We had a parent who was a very good club cricketer, good enough to be picked in the state squad one season. We had a mother whose father captained the Australian Test team. We had Lynn Fuller, a good country cricketer, who coached us. I had a coach at St Leonard's Primary School who was smart enough to know I already had a coach and didn't try to influence my batting technique.

Then when I went to Prince Alfred College [PAC] in Adelaide there was a magnificent cricket environment. The headmaster, John Dunning, was a former New Zealand cricket captain. Former South Australian player Bill Leak coached PAC Firsts for a year, then I was fortunate enough to come under the influence of a new coach, Chester Bennett, who played for Western Australia. There was Ray Smith at the school, who played for Kensington in the days of Bradman and Grimmett.

I can see where Phil was coming from in that he figured that the Waughs would have always had a batsman and bowler to battle it out in the backyard because they were the same age. However, Greg and I were only five years apart and we grew up in such a brilliant cricket environment where there was constant encouragement and support. Every time there was a family function, people would be forever talking to Vic about cricket, the old days, the players of his time.

School master and PAC First XI coach Chester Bennett had a significant calming influence on Ian, as he did later on the other two Chappell boys when they attended PAC. Bennett was a man of solid character. He was a good talker and a good listener. He didn't rant or rave and he didn't attempt to instruct Ian in batting technique, for he knew he was already being tutored by Lynn Fuller, but he was able to help in other ways. In 1960, Ian's last year at PAC, he was made First XI captain. This was at a time when the PAC Firsts played in the South Australian Cricket Association (SACA) district B-grade competition. It helped to bring good young players on very quickly.

I recall, in my last year, captaining Prince Alfred College against Kensington Bs. They had a pretty strong and experienced team, and we very nearly beat them, losing by only three or four runs in the first innings. I remember being furious that we just missed out and I was still cranky and upset as I sat with the pads on as number three waiting for a turn in the second dig. There were only a couple of hours to go in the match, not sufficient time for an outright result.

When the first wicket fell, I stormed onto the field, determined to rip the Kensington attack part. But I only scored a few runs then holed out. I angrily stormed off the field and into the dressing-room. There I threw my bat in my bag, pulled out my box and hurled it at the wall and swore my head off. Then I received a gentle tap on my shoulder. There standing behind me was Chester. I thought I was 'in for it' for having sworn and carried on, but Chester just stood there, his hand on my shoulder.

'Ian, I know exactly how you feel. You've thrown your wicket away because you're upset at the fact that we didn't win. Just remember Ian, nothing is ever achieved in anger.'

I acknowledged his words with a nod of my head and he carried on: 'You are right to be upset by that, but you'll learn that it doesn't do any good. Just remember one of the big things with this game is to keep persevering. The game will get to you at times, but never forget that perseverance is a great thing.'

Chester was dead right. I never forgot his words. It was a great lesson in having the right attitude.

The Chappells' famous grandfather, Vic Richardson, did not seek to have a hands-on role in the coaching of the boys.

Vic would say, 'I'm not going to have anything to do with coaching you, Ian. You've got Lynn Fuller. You should only have one coach, otherwise you can get mixed up. Each coach has different ideas from the next and it would be easy to become confused.'

Vic took a back-seat position with our cricket. Sometimes I'd come home from a game and Mum would ask whether I had seen Vic at the ground. I'd say 'no' and she'd tell me he had been there, parked in the shade of a tree watching from a distance. Then he would ring, but he wouldn't stay on the phone long — he hated telephones. He would say, 'Well done,' and the phone would go dead. He'd hang up, just like that.

Occasionally he would talk cricket and I remember three things he told me: 'If you can't be a good cricketer, at least look like one,' something I think rubbed off better on Greg than me. Another time — I reckon it was after I became vice-captain of Australia — he said, 'If you're lucky enough to captain Australia, don't captain like a Victorian.' I don't think Vic was aiming at Bill Lawry when he said that, I suspect he was referring more to Lindsay Hassett than anyone else. The other thing which I recall Pop telling me was round the time I was vice-captain for both South Australia and Australia: 'Just remember, when you win the toss, nine times out of ten you bat first . . . on the tenth time you think about putting the opposition in, but you still bat first.'

I guess I always regret not having gotten to know Vic better. It was only in the last years of his life that we had much to do with each other. I used to love the stories of the old days, and after I had become a Test player he introduced me to the old New South Wales and Test batsman Allan Kippax. That was a special moment. I was very proud to be Vic's grandson and whenever I did anything wrong I used to say to myself, 'I wonder what Vic would think about that.' He once advised me never to abuse umpires and I've always felt guilty about the times that has happened. But if I ever get the chance to meet up with Vic, wherever that might be, I would like to think that we could sit down over a cold beer and he would say to me, 'Well then, Ian, there were three or four things you did that I didn't agree with, but on the whole I thought you did a pretty good job.'

Two

Fearless at the wicket

I have always said the season with Ramsbottom in 1963 improved my drinking and swearing and set my cricket back a couple of months. I went from never being more than twelve stone when I left Australia to being 14 stone-plus upon my return.

By the summer of 1961/62 Ian Chappell had just turned 18, but his batting had greatly matured. He was touted as the rising star of South Australian cricket. Success at A-grade level doesn't necessarily guarantee a state berth. Cricket selectors don't always get it right, but the astute ones look beyond a player's ability to score runs and take wickets; they look closely at a player's ability to cope under pressure. In addition to his ability to perform consistently, the player needs a good temperament to have a chance in succeeding in the first-class arena. Selectors Don Bradman and Phil Ridings saw all those qualities, and more, in young Ian Chappell. They had been hearing glowing reports from the school and from Ian's club, Glenelg, for some time.

Because Ian was playing for Prince Alfred College (PAC) in B grade, he didn't play A grade for Glenelg until he left school. At 17 he left PAC and played the last half of that season in the Senior Colts team. During his stint with PAC in the B-grade competition, Ian faced the leg spinners and wrong 'uns of West Torrens's Brian 'Banger' Flaherty, who claims to have clean bowled Chappell twice for a duck: 'I was about 17. Martin Chappell was then captain of the Glenelg Bs and Ian shouldered arms to my wrong 'un. I got him out the same way for a duck in both innings. Next time I caught up with Ian was in an A-grade match about a year later and he belted the hell out of me, and the rest of the West Torrens attack.'

The Colts team was disbanded before the next season so I played for Glenelg [in 1961/62] and after about ten matches I was chosen to play against Tasmania, then New South Wales, then Victoria in the final game of the Shield season. I guess I first got the feeling that something special was round the corner in my sixth or seventh A-grade match for Glenelg. I scored a century against a West Torrens side that included state bowlers Alan Hitchcox and Peter Trethewey. The state selectors were about to pick a Second XI to play a combined country team at Mount Gambier and I thought I might have a chance of getting into that side. Each Sunday I used to go to the beach with a few of my cricket and baseball mates and it was there that I found out I had been selected not for the second team, but for the South Australian Sheffield Shield side.

Glenelg keeper Des Selby, who batted with Chappell during the century against West Torrens, remembers the innings: 'Ian must only have been 17 or 18. He was aggressive even then and he was really serving it up to the fast bowlers. This pair [Trethewey and Hitchcox] opened for South Australia and they both chucked. Chappelli and Hitchcox especially were at it. West Torrens took the new ball and Hitchcox immediately bounced him. He hooked his first ball for four, with the rejoinder, "Fancy you opening the bowling for South Australia." The quick bowler was fuming and he bounced him another three times in succession. Ian hooked all four in a row for four, to move from 84 to a hundred. It was magnificent cricket. For a bloke so young to serve it up to the experienced guys was one thing; for him to be able to hook so brilliantly was another. I was at the other end. I saw the whole thing. Here was a guy who was special, ready to play big cricket. Phil Ridings [a South Australian, and later in 1971 an Australian selector] was at the ground and could not have failed to be impressed by that superb knock.'

Glenelg stalwart and successful businessman Jack 'the Flea' Butler, a sprightly bloke who looked a bit like diminutive cigar-smoking Danny DeVito, was over the moon about Chappell's state selection. A long-time member of Glenelg Cricket Club, Butler wrote to Chappell:

Dear Ian,

On an occasion such as this I feel that it is much nicer to write to you than call you on the telephone. I cannot remember being so thrilled over an Interstate selection as I am right now. Firstly, you have earned state selection, and more important, you are ready to play state cricket, and I am confident that you will handle the situation very successfully.

Confidentially, the selectors at the moment have in mind to play you and make Rex Sellers twelfth man. Do not be too disappointed if they change their mind between now and Friday, because they do this sort of thing occasionally.

Good luck on Friday, and I know that everybody at Glenelg will be with you.

Meanwhile, Ian was trying not to get too far ahead of himself.

I was twelfth man against New South Wales when Sobers made 251 and then he had to return to the Caribbean to play in a Test series, so I came into the eleven against Victoria—hence I always say I replaced Sobers in the South Australian side. Against a Victorian attack of Meckiff, Guest and Connolly I made two and 59. South Australia was murdered in that game, but I remember Bill Lawry coming to the door of the South Australian dressing-room as he was leaving the ground and he said, 'Where's young Chappell? I guess he's already left. Tell him well played.' I was sitting in the dressing-room having a beer—Bill didn't know me too well at that stage.

Garry Sobers had left the country by the time Ian had completed his gritty 59. However, Chappell later played a number of matches with Sobers and he has an enduring admiration of Sobers the cricketer and Sobers the man. Ian calls the champion 'Sobey'.

I learnt a hell of a lot by just watching Sobey, but he was always helpful. One of the things I admire about Garry, apart from his ability and that he was the senior man in the side, he always treated me as an equal. Here was this 18-year-old nobody and he's just arrived as the best cricketer in the world, and yet he was happy to give me some advice.

The next summer Ian lost his leg stump to a ball from Ian Meckiff, the Victorian and Test left-hander. He had obviously moved too far across his stumps.

I said to Garry in the dressing-room, 'I've obviously got a problem, do you have any suggestions.' He said, 'Go and get a bottle of beer son and we'll talk about it.'

He asked what guard I took, which was middle, and he then suggested that I take leg stump because, he said, 'Like me you have a back and across movement and so it's better to start from leg.' He also said it would help my on-side play because, 'You know anything at the pads is going to miss leg stump.'

Sobey also suggested I bat with both feet outside the crease to the quickies, because my first movement was back and across. I followed his advice and never changed guard again, and always batted with both feet outside the crease to the fast bowlers.

The game in which Chappelli made his first Shield century, Sobers showed the way against hostile spin from Richie Benaud in the South Australian second innings:

We were chasing just over 200 in the second innings and we needed them in a hurry. Whereas in the first innings I had played Richie fairly comfortably by jumping down the track to him, it was very different in the second dig. Benaud came around the wicket and bowled into the footmarks. I wondered what the hell had hit me. I played and missed a few from Richie, and at the end of the over Sobey came down and said, 'Don't worry son, it'll soon be over.' I thought, 'Yes, you're right. I'll be out soon.' Sobey then hit four fours and took a single off Johnny Martin, hit a couple more boundaries off Richie and then got another single, and then he belted the winning runs off Martin and it was over in a hurry. We put on 45 of which I got nine.

Garry Sobers's immense skill and confidence rubbed off on the South Australian players. The captain at that time, Les Favell, also had a lasting effect on his men. Favell was all-out attack and his confidence was such that he thought absolutely no one he came up against could bowl at all. 'In addition to Les [Favell], Garry did a lot to change the "underdog feeling" in the SACA dressing-room, especially when we played New South Wales with their near-Test line up,' Chappell says.

And what did Sobers think of Ian Chappell? Mike Coward quotes Sobers in *Cricket in the Seventies* as saying:

I watched Ian in the South Australian dressing-room before he even played for South Australia. He used to come in and sit down and listen for hours and hours . . . listen to the fellows talk about the game and their jokes. Ian was always a student of the game and was always going to be a good captain. To me he was a good leader of men, one of the best.

Ian played three matches in 1961/62, scoring 92 runs at 18.40 with a highest score of 59—that courageous knock against Victoria which so impressed Bill Lawry. Then in 1962/63 he played in ten matches for South Australia, scoring 491 runs at 35.07. He hit a brilliant 149 against the strong New South Wales side at Adelaide Oval in December 1962, only his fourth Shield match.

Richie Benaud, then New South Wales and Test captain, was intrigued by Chappelli's facial expressions when facing him. According to Chappell, in the wake of Chappelli's brilliant century, Benaud said to Barry Jarman over a beer in the dressing-room:

'What's young Chappell like? He's not a smart-arse is he?' Jarman immediately assumed that I had said something to Richie, which I wouldn't have done, and Richie said, 'No, he didn't say anything. He just kept grinning at me while he was facing up.' Jar laughed and explained that I always gritted my teeth when I was batting and it looked like a smile.

Martin would have been happy because he often told me, 'Grit your teeth son and do your best.' I must have taken him literally, although I think I got out of that habit after that episode.

At the end of that first successful Shield summer, Ian headed to the United Kingdom, playing for Ramsbottom in the tough Lancashire League. He made 510 runs and took 60 wickets, but the team finished last and at the end of it all he was glad to be going home. Ian did not believe the Lancashire League experience provided him any great benefit, in the cricketing sense. However, it was an experience overseas and he got to know a little more about England and the attitudes of English cricketers. He did not think much of the English club cricket experience:

I have always said the season with Ramsbottom in 1963 improved my drinking and swearing and set my cricket back a couple of months. I went from never being more than twelve stone when I left Australia to being 14 stone-plus upon my return. It took me a couple of months to shed the excess weight. Glenelg played Sturt first game of the 1963/64 season and I had been batting for about an over when Jack Lill asked Murray Sargent, the Glenelg captain, 'What happened to young Chappell who used to bat at number three?', and Sargent said, 'That's him up the other end.'

In the 1963/64 season Chappell established himself in the South Australian team and his name was high on the list of emerging Test cricketers. He scored 596 runs at an average of 54.18, with a personal highest score of 205 not out against Queensland in Brisbane, the first time he batted at number three for South Australia. In all first-class games he hit 662 runs at 60.18. That summer the Test selectors were to pick an Australian Eleven to play the visiting South Africans at the Melbourne Cricket Ground (MCG). Chappell believed he had the form to win selection for that game, a golden chance to press claims for higher honours.

I thought I was a real chance to play, but they went for Terry Lee, a New South Wales all-rounder. I was annoyed because Lee had only played a couple of games. I had been around a lot longer, was batting number three for South Australia and had scored a double century for my state.

That winter, when Bob Simpson led Australia's 1964 team in England, Ian played Claxton Shield baseball and at the completion of the national carnival he was picked in the All-Australian base-ball team. Chappell played in three successive Claxton Shields and again won Australian selection in 1966.

Starting the 1964/65 cricket season with a flurry of runs, Ian reckoned he would be a real chance for the tour of the West Indies at the end of the Australian summer. He was picked in the one-off Test match against Pakistan at the MCG. He heard of his selection on the radio and the Chappell family celebrated quietly with a few drinks at home. Martin, Jeanne, Greg and Trevor were immensely proud of Ian's achievement. Also selected in that one-off Test was Chappell's Glenelg and South Australia team-mate David Sincock.

Chappell was soon to discover how tough it would be to juggle work and cricket commitments. In those days Test cricket was largely an amateur exercise and all players needed a job to sustain their lives while playing cricket. His working life had begun in 1961 as a share clerk with stockbrokers Walkley, Todd & Co. in Adelaide. He stayed there until 1963, when he joined Nestle Australia as a public relations consultant. Later, in the late 1960s, he would join the promotions and public relations department of WD & HO Wills, but during the early years of his working life he was struggling to establish himself in the team.

Batting at number three spot, he was out for eleven in his first Test, the hook proving his downfall, but he took three catches in the Pakistani first innings and one in the second, and bowled in both innings, conceding 49 runs off 15 overs in the first and 31 off eleven in the second, without taking a wicket. The match was drawn. His team-mate David Sincock took 3/67 and 1/102, a fair wicket haul operating against a good batting line-up on a flat MCG track. Sincock says the match was a good pointer to Chappell's ability in the slips. But Sincock also gleaned that his good friend was harbouring some self-doubt: 'Early in his career Chappelli was not sure whether he was good enough to play at that level,' Sincock says. 'At least he was asking himself the question, "What do I need to do to be good enough to succeed at Test level?" He never lost sight of what he wanted to achieve. He always challenged himself at the nets. Chappelli didn't merely go in to the net for a hit; he always tried to simulate a game situation in his head. "Play yourself in, move the score along, find the gaps."'

While Chappell's overall summer of 1964/65 with the bat was a good one—he scored 678 runs at 52.15—he was overlooked for the tour of West Indies. It was a bitter disappointment:

I was with the state side in Brisbane at the time the touring side was announced. We were sitting about in the team motel, waiting for the names to be read out over the radio. When I realised that I had missed out I was very angry and terribly disappointed. I excused myself from the group and went to my room and I shed a few tears that night.

As it turned out Bob Simpson's team got belted by the West Indies two to one. Fast bowlers Wes Hall and Charlie Griffith bowled like the wind and made batting in the middle decidedly uncomfortable, but had Chappell gone on that tour he might have made all the difference to Simpson's men, for he certainly would have taken the attack to the fast bowlers. However, he shrugged off his disappointment and worked hard in the off season, and the hard work paid off, for in 1965/66 he enjoyed his best batting year so far, hitting 1019 runs, including four centuries and five 50s, at an average of 59.94 in all of the first-class matches. But it was still not happening for him on the Test arena. In two Tests against England that year he struggled, returning a modest 36 runs in two completed innings. However, he had done enough to convince the Test selectors that he was a batsman of quality and a man of substance.

It was around this time that Ian suffered an injury at work.

I was working with the Nestle company and was putting up a display at a shopping centre in Somerton. Using a Stanley knife—and using it very badly—I sliced back towards my hand, exactly as I had been told not to do, and took off the top off my left index finger. I soon realised I had done a fair bit of damage and went to the bathroom to put my left hand under the cold water tap. When the blood cleared I could see a bit of white stuff in the deep cut so I went back to the area where the accident happened and found the missing piece of white flesh on the floor. I took it to the doctor and asked him to sew it back on because I had to play a semi-final against Woodville the next day. The doctor told me I'm mad because if it gets hit it won't 'take' a second time. I figured Glenelg was playing at the Adelaide Oval and the pitch was true so I probably wouldn't get hit.

When Glenelg's keeper Des Selby heard about Ian's accident he said, in his dry, laconic way, 'What's Ian Chappell doing working on a Friday afternoon?'

Ian's bumper harvest of runs in the summer of 1965/66 led to his being picked for his first overseas tour, to South Africa with Bob Simpson's Australians in 1966/67. But it proved an unhappy time; he scored only 196 runs for the five-Test series at a modest average of 21.77. During that tour Bob Simpson, the team captain, encouraged him to look upon himself as an all-rounder, batting number six and bowling his leg breaks.

I had always bowled a fair bit in the backyard and at Princes [Prince Alfred College]. Dad encouraged me to bowl, saying, 'You may as well learn to bowl well, because you'll have to spend a lot of time in the field and it will pass a lot easier if you can bowl now and then.'

In the PAC under-13 team I used to run in and bowl as fast as I could, then I switched to bowling off breaks. At that stage there was controversy in Australian cricket about chucking; I saw a bit of a game at the Adelaide Oval one day and I thought, 'If it's good enough for them, it's good enough for me.'

Being a baseballer and possessing a fairly strong arm I figured I could ping them as quick as most and, with this in mind, I set about working on my bowling style. In the summer schoolboys' carnival I opened the bowling and occasionally I'd chuck a quicker one. Then I would bowl some offies, with the odd round-arm throw. The ball would curve away from the right-hander and then spin back at him.

At the end of that carnival I was picked in the metropolitan team to play the country side and was very surprised when I didn't get a bowl for the entire match. When I asked the captain why I didn't bowl, he said he had been instructed by the manager, Howard Mutton, not to bowl me because of my suspect action. While I was highly browned off by that, I thought, 'There's only one thing to do and that is to go back and bowl leggies because there is no way you can chuck a leg break.'

Overnight I made the change and in the very next match I played for PAC, I took five wickets in an innings. I pushed them through because that way I actually imparted a bit of spin. I don't think I was ever a flat spinner but quicker, probably about the speed of Shane Warne's quicker leggies, without his turn.

In South Africa in 1966/67, Chappell's chance to survive on the Test stage appeared to hinge on his all-round ability. For some time the Test selectors had pursued a policy of having batting all-rounders. They were seemingly desperate to discover a spinning all-rounder, or so it seemed, given that they were also encouraging Victorian Keith Stackpole to bowl his leg breaks to complement his middle-order batting. Ian tried valiantly to improve his bowling.

I worked hard on my bowling and approached Richie Benaud, who was covering the tour for the newspapers, for his help. He suggested that the best way to train was to get eight balls and bowl them one after another in the nets and, having bowled all eight, to retrieve them and go through the process again.

I practised this way for hours on end. Sometimes I had our keeper Brian Taber behind the stumps. For all my effort I didn't have much success. Anyway, I wasn't convinced that I wanted to be a number six batsman who bowled leg spinners. I always had in my mind, 'Bowling's fine, but I want to become the number three for Australia.' Later, when I had become established as Australia's number three batsman, people used to encourage me to bowl more, but I felt bowling took the edge off my batting.

After I became captain of Australia I reckoned that if I bowled too much it took the edge off my captaincy. I found that halfway through an over I'd still be angry about something that had happened in the previous over. So instead of thinking about field placings and the other bowler, I'd still be thinking about my own over.

I was probably a bit unlucky [in South Africa] because I got 30 odd in each dig in the first Test at Jo'burg, and was on 49 in the first innings at Newlands in the second Test and got a shocking decision, which wasn't unusual in South Africa at that time. I got an inswinger from Trevor Goddard, going down leg and tried to glance. It missed and hit me on the calf of the back leg and I was given out, caught behind. A big score in that innings might have meant a different tour because I didn't do a lot after that innings.

On advice from Bob Simpson in South Africa, he also shelved the hook shot. But sometimes when a batsman who is a good hooker puts that shot on the shelf he can get into all sorts of trouble with short-pitched pace bowling. Sir Donald Bradman later said to him, 'Ian, you used to be a good hooker. I'd like to see you playing that shot,' so he started using it again.

While big brother Ian was away on Test duty in South Africa, Greg Chappell began his first-class career with South Australia. Immediately Greg impressed, especially with his stylish on-side play. But having two Chappells in the side proved a headache for the Adelaide Oval scoreboard staff. How would they differentiate between the two? Simple—Ian Chappell became Chappell I and

Greg Chappell became Chappell G. Their new scoreboard names were first seen at Adelaide Oval on 27 October 1967, the first day of the Sheffield Shield match against Victoria. From that day on Ian Chappell became known as 'Chappelli'.

And both Chappells were brilliantly stumped by keeper Ray Jordon, standing up to the medium-fast Alan Connolly. Ian scored 67 and Greg twelve. In the second innings Ian fell to Connolly again for ten and Greg scored 75. Ian bowled well in the Victorian first innings, taking 4/87 off 23 overs. The 1967/68 season loomed as a make-or-break summer for Ian. He needed to succeed at Test level. India was making its second tour of Australia, their first since Lala Amarnath's side battled Don Bradman's Australian team in 1947/48. The Indians did not possess any fast bowlers with much venom, but they did have a great little off spinner in Erapally Prasanna.

Against New South Wales, Ian Chappell scored a splendid 128—this time batting at number three—and he took 4/53 off 19 overs to help South Australia to a comfortable win. Then South Australia played New Zealand and he scored 50 and twelve. He was clobbered by Kiwi tailender Dick Motz to the tune of 62 runs from only four overs in the New Zealand second innings. His full figures were: four overs, one maiden, zero wickets, 62 runs. (This was my debut for South Australia. I made eight not out and zero, and the Mallett bowling figures were only a little better than Ian Chappell's: 0/24 from eight overs and 0/12 from four overs.)

Chappell's century against New South Wales won him a berth in Australia's team for the first Test in Adelaide. But this Test was again an unhappy one for him as he was bowled by Prasanna for two in the first innings and bowled by Rusi Surti for 13 in the second. His bowling efforts brought no reward; time was running out, but the selectors showed their faith and kept him in the side for the MCG second Test. He was decidedly nervous before the match.

I hadn't batted as well as I would have liked in the nets the day before the Melbourne Test against India. When we got back in the dressing-room, I asked if anyone wanted to stay behind and have a bowl after lunch because I was interested in another hit. Barry Jarman grabbed me and said, 'You're not going anywhere near the nets, you're coming with me.'

Jarman took it upon himself to take his South Australian and Test team-mate to what he euphemistically called the 'Scout Hall'—the Carlton United Brewery. There, Jarman, Chappell and New South Wales fast bowler Dave Renneberg had more than the odd beer.

I said I definitely wasn't going there and that I needed another hit because I wasn't happy with my batting. Jar told me that the last thing I needed was another net, that I was too uptight and I needed to relax. We went to the brewery.

I escaped Jar's clutches at about 6 pm and staggered back to the Windsor [Hotel]. I was in bed when Kay [Chappell's first wife, whom he had married in Adelaide in 1966] arrived at the hotel. She had driven over with Martin and luckily had declined Martin's offer to help her take her bags up to the room. If he'd seen I'd been drinking before the Test he wouldn't have been too happy. We fielded the first day and I made a hundred when we batted, so Jar was right. I think it was that episode that helped me to relax more. It also helped me later on as a captain because I realised there are times when guys need to work hard, but equally there are occasions when they need to get away from the game a bit and relax.

I think it may have also changed my attitude to practice. After that I went more for quality rather than quantity in the nets. I spent extra time at practice only if there was something specific I was trying to fix, and that would usually be off in a side net with someone throwing the ball to me rather than an extra hit. I also worried less about hitting them well in the nets before a match, and I think I developed more of a planned approach to batting in the nets.

And so Chappell scored his 151 off 224 balls, with 21 fours, occupying the crease for 252 minutes. His footwork against Prasanna was impressive and, although the little spin wizard took 6/141 off 34 overs, this time he did not dismiss Chappell. That first Test century confirmed Chappell's class. It would also have eased the minds of the Test selectors, Sir Donald Bradman, Jack Ryder and Neil Harvey.

Perhaps Harvey more than the other two selectors was aware of Chappell's appeal to the players for, although Harvey didn't drink until the 1961 tour of England, he was a down-to-earth, knock-about sort of bloke who came to love a glass of beer and the camaraderie of his mates. Ryder, on the other hand, was a tee-totaller and Bradman would no sooner walk into the front bar of a hotel than fly to the moon. Harvey saw in Chappelli a natural leader, a man's man with the common touch, and it wasn't long before he was pressing for Ian Chappell to be the Australian captain.

In the first-class matches in 1967/68, Ian Chappell scored a total of 728 runs at 40.44, including two centuries and five 50s. While his figures were not sensational, he felt he was finally on his way.

The big turning point for me was not so much the century I hit against India, but my batting in the last Shield match of the season against Victoria at the MCG. I was in very good form and got 52 in the first dig before being stumped by Bob 'Wallaby' Cowper—I must have been looking the other way when Cowper bowled—and then ran myself out for 79 in the second innings. I was really angry with myself after the run-out but I thought about it and I decided that if I made the tour to England I would relax and enjoy myself. It was the best decision I ever made because I began to play a lot better in Test cricket.

In fact, Chappell was an automatic selection for the England tour, the first of three such tours for him, although he missed the connecting flight from Adelaide to Sydney when Kay and Ian's six-week-old baby girl, Amanda, was not quite the alarm clock they assumed she would be.

Despite a wet start, the sun finally came out as the tour wore on and the runs began to accumulate. Chappell hit 1261 tour runs in 20 matches in 1968, with a top score of 202 not out against Warwickshire at Edgbaston and a season's average of 48.50. It wasn't merely compiling 348 runs at 43.50 in the five Tests that stamped him as a class act for they are not startling figures in themselves, but rather countering the great threat of left-arm medium-paced spinner Derek Underwood, England's best bowler.

Australia won the first Test at Manchester then, after a hail-storm at Lord's, was knocked over for 78. Australia escaped with a draw, but the weather and the dourness of the English team conspired to make it a colourless series, which England squared by winning the fifth Test by 226 runs. (I had the good fortune to be selected for this tour, and made my Test debut in the fifth Test at The Oval, taking 3/87 and 2/77, including the wicket of Colin Cowdrey in each innings.)

Chappell batted down the order in England, but the following summer he slotted into his favourite number three spot in the first Test against the West Indies at Brisbane. Chappell made 117, but Australia lost that match by 125 runs. However, they went on to win three of the next four matches and to take the series con-vincingly with three to one. This was to be Chappell's best season of first-class cricket, producing 1476 runs at 82 with six centuries and five 50s. He also grabbed 27 catches, mostly at first slip—again his best catching haul of any season. In the Test matches against Garry Sobers's men he hit 548 runs at 68.50—including a high score of 165, a second hundred and three 50s—and took ten catches. He was appointed vice-captain of Australia before the last Test in Sydney in early 1969, replacing Barry Jarman who had indicated that he would not be available for the forthcoming tour of India. Ian's appointment left the South Australian administration no choice but to make Chappell the state vice-captain, again replacing Jarman.

In the 1968/69 season, Chappell had especially loved the challenge of batting against West Indian fast bowlers Wes Hall and Charlie Griffith, as well as playing against one of his heroes, Garry Sobers. He ended off the season ready for India and his renewed battle with Prasanna.

Watching Ian Chappell bat, observing his technique and seeing him perform day in and day out under extreme pressure was both educational and inspirational. He loved to talk while he waited to go in to bat. The instant an opener was dismissed he would invariably be chatting to those of us watching in front of the dressing-room. Even as he adjusted his cap and grabbed his bat, Chappelli would be finishing off a story. He was in his element spinning yarns or belting the hell out of an opposing bowling attack.

Yet, whatever the state of the game, he never dawdled to the crease and always made it his business to cross with the outgoing batsman on the field and get to the middle as soon as possible. As a bowler, you just knew he was bringing the attack to you. There was nothing subtle about his batting strategy. Ever on a mission to dominate an opponent, he would ensure he had the psychological edge before he faced the first ball. The message was clear—he was here to play.

Ian took the fight to the bowler. He believed that a batsman had to make a statement at the crease. The opposing side might have appeared nonchalant enough as he walked towards them, but they feared his batting. He would look up and around him as he walked to the batting crease (looking up helped him adjust to the light). His collar upturned, he would take guard and mark his crease. While prodding the pitch with his bat in his right hand, he would fiddle with his box and thigh pad, and tug at the peak of his cap with his left. Soon he would be ready, but not before going through the motions a second time for good measure. Sometimes he would run on the spot to get his legs moving. There may have been a hint of nervous energy at work, but the bowlers knew a ball too full or too short would be for it— first ball or not.

The quick bowlers were aware that Ian would take up the challenge and hook the short stuff; the bitter-sweet joy of this battle was that you knew you had a chance of getting him out. And there was also that nagging question at the back of any fast bowler's mind, 'What if he gets going?'

Chappelli once described himself as the 'happy hooker'. While it often contributed to his downfall, the hook also brought him many runs. A master of the horizontal bat strokes—the cut, the pull and the hook—Ian's footwork was swift and efficient, he was always there in a good position and his eyes were glued to the ball all the way. Bat-pad fieldsmen took cover when Ian rocked onto the back foot. Against the slow stuff he used his feet to get to the pitch of the ball, also utilising the sweep, the pull and the cut to frustrate spinners and disrupt their rhythm. His peers always said that if they ever wanted a man to bat for their lives, Ian Chappell was that man.

I looked to score at every opportunity. I believe a batsman must be able to dominate the bowler, and to do that he has to show intent. The bowler must know that if he makes a mistake he will be punished. That way, I believe, he is more likely to make a mistake.

Making runs is also critical because it is one of only two ways in which to win a match—by so many runs or so many wickets. I believed it is a batsman's job to score his runs as quickly as possible so as to give the bowlers time to take the 20 wickets. I always loved the challenge of pitting wits with the bowler. I guess that is why I loved batting against blokes like Prasanna and Pakistani leg spinner Intikhab Alam.

With fast bowlers it is generally more a test of courage, although up against the likes of John Snow, Andy Roberts and Joel Garner you knew they were thinking about their bowling, and this was also a big challenge. I always thought that if a batsman is tied down it is his duty to do something to correct the situation rather than wait for the bowler to make a mistake. The good ones don't make too many mistakes unless you provoke them.

I had two categories for spinners: those I wasn't looking to hit for fours and those I targeted to hit boundaries off. Against the really good spinners, I tried to work the ball and if the odd boundary came that was a bonus. You need to think aggressively when up against a good spinner and that means looking for runs all the time. You don't necessarily try to hit boundaries. Against the average guys, on the other hand, I thought there was a four coming and if I didn't get one that over there would be two the next over.

Manipulating the spin bowler's field placings was important. If you could dictate the field changes with your placement then you were winning the battle. I always felt I could score a century by hitting the ball along the ground. Placement is paramount. I think too many batsmen don't work hard enough on this and rely too heavily on hitting the ball in the air. Having a plan is critical against spinners—just as important as it is against fast bowlers. I think a lot of batsmen forget this aspect against spinners.

The Australians had two weeks in Sri Lanka, playing two unofficial Tests, before arriving in India. Bill Lawry led the team, with Ian Chappell as his deputy.

It took the players some time to adjust to the noise, the dust and the poverty of this fascinating and often beautiful land of contrasts. In Calcutta they saw the emaciated figure of a leper, covered in weeping sores, too feeble to brush away the swarm of flies that gathered about him in a cloud. He stood beside an open sewer, where two young girls playfully splashed each other. The monsoon season is especially dreaded by locals, for the open sewers cannot contain the rain and sewage spews onto roads. Then the smallest scratch festers. In the main, however, Lawry's men stayed relatively fit and well, apart from the odd case of 'Delhi belly' and the usual variety of stomach complaints.

Chappell continued his good form and emerged from the tour with Bill Lawry telling the cricket world: 'Ian Chappell is the best batsman on the planet.' He certainly batted brilliantly on those spinning tracks and against Prasanna, arguably the greatest off spinner to draw breath (Ian certainly regards Prasanna as the best spinner he ever faced). Prasanna was fairly short and stocky and had rather short fingers; but no matter, he could make the ball buzz. Shane Warne gives the ball such a rip the batsman, keeper and close fieldsmen are able to hear the ball fizzing through the air. Prasanna did the same, and he managed to achieve an amazing amount of purchase on the ball. With the left-hand slow-man Bishan Bedi—who didn't spin the ball as much as Prasanna, but was all rhythm and subtle change of pace—he formed one of the game's great bowling partnerships. Chappell says:

I thought Prasanna was a genius. He had beautiful flight with his off-the-shoulder style action. So many times when the ball left his hand, it appeared to be an invitation to a juicy half-volley, but it never kept the appointment. I used to wonder if Pras had the ball on a string that he tugged just as you were about to play the shot. Pras was equally adept at spinning a web of confusion on both the hard Australian pitches and on the more receptive surfaces in India.

Prasanna was such a good bowler that he could force a batsman onto the back foot, then lure him forward at the precise moment he wanted the batsman to advance toward him. Sometimes he trapped batsmen playing across the crease. He mixed his pace cleverly and was ever at the batsman. He didn't mind giving away a few runs; he was a wicket-taker. Prasanna would have enjoyed today's cricket where there are so few really good players of spin bowling.

In Bombay, Ian scored 31 (bowled by Prasanna) and 31 not out during the first Test of the 1969 series. The Indians put up a good fight and it was Prasanna (5/121 off 49 overs) and Bedi (3/74 off 62.4 overs) who kept the team in the match. Keith Stackpole hit a first innings of 103. The match was marred by a riot caused by the lower-order batsman Venkataraghavan (later to become a good Test umpire) being given out, caught behind off the bowling of Alan Connolly, when he clearly missed it. The situation was not helped by a commentator on the radio saying, 'Venkat was not out and Lawry is a cheat.' All hell broke loose. The people in the outer stacked deck chairs and set them alight, the tennis court next door was on fire and two cars in a nearby street were turned over by the angry mob and set ablaze, but the game continued.

Then a gang of armed policemen in riot gear stormed onto the field. People had been hurling bottles over the cyclone fence which surrounded the ground, trying to hit any Australian player within reach. The burly police chief spoke to the players as they gathered in the centre of the ground. 'If the people break down the fence,' he said, 'you are in trouble. Grab a stump, grab anything, but take a few down with you.' At that point black smoke surged across the ground and out of the smoke ran a small man with an agitated look on his face. 'Mr Lawry, Mr Lawry, I am the scorer,' he cried, 'I cannot see for the smoke. I am going home. All will be well,' he added, as he rushed away, 'the radio commentator will keep score . . .'

Ian Chappell sidled up to Lawry as they watched the riot squad leave the ground. 'Bill,' he said, 'I think it will be safer if we all gather as a group and leave the field together at the end of the day's play. What do you think?'

'Gee, Chappelli, we need a wicket bad.'

Bottles rained down on the Australian players when they left the field and the Australian dressing-room was a shambles, but Doug Walters must have pre-empted trouble for he had a bath full of ice and cold Aussie beer in the room where the players were huddled. Team manager Fred Bennett arrived, red faced and breathless. 'Fellas, there are ten thousand people in front of the main grandstand, calling for Bill Lawry's blood,' he said. As ever, Doug Walters's timing was perfect.

'C'mon Fred,' he said, 'give 'em Lawry and let's get on with the drinking.'

Although India had some outstanding accommodation, Bill Lawry's Australians stayed in places that were more hovels than hotels. In Gauhati, a town in the state of Assam, mosquitos pervaded the hotel and the place was disgustingly damp and dank. The dining room was no place for faint hearts. One night a group of the players ventured into the kitchen in search of bread to toast in Doug Walters's room. They were greeted by a sea of cockroaches swarming over the wet floor and several cats dancing on the salads in the fridge. Armed with bread and forks they returned to the hotel room. The floor was concrete, so a small fire wasn't going to do much harm. Wooden struts from mosquito nets fuelled the flames.

The beds at Brabourne Stadium [in Bombay] had no inner springs: wooden slats supported a thin, hard horsehair mattress. Doug Walters removed some of the slats to make a more comfortable bed for himself, but the slats gave way and Doug later improvised by removing all the slats and hanging the horsehair mattress in the fashion of a hammock. The day before we left for South Africa we stayed at the luxurious Taj Mahal Hotel in Bombay, but it was only for one night, and that only increased our anger because we knew that there were good hotels in India, but our board wouldn't book us in at them.

Around this time, the team learnt that their lives had been insured for a figure somewhere in the vicinity of $400. Conditions were dreadful and the Australians were in a dark mood. Gauhati proved the perfect place to hold a meeting for the players to get their anger at the board off their chests. Bill Lawry called a team meeting with the idea of listing all the players' grievances, which he planned to put in a letter to the board. Ian advised Bill to have all the players sign the letter, as a collective was far better than a lone voice in this matter.

I said to Bill, 'Look mate, when you write the letter get all of us to sign it for it is not only you who is annoyed with the board over the arrangements here—it's the entire squad of 15. We must all sign the letter. If we don't all sign it you know what the board will do—they will put a black mark against your name and wait for an excuse to get rid of you. Any loss of form and they will drop you.'

That's exactly what happened. I guess Bill felt that it was his responsibility to sign the letter himself. As far as I was concerned that was the end of Bill Lawry as captain of Australia. Once he put the letter in, it was just a matter of finding any excuse they could to get rid of him.

To this day Bill Lawry feels he did the right thing in the wake of the players' meeting in Gauhati. 'I saw signing the letter as my responsibility as captain. No one influenced me. I think Ian Redpath mentioned something about the guys signing the letter and maybe Chappelli did, but I felt that I alone had to make the point. It was my responsibility. I was the captain. In hindsight I can see that it rebounded on me, but at the time I felt I was doing the right thing.'

Another incident in India was to have repercussions later in Chappell's career. During a match against South Zone at Bangalore, wizard Indian off spinner Prasanna was facing the bowling of Alan Connolly and, as was his habit to Connolly, Australia's second keeper, Ray Jordon, was standing up to the stumps. Prasanna had scored nine when he appeared to miss a ball from Connolly and his off stump was knocked forward. Prasanna was nonplussed. He was convinced the ball had missed the stumps, but Jordon appealed loudly. Ian Chappell was at close quarters and he suspected foul play: 'The umpire never gave Pras out—he eventually walked because, Doug Walters told me afterwards, Jordon had kept telling him, "Piss off, you're out mate."'

The consensus was the ball had missed Prasanna's stumps and rebounded off Jordon's pads to break the wicket. Afternoon tea was taken soon after Prasanna's dismissal, and Chappell sat in the corner of that tiny Bangalore dressing-room, seething. 'It was all boiling inside of me and after about ten minutes I couldn't help myself. I just erupted, "Listen you cunt, if you are going to cheat blokes out . . . we are playing for Australia. We don't have to cheat blokes to win. If we have got to be cheating fellas out we shouldn't be playing for Australia."' This dismissal was reminiscent of an earlier incident in the 1967/68 Sheffield Shield final match against Victoria, again with Jordon standing up at the stumps to Alan Connolly, when South Australian wicket-keeper Barry Jarman was seemingly dismissed in the same way.

Ian Chappell is still convinced that Jordon dismissed Prasanna by foul means that day in India.

I asked Doug Walters, an honourable person and cricketer, who was fielding square of the wicket at point and had a good view, and he told me the ball bounced off Jordon's pads onto the stumps. In the dressing-room exchange with Bill Lawry [who played for Victoria with Jordon] Walters said, 'Everyone knows Slug's [Ray Jordon] a cheat!'

I was watching in the stand, side-on to the action, when the incident occurred. Connolly was bowling and Prasanna shaped to leg glance. I could not see the flight of the ball after it passed Pras's pads, but I did see the leg stump fall forwards. That seemed odd. Usually when a ball hits the wicket a stump tends to fall in the opposite direction. Jordon appealed straight away and Connolly looked up after having followed through, his body language telling all and sundry that he had bowled the batsman. The ball had flown to fine leg, Jordon's arms were outstreched in appeal and Prasanna stood shaking his head in astonishment. I suspect the blokes on the field saw at close hand what we couldn't see from the pavilion, yet even from that distance those of us in the stand thought something was very wrong out there on the field.

Originally the board wanted the Australian team to tour India and then go on to Pakistan, but it could not come to a satisfactory financial deal with the Pakistanis, so the proposed tour of Pakistan was cancelled.

South Africa was keen to expand its international cricket involvement and immediately put forward a proposal to host the Australian team following their tour of India. The board agreed, but while the deal may have been financially sound, it was less so in a cricketing sense. Whereas going to Pakistan from India was logical—playing conditions were alike and there would have been little adjustment involved for the players—playing conditions in South Africa compared with India were always going to be a major concern. In India the wickets were notorious 'turners', the ball bouncing and spinning, and there was little grass to help the fast bowlers. In South Africa, the wickets were perfect for seam bowling, hard but with more than a tinge of green. Poor food and conditions in India also made it tougher for players to adapt in South Africa.

Revolt was in the air. Sub-standard food, squalid hotels and hopelessly confused travel arrangements rendered the Indian tour a disaster in one sense. But, despite the trials and complications, Chappell played magnificently. The wickets were simply made for spin. They spun and bounced, and Chappell excelled in combating the Indian spinners. Only Prasanna worried him. At Kanpur, where the wicket was benign, Chappell was lbw to Prasanna for just 16. Ian Redpath hit 70 and Paul Sheahan scored his maiden Test century. At Feroz Shah Kotla in Delhi the Australians trained on a shocking wicket—the bounce was horrendous, the ball either searching for the throat or scuttling along the ground. Australia batted first and scored 296. Ian Chappell hit a brilliant 138, using his feet to the spinners and placing the ball to perfection. Only Stackpole (61) and Taber (46) provided any support as Prasanna (4/111) and Bedi (4/71) again called the tune. India replied with 223, but then Australia was bowled out for 107 in the second innings while India lost only two more wickets in scoring the necessary 181 runs for victory.

Ian Chappell hit 99 in the fourth Test at Eden Gardens, Calcutta. Again, he batted beautifully and was the main reason Prasanna failed to take a wicket in the Australian first innings. In the final Test at Chepauk, Madras, Ian failed in both innings—bowled by Prasanna for four in the first and by Amarnath for five in the second. Variable bounce in the Chepauk wicket plagued every batsman, although Doug Walters played a masterly hand in scoring 102 in the first innings. The batting of Chappell, Walters and Redpath against the combination of Prasanna and Bedi was a

major factor in Australia gaining the upper hand in the series, which Australia won three to one with one Test drawn.

The next day Bill Lawry's team flew to Nairobi, Kenya, en route to South Africa.

Three

Born leader

Bill, you are the captain and you can pick whatever team you like,
but if you are going to pick Ray Jordon in the Australian cricket
team please don't consider me for selection. I'm not available.

In August 1968, Cape Coloured all-rounder Basil d'Oliveira hit a career-best 158 for England against Australia at The Oval. A day later he found himself out of the English team, only weeks away from touring South Africa. When Tom Cartwright subsequently withdrew from the tour through injury and the selectors picked d'Oliveira, South Africa's prime minister, John Vorster, who had been interned during the war years as a Nazi sympathiser, told the English cricket authorities that an English team that included d'Oliveira was 'not welcome in South Africa'. England subsequently cancelled the 1968/69 tour.

Before Bill Lawry's 1970 Australian team arrived in South Africa, each member of the team received a letter from anti-apartheid campaigner Peter Hain. Hain, who later became a Labour MP and Leader of the House of Commons in the United Kingdom, was a 19-year-old white South African, studying engineering at Imperial College, London. Brought up in a liberal family in Pretoria, he had been in the United Kingdom for only three years when he became a leader of the Stop the Seventy Tour Committee in September 1969. Hain urged every member of Lawry's team to think carefully about the injustices of apartheid and to boycott the South African tour. While the tour went ahead, the movement driven by Hain eventually caused the cancellation of South African rugby and cricket tours to England and Australia. There were images of barbed wire protecting the pitch at Lord's leading up to the northern summer of 1970, and a South African cricket tour of England was thought to be impossible. The pundits proclaimed that if rugby could be stopped by the protesters, cricket had no chance.

Australia's first match of the tour was against North-Eastern Transvaal at Berea Park in Pretoria. While the contest was notable for Ian Chappell hitting his 25th first-class century, more noteworthy was the fact that no coloured-skin person was permitted to attend. Travelling in Northlands, the Australians stared in disbelief at a group of black men chained together at the side of a busy road near the Wanderers Cricket Ground. At the whistle the blacks raised their picks. A second whistle signalled the downward swing. The scene was right out of the American South in the days of slavery. The stigma of apartheid was everywhere. The blacks' collective spirit cowered under the inhumane whip of apartheid. Separate toilets, buses, beaches, the Group Areas Act, and the dreaded pass, which designated a black person as 'second class', were all huge psychological and practical burdens.

The Afrikaaner was in control of this nation and it was the Afrikaaner who interpreted the good book to suit his own purpose. The black man as a 'hewer of wood and a drawer of water'. The day before the first Test match in Cape Town, a left-arm spinner named Baboo Ebraheim turned up at the nets. The South African Cricket Union had offered Ebraheim to Lawry as a net bowler, yet this slim young man was easily the best spinner in South Africa—a much better bowler than the two spinners in their Test line-up, Graham Chevalier and Mike Seymour. And only a few miles across the water from the Newlands where the Australians were training, Nelson Mandela sat in a cell at Robben Island in the sixth year of a 27-year incarceration for his alleged treason.

South Africa had a powerful line-up, including Graeme Pollock, Eddie Barlow, Trevor Goddard, Barry Richards and Mike Proctor. The Australians were unhappy with the umpiring in the first Test, which they lost by 170 runs, but they played so poorly they deserved to lose.

There were three on-field incidents during the series which upset the Australians. Long before play began in the second Test at Durban, Ali Bacher asked Bill Lawry to toss. Bacher won and elected to bat. Bill didn't mind, as the wicket had a crew cut of green and the grass appeared fairly long and would suit the pace of Graham McKenzie. But just as Bill reached the dressing-room there was a flurry of commotion and Lawry watched in horror as a gang of men in blue overalls, each pushing a lawnmower, rushed onto the ground and raced up and down the wicket, stripping it of its green grass.

'Shit, they can't do that . . . we've just tossed,' exclaimed a heated Lawry. He rushed to the centre of the ground, demanding an explanation. To his annoyance he learnt that Bacher had tricked him—the good doctor knew that the small print in the rules allowed for the pitch to be mown up to 30 minutes before the start of play. Bacher's ploy was within the rules, but it was not within the spirit of the game.

The South Africans, thanks to a punishing double-century from Graeme Pollock and a century by Barry Richards, carved up the Australians. Bacher declared at 9/622, then the Springboks blasted Australia out for 157. In the second innings, Lawry's men did better, scoring a total of 336. Chappell, who had failed twice in Cape Town, failed again, but Keith Stackpole scored 71, and Ian Redpath (74 not out) and Doug Walters (74) were in the middle of a productive and face-saving partnership when Walters was declared out in controversial circumstances. Egyptian-born South African off spinner John Traicos dropped one short to Walters and the umpire, John Draper, stuck out his right arm and yelled 'No . . .' There was a definite signal of the arm and a definite call. Walters tried to hit it into the stands over mid wicket but got it a bit high on the bat, and Graeme Pollock at deep square leg ran some 30 metres to his left to take the ball cleanly about a metre inside the fence. Redpath and Walters were astonished to see Umpire Draper with his finger in the air. Walters was given out. Placid Ian Redpath hurled his bat onto the ground in disgust. Ian Chappell recalls:

I was really pissed off with Ali Bacher . . . he did three things which really annoyed the hell out of me. The first was when he came in and asked Bill to toss early. That was definitely underhanded. Then there was the time Dougie was cheated . . . Redders said to him, 'You said "No," so it is a no-ball' and the umpire replied, 'No, I thought it was going to be a no-ball and I did not carry on with the call.' Ali Bacher should definitely have stepped in, refuted the appeal and called Walters back.

The third incident involved Ian Chappell in the third Test, at the Wanderers in Johannesburg. In the previous two Tests he had scored nil and 13 (Cape Town) and nil and 14 (Durban). He got to 34 in the first innings at the Wanderers and was batting really well, like the batsman Lawry had so lavishly praised at the start of the tour. Left-arm medium-pacer Trevor Goddard was bowling. He had resorted to negative tactics, bowling wide down the leg side, with the occasional one thrown wide of off stump. The tactic was to try and lure Ian into playing a rash stroke. Eventually, frustration got the better of him and he launched into a cover drive. The ball was very wide of off stump and he lifted it towards Tiger Lance, fielding at backward point. The Australians had a good view from their dressing-room and clearly saw Lance accept the ball on the first bounce, the ball landing so far short of his hands that it almost bounced twice before it got to him. However, unfortunately for the Australians there were no slow-motion TV replays or third umpires in those days.

Chappell asked, 'Did you catch it, Tiger?'

'Ja,' said Tiger. 'I caught it Chappelli. I caught it.'

Now, normally if you are caught at point you don't hang around because you are only embarrassing yourself, but the reason I hesitated and asked Tiger was because the umpire wasn't doing anything. If the umpire was uncertain whether Tiger caught it or not he should have been having a chat to his colleague. But I sensed the umpire at the bowler's end wasn't going to do anything . . . he was like a rabbit caught in the headlights . . . he just froze.

That night Eddie Barlow, whom I always had the highest regard for as a cricketer and an opponent because he played the game hard and was one of the South Africans I always thought would play the game fairly, apologised to me. He was the only South African player to do so. He came into the room, straight over to me and said, 'Ian, I am sorry about what happened out there today . . . The ball bounced.'

'Well, what did happen, Eddie? I'm not too bloody sure, it looked strange to me.'

'Yeah, Chappelli. The ball bounced. When we quizzed Tiger he said, "Chappelli didn't ask me how many times it bounced." '

To me that's a disgrace. Ali Bacher should have got involved . . . I didn't have a lot of respect for Ali as a captain in that series. However, I do admire what he has done with South African cricket in trying to integrate the game.

Soon after that series South Africa was ostracised from the Test stage. Bacher was the man who drove South Africa's return to the Test arena, but it would take him more than 20 years to do so. A medical doctor by profession, Bacher became the managing director of the South African Cricket Association and, while the South African Government chose to circle the wagons and retreat into the laager of an isolation of their own making, Bacher worked towards introducing cricket to the Black majority during the latter years of the apartheid scourge. With Nelson Mandela's blessing—Mandela instructed the African National Congress's military arm to guarantee Bacher and his coaches safe passage—Bacher took cricket into the black townships.

Apartheid ruined the Test careers of the likes of Graeme Pollock—the man Chappell ranks second only to Sobers as a batsman he played with or against—Barry Richards and Mike Proctor.

Barry Richards batted brilliantly at Durban in 1970. Had Bill [Lawry] not stopped to do his bootlaces up and cheat him of another over, Richards would have scored a century before lunch. The crowd was abuzz with Richards. At lunch Barry was on 94. He had been joined by Graeme Pollock and when the pair returned after lunch, the crowd was still abuzz with Richards—this was his home ground. Alan Connolly was bowling and Pollock smashed two or three fours off the remaining four balls of his over, and he didn't even look to get a single off the last ball. You immediately knew something was amiss when he did that and at the end of the over he put his hand on his hip and he looked around the ground.

I said to Stacky, 'Mate, we have a huge problem.'

'Oh, Chaps, what's that?'

'Well, the crowd are all buzzing for Richards, but this fucker's going to see how many Richards gets and he's going to get twice as many, just to shut these people up and show them there's another player here as well.' I was wrong, Barry got 140 and Graeme only got 274.

Australia, already two down, lost the third Test by 307. On the eve of the fourth Test, the Australians were training at St George's Park in Port Elizabeth when Lawry approached Chappell.

'Ian, can we go out to the middle, just you and me?' he asked. ' I want to have a meeting before we have a selection meeting.'

'Sure mate,' I said.

We went out to the middle and Bill said, 'Look, we are not getting a lot of runs down the order and I'm thinking of playing Ray Jordon in place of Taber. I think he might make a few more runs than Tabsy.'

'Bill,' I said, 'you are the captain and you can pick whatever team you like, but if you are going to pick Jordon in the Australian cricket team please don't consider me for selection. I'm not available.'

'What do you mean?'

I explained that I felt Jordon was a cheat. I did not want to play with a cheat. If we picked a bloke and found out that he was a cheat later, that was a different matter. But to knowingly play a bloke we knew cheated, that would be unacceptable to me. To knowingly select a cheat for Australia, I couldn't be part of that . . . You could quite easily drop me anyhow because I'm not making any runs and it is not going to be a problem. If you want Jordon that's fine, you are entitled to have the team you want; just don't consider me for selection.

Bill said, 'Shit, I didn't realise you felt so strongly about it . . . We'll forget about it. Taber plays.'

Taber played, took five catches in the South African first innings and scored three and 30 not out in yet another losing Test match for Australia. It proved to be Taber's last Test, as Rodney Marsh took over as Australia's Test keeper in the next Test, against Ray Illingworth's England at the Gabba in November 1970. Ray Jordon subsequently played a lot of first-class cricket in Australia and on tour in India and South Africa, but he never played a Test match again.

Halfway through the South African tour, after South Africa had won the first two Tests, the South African Cricket Association suggested that a fifth Test be played. The South Africans wanted to swell their coffers; the extra Test was to be played in Johannesburg, where a full house was likely on most days. Fred Bennett and Bill Lawry explained to us that the South African proposal had been agreed to by the Australian Board of Control. The last two remaining first-class games (against Western Province and Orange Free State) would be scrapped and the fifth Test played in their stead. Ian Chappell was unimpressed.

I think we all thought that we were sold up the river by the board, being sent straight to South Africa after India. As vice-captain of the team I told the players that this was an opportunity not to be missed. 'Look you guys, we've got the bastards over a barrel.'

It meant we had to sign a new contract, because it went three days longer than the period we had signed for in the first place. And I remember saying, 'Look, this is our chance. We've got the bastards. Let's fucking let them know we are not going to be pushed around.'

The board were going to pay $200. Then [we asked for] $500. The board wouldn't pay $500, but the Wanderers Club offered to make up the extra $300. One player said he could use the money and they should go ahead and play the match without the dissenters.

Ian Chappell took his chequebook out and banged it on the table. 'Look,' he said, 'if you want the money so badly I'll write out a cheque for you now. We've got this opportunity to stand up and be counted, and we'll fucking well tell them we are not playing. Look at the fucking itinerary they've given us—India then South Africa. Do they care about us? No, they don't.'

Then Bill Lawry stepped in and said, 'Righto, it's either all-in or all-out. It's obvious that some of you don't want to play, so it's all over, forget it.' The fifth Test match was not played because Lawry would have only accepted a unanimous decision.

Chappell's strong leadership unquestionably influenced many of the players in the room. The board didn't like it; Bill Lawry would undoubtedly have had another black mark struck against his name. The South African Cricket Association was peeved, for it was banking on a bumper crowd and a handsome profit. But how much more upset would they have been had they known that South Africa would have to wait 21 years to play another Test match . . .

The proposed 1970 South African cricket tour of England was cancelled. It was replaced by a tour by World XI, led by Garry Sobers and including Graeme Pollock, Rohan Kanhai, Mike Proctor, Intikhab Alam, Barry Richards, Mushtaq Mohammad and Eddie Barlow. The England side was led by Ray Illingworth, a magnificent captain and the man likely to get the best out of his men—even moody fast bowler John Snow. A tough series against World XI in England was ideal preparation for Illingworth's Ashes tour of Australia in 1970/71. England had a strong batting line-up headed by Geoff Boycott, John Edrich, Colin Cowdrey, Basil d'Oliveira and John Hampshire.

Chappell returned to form with a solid 59 in the drawn first Test in Brisbane, Doug Walters got a first innings century and

Keith Stackpole hit a career-best 207. Ian Redpath made 171 and Greg Chappell hit a debut century in the second Test (the first Test match ever to be played in Perth). The second Test was also drawn and the third Test, scheduled for Melbourne, was abandoned without a ball being bowled, so the administrators decided to play a one-day match to appease spectators who had paid for their Test tickets. It became the first one-day international and was won comfortably by Australia.

The fourth Test, at the Sydney Cricket Ground (SCG), saw Boycott and Brian Luckhurst put on 116 for the first wicket in an English first innings total of 332. As the players left the field, Lawry said to Ian Chappell, 'You strap 'em on. You're opening with me.'

Keith Stackpole, who scored five and nil in Perth, was relegated to bat at number six. Ian was not happy. He made twelve and nil, falling both times to Snow, who took 7/40 as England won by 299. Lawry carried his bat for 60 in an Australian second innings total of 116.

Back at number three in Melbourne, Ian hit 111 in another drawn Test and then scored a second-innings 104 in the sixth Test in Adelaide—his partnership with Stackpole (136) crucial to Australia battling it out for another draw after Illingworth decided not to enforce the follow on. Bill Lawry scored ten and 21 in Adelaide in what was to be his last Test match.

After the third Test was washed out, the Australian Cricket Board organised a seventh Test. With England ahead one to nil, the Ashes, held by Australia, were in the balance. The Test selectors responded to Australia's recent failures by making wholesale changes, and Bill Lawry was sacked as both captain and player. To add insult to injury, he heard of his sacking from his friend and Test opening partner Keith Stackpole, who rang Lawry after hearing the news over the radio. Victoria's Ken Eastwood replaced

Lawry as opening batsman. New South Wales leggie Kerry O'Keeffe was picked along with South Australian leg spinner Terry Jenner in place of Gleeson and Mallett, and big Queensland left-arm fast bowler Tony Dell came in for Alan 'Froggy' Thompson. Chappell was made captain.

My original thought when I found out I was going to captain Australia was that I'd be given a tough task. However, I then sat down and thought about it a little more deeply and realised it wasn't so difficult at all—Lawry hadn't been winning, so if I didn't win people weren't going to blame me and if I did happen to win they would think I was a genius. Once I had rationalised the job that way I was pretty calm about it all.

Big Queenslander Tony Dell had been picked to open the bowling with Dennis Lillee. Dell was a bundle of nerves and wasn't sure how he was going to fit in. 'I didn't even own a pair of pads,' Dell recalls. 'I'm in the deep end, nervous as hell and I start off bowling crap—as did Lillee! I had heard a lot about Chappelli and his blunt manner, but that wasn't his captaincy style. He calmed me down and we worked through the nerves. This gave me confidence and I got two wickets for not many runs.'

Chappell considered himself to be reasonably calm on the first day of his first Test match as captain.

I think fielding first helped me because I had to actually captain straight away rather than sit around for a day thinking about it. However, I also decided very early in my career that it was important to keep my emotions in check and not get too high or low as otherwise the players would fluctuate with me. Consequently, I tried to keep an outward calm even when I was inwardly worried. This approach came from a story Lyn Marks [the New South Wales and South Australian left-handed batsman] told me when I roomed with him during his 1965/66 season with South Australia.

Lyn said the reason for Richie Benaud's success was the players believed he would always have the answer. Even when the opposition was 0/200 Benaud would be calmly standing in the gully with his arms folded. Then, suddenly he would change the bowling and move a couple of fielders and everyone in the team would think, 'Ah, this is the big move that will change the game.' Because Richie was so calm and the players believed in him, his move would often turn out to be pivotal.

I always remembered this story and that is why I tried never to yell at players and to only use moderate hand signals rather than frantic arm waving out in the field. I always tried to exude calm, even when things weren't going so well. Folded arms in the slips is a good way to create the impression that all is well.

Chappell won his first toss on a pitch that was likely to be lively after some wet weather, and England were bowled over for a paltry 184. On the second day, Chappell almost won his first Test as captain on a forfeit when Ray Illingworth took his men from the field. Tailender Jenner had been struck on the back of the head when he ducked into a John Snow bouncer. Snow was warned by Umpire Lou Rowan for 'bowling in an intimidating manner'. At the end of the over, Snow, a volatile fast bowler who took 31 wickets in the series, snatched his hat from umpire Rowan and stormed down to his position at fine leg. There he copped the wrath of the angry crowd, ducking a hail of empty and partially filled beer cans. A drunk spectator lunged at Snow and grabbed him by the shirt sleeve. It was an ugly and potentially dangerous incident; Illingworth called his men together and they swiftly left the field to the accompaniment of the heckling crowd. Sacked Test skipper Bill Lawry, commentating on radio, claimed that the English walk off constituted a forfeit and the match would be awarded to Australia. He said he had won a bet with Richie Benaud that Australia would win the match.

But that was not to be. Illingworth and his men were holed

up in the visitors' dressing-room for a few minutes until Umpire Rowan walked into the room and delivered Illingworth an ultimatum: either return to the field immediately or England would forfeit the match. Illingworth reluctantly agreed to the demand, and resumed the drama on field. Coming into the final day's play Australia, needing 223 for victory, was 5/123. Victory was in sight, but Australia's last five wickets fell for 29 runs and England won back the Ashes.

In the six Test matches of the series, Ian Chappell scored a total of 452 runs at 37.67, with two centuries and in all first-class matches in 1970/71, he scored 1210 runs at an average of 48.40. That year Chappell collected another feather in his cap when South Australia won the Sheffield Shield in his first season as state captain. Ian played seven matches for South Australia that summer, scoring 648 runs at 58.80. Brilliant South African batsman Barry Richards played for South Australia that year too, hoping to gain experience of Australian wickets in readiness for the proposed South African tour of 1971/72. Over the course of the season Richards scored a Bradman-like 1145 runs at 104.09, including a great 356 against Western Australia in Perth, against an attack which included Graham McKenzie, Dennis Lillee and Tony Lock.

At the end of the first day's play in the deciding Sheffield Shield match against New South Wales, South Australia was 3/513, with Richards unconquered on 325. Ian Chappell scored a century in 144 minutes that day and a local reporter later described the knock as 'sluggish'. South Australia needed to beat New South Wales outright in Adelaide to ensure the Sheffield Shield was in its grasp. Richards batted in the second innings with a broken bone in his right hand, an injury sustained when hit by a ball from Dave Renneberg. Despite the injury, Richards hit New South Wales leg spinner Kerry O'Keeffe through the covers for three consecutive boundaries with only his left hand on the bat.

Ian declared and South Australia wrapped up the game, taking the shield.

As expected, the South African tour of Australia was cancelled. In its place a World XI was selected. The team included South Africans Graeme and Peter Pollock and Hylton Ackerman, West Indians Rohan Kanhai, Garry Sobers and Clive Lloyd, Indians Sunil Gavaskar, Bishan Bedi and Farokh Engineer, Pakistanis Zaheer Abbas and Asif Masood, Englishmen Norman Gifford, Tony Greig, Bob Taylor, Richard Hutton and the Kiwi Bob Cunis. Ian Chappell was eagerly looking forward to the challenge, thrilled that his first full series as Australian captain was against a team led by Garry Sobers.

After a draw against Victoria and a comfortable win over Queensland, the World XI was ready to face Ian Chappell's Australians in Brisbane. Australia batted first with Chappell hitting a dazzling 145. Stackpole also hit a century and Ian called a halt to the slaughter with his team just four down for 389, Doug Walters not out on 75. Centuries to Kanhai (112) and Ackerman (101) saw the World XI declare, also just four down. Both Chappell and Sobers were keen to play attractive cricket and go for a victory. In the end the weather beat them and the game was drawn, but not before Chappell had stamped his authority on the team with a second hundred.

The second big game against the World XI was in Perth. Australia again batted first on the pacy WACA wicket and Ian Chappell (56), Keith Stackpole (55) and Doug Walters (125) were the main scorers in Australia's 349. Then Dennis Lillee cut loose, bowling like the wind to take an incredible 8/29 (his last six wickets for none), demolishing the World XI for 59. Ian learnt a good deal about the character of his spearhead that day: 'Dennis had 2/29 and even though he told me he had just about had it, I asked him for one more over. I never regret having done so, because he kept bowling and took another six wickets to end up with a career best 8/29.'

In later years Chappell was criticised for over-bowling Lillee. 'There may have been a bit of truth in that,' he concedes, 'but I'd prefer to believe that on all occasions I went to Dennis I asked him how he felt. The real problem was that Dennis didn't know how to say "No" to an offer to bowl. I guess, however, there were times when I asked him for one more over, knowing that he was tired.'

Ian Chappell had always held Garry Sobers in the highest esteem, and the innings the West Indian maestro played in the third international at the MCG, after getting a first-ball duck in the first innings, is generally credited with being one of the greatest of all time.

'We were three down for next to nothing in the first innings when I came in to replace Graeme Pollock, who had just gone to Lillee,' Sobers recalled. 'First ball, Dennis dropped it short and, probably conditioned by Perth, I played my stroke too soon and Keith Stackpole caught me down by his ankle in the slips. Out first ball—to Lillee again. In the dressing-room afterwards I told Ian Chappell, within earshot of Lillee: "What's up with this fellow, Ian? I've met him in three innings now and every time he's let me have a bouncer first up. Tell him I can bowl them too."'

Lillee, buoyed by an early wicket, tried to york Sobers's first ball in the World XI second innings, but the great man thrashed the ball straight down the ground. That was the beginning of an extraordinary exhibition of batting. In the first three overs from Lillee and Massie, Sobers raced to 30. At stumps he was 139 not out. After breaking for a rest day, he resumed his knock, hitting a magnificent 254 in a total of six hours and 16 minutes, carving up the attack to the tune of 35 fours and two successive sixes off Kerry O'Keeffe. Don Bradman was moved to say that Sobers's innings was the greatest he had seen from anyone in Australia.

Chappell ranked Sobers's innings with the 251 he scored for South Australia against New South Wales and Barry Richards's extraordinary 325 in a day for South Australia against Western Australia in Perth.

Some of Garry's shot-making was unbelievable, especially his square cutting. When I looked back at film of that innings I kept asking myself why on earth I retained two slips and a gully for Sobers. I spoke with Richie Benaud after that match about captaincy and he told me not to worry—that I couldn't contain Sobers. Richie said, 'Nobody can, and I had plenty of experience trying. The only advice I can give you is not to bother with a gully fieldsman. He does hit the ball a little in the air in that area, but the cricketer hasn't yet been born who can catch what he hits there.'

Chappell is often asked about what was said on the field in his time. 'The lower the grade of cricket, the more likely there are angry verbal clashes.' He explains:

There is a bloody good reason for that because you don't upset good players, and I always use Garry as an example. If you are playing against Garry Sobers you hope that he gets a hundred and he gets bored with it. You don't want to upset him and guarantee that he'll get 200. When he got the 254 in Melbourne in the World XI series, he was 139 not out on the night before the rest day. We were in the World XI room that night and Garry was sitting alone having a beer. That was unusual for Garry to be by himself. He was always in the thick of things. He called me over and he said, 'Ian, Prue's [Garry's wife] left me.'

'Shit Garry, if that's what's annoying you, give me her phone number, I'll ring her and tell her to come back to you immediately.'

To me he was that sort of bloke. The last thing in the world you wanted to do was to annoy Garry. He had the ability and the temperament to perform and was at his most dangerous when he was annoyed.

You know I always appreciated Garry treating me as an equal from day one. As an 18-year-old kid coming into the South Australia side he just treated me as an equal. He wasn't doing me any special favours, he just treated everyone the same. Not only was he a great cricketer, but he is a great human being.

Forty years after South Australia won the Sheffield Shield in 1963/64 a team reunion was held in Adelaide. The players present remembered a special piece of play by Garry Sobers.

All the blokes at the reunion vividly remember it. I think we all pinched ourselves and wondered whether this really happened. Anyway, it was just before lunch and [South Australian leg spinner] Rex Sellers was bowling to the left-hander Ian Huntington. The outcome of this game would determine who would win the Shield. South Australia in those days rarely beat Victoria and we had them right in the cart at lunch. I think they were five or six down and in the last over before lunch. Huntington had obviously decided to play for lunch. And he played one or two defensive prods and Garry is at backward short leg. He's seen him play one or two balls and the very next ball Garry moved forward as the ball was delivered and he put his hand down on the pitch and Huntington played it straight down into his hand.

We were all thinking, 'Did this really happen?' It was just a brilliant piece of cricket thinking.

Thanks to Sobers's amazing 254, the World XI reached a total of 514, then bowled Australia out for 317, Bedi and Intikhab getting 4/81 and 3/83 respectively. With all the excitement of Sobers's stunning 254, few remembered Doug Walters's splendid 127 in the Australian second innings, in which he completed a century in one session. The World XI won the match by 96 runs. The Sydney match was drawn and the World XI took the series two to one by winning in Adelaide, where Ian Chappell and Graeme Pollock made memorable hundreds.

Soon after, the team for the 1972 Ashes tour was named, with Ian Chappell as captain and Keith Stackpole as his deputy. Chappell had a scare when, during a medical check before the tour, a small lump on his chest was diagnosed as cancerous. However, it was cut out under a local anaesthetic and he was relieved to be given the all clear. He was about to lead an enthusiastic young side to England in the quest to regain the Ashes.

Four

1972: The defining tour

Ray Steele held up a newspaper: 'Aussies take loss lying down' . . . He looked about the room and said loudly, 'Pig's bloody arse we do!'

Ian Chappell and Doug Walters flew out of Australia a few days before the rest of the 1972 team. They headed for Kingston, Jamaica where they were to play in a two-day double-wicket tournament that had been arranged as a testimonial for Garry Sobers. Chappell was grateful to get the chance to help make the benefit a success. They then flew on to London, arriving some twelve hours before the rest of the side flew in from San Francisco. Ian was wearing a mauve safari suit, which raised a few eyebrows among the more conservative cricket correspondents assembled at Heathrow.

Although new to captaincy at this level, Chappell learnt

quickly, and from the outset argued that eleven heads are better than one. He empowered his players and encouraged them to play with flair. Back in Australia, Labor's 'It's Time' election campaign was gaining momentum and a change in government seemed inevitable. Time indeed: time for Gough Whitlam to become the first Labor prime minister in 23 years and time for the Australian cricket team to start winning Test matches. New South Wales opener Bruce Francis had replaced Lawry, Western Australian batsman Ross Edwards was there in place of Ian Redpath, and New South Wales all-rounder David Colley had replaced McKenzie. All three of the new members deserved their chance and, although Australia might well have won back the Ashes with Lawry in the team, Chappell never once lamented the loss of the three men who missed selection. He was hell-bent on creating an environment of trust within the collective; a philosophy which worked brilliantly, for the players respected being given the freedom to play the game the way they wanted.

Tired after a long flight, the Australian side attended a press conference where Australian team manager Ray Steele likened the 1972 team to the 1930 side—the last Australian touring team to win back the Ashes in England. Steele drew parallels between Chappell and Vic Richardson (vice-captain of the 1930 side), whose attacking style of leadership for South Australia and later for Australia in South Africa in 1935/36 won universal acclaim. Steele said Richardson's grandson, Ian Chappell, had a similar style.

'We have come here with two aims,' Steele said, 'to win the series and reclaim the Ashes and, if we are good enough, to do something for the game of cricket. It is our dearest wish to do this. The game still has tremendous support and the affection of millions of people and we shall try to play the type of cricket that will please them. We are aiming to win every game we play. We'll always be there when the whips are cracking and we hope that this will be one of the great series.' Steele then paused and grinned, his whole tanned face lit up, 'But I would add that it always takes two to tango.'

The English press had already written this young Australian team off; the theme that it was 'the worst Australian team to reach English shores' was catching and, to the team at least, amusing. To a man, they were sure they would be able to show the Poms that they could actually play good, attractive cricket. Early in the tour, Bill Edrich (former Middlesex and England all-rounder) was one of the few English critics to give Ian Chappell's 1972 Australians any chance of winning back the Ashes. Writing in *The News of the World*, Edrich lauded the Aussies:

They have already shown against Worcestershire, Hampshire and the MCC that given the half-chance they are going all out to win by aggressive stroke play. They love to hit the ball, from opener Keith Stackpole, through to the two Chappells, Doug Walters and Graeme Watson, down to wicket-keeper/ batsman Rodney Marsh at number eight. If we don't adopt an aggressive policy, then I'm afraid the Aussies will regain the Ashes.

It was a case of Australia's youth pitted against England's old guard. Even before the first Test at Manchester got under way Ray Illingworth, who had just turned 40, was leading a team dubbed 'Dad's Army'. Illingworth was often seen at Lord's sizing up the opposition. He had been keen to see Dennis Lillee, and the new boys such as Hammond, Colley, Francis and Edwards in action. He also wanted to assess the form of key batsmen such as the flamboyant Stackpole, the enigmatic Walters, the stylish Sheahan and, most importantly, Ian and Greg Chappell—the backbone of the Australian batting. Ray Steele was a bit warlike in his praise of the young team, claiming, 'We have youth on our side. We have a good captain and all our batsmen like to hit the ball. We have three young bowlers of genuine pace and a fourth who moves the ball about in the air.'

Ian Chappell's words, unlike his fashionable clothes, were more circumspect. 'Australian cricket is stronger than when England came to our shores more than a year ago. Then we had a number of players who were establishing themselves in their Sheffield Shield sides. Now there is nobody who has not had three or four seasons' experience.' The English people liked Ian's style. They saw him as a straight shooter and he won them over immediately. The public sensed a refreshing openness, warmth and honesty in Ian.

When England won the Ashes 'down-under' in 1970/71, it was the pace and fire of England's John Snow that turned the tables on Australia. Ray Illingworth wrote in *The Evening News*:

> Whatever happens on the field in the Tests, especially between the Australian batsmen and John Snow, I fancy there will be another little battle going on off the wicket— between John and Aussie skipper Ian Chappell. A colourful one too. Ian has always been a snappy dresser and he looks as though he has brought with him a neat line in mauve and purple suits. Ian even surprised his colleagues the other day when he appeared in a red velvet jacket with black and yellow striped trousers! That's enough to make Snowy envious, for he has picked up some fancy items himself on various trips. It should be quite a meeting when they come face-to-face off the field.

Within days of their arrival in England the Australians had formed a tight unit, with a collective resolve to prove themselves to their supporters and their detractors alike. They gelled. In London, the Australians stayed at the Waldorf Hotel, a couple of hundred yards from Australia House, near Fleet Street and The Strand. The players loved the atmosphere of the theatres and the old market area of London, awash with people and always buzzing. The team room, with its first-floor bay windows, provided a superb view of The Aldwych—a one-way horse-shoe-shaped traffic way—with its non-stop parade of cars, trucks, cyclists, black cabs, red double-decker buses and pedestrians.

The team room was very much the hub, but there was always a good turnout in the front bar of the hotel as well. Chappell had his captain's allowance and it was hard for anyone else to buy a beer when he was at the bar. His company was enjoyable and there was always something to learn, not just from his string of funny yarns, but from his cricket knowledge and his respect for the game and its traditions. It was all a bit surreal; they rubbed shoulders with the likes of Mick Jagger and the actor Ed Devereaux. Jagger loved a pint of ale and he enjoyed mixing with Ian and the young emerging star fast-bowler, Dennis Lillee. Devereaux, probably best known for his role in *Skippy the Bush Kangaroo*, was one of the Australians' greatest supporters and he liked the team's company as much as they liked his. An admirer of Ian Chappell, Deveraux said, 'He reminds me of Paul Newman; he has presence. The guy walks into a room and everyone looks up. You either have that sort of charisma or you don't.'

Chappell jealously guarded his right to relax in the bar and refused to sign autographs there. He would say, 'Look mate, this place is our home away from home. It is our lounge-room, if you like. Now you wouldn't barge into my lounge-room demanding autographs, so don't do it here.' Some of the players, including Ian's brother Greg, were uncomfortable with Ian's attitude to the bar-room autograph hunters, as the odd one would persist and become demanding and Chappell would get his back up and tell the bloke to piss off. Greg Chappell reckoned it was better to spend 30 seconds signing an autograph than have a five-minute argument. Yet at the cricket ground, Ian was always willing to sign a bat, a cap or book for a cricket follower. He was always generous with his time with kids—a sure acknowledgement of his roots and how tough it was making his way in the game as a youngster.

There was always a cassette playing on the team bus: Don McLean's *American Pie*, Johnny Nash's *I Can See Clearly Now*, Elton John's *Crocodile Rock*, Helen Reddy's *I Am Woman*, Roberta Flack's *The First Time Ever I Saw Your Face*, Billy Thorpe and the Aztec's *Most People I Know Think that I'm Crazy* and John Lennon's *Imagine*. At the team meeting on the eve of the first Test to be played at Old Trafford, Manchester, Greg Chappell, Paul Sheahan and Ross Edwards performed a song for the side. Edwards was on guitar accompanying Chappell and Sheahan as they sang the lyrics to a song the threesome had composed during coach trips between venues. It became the team song, the first verse reflecting the wet start to the tour:

> *My eyes are dim, I cannot see.*
> *The rain is pissing down on me.*
> *The rain is pissing down on me …*
> *There was Ian, Ian, in their pockets peeing on the tour, on the tour.*
> *There was Ian, Ian in their pockets peeing on the Aussie–England tour.*
> *There was Stack, Stack, needing saunas front and back, on the tour, on the tour.*
> *There was Stack, Stack, needing saunas front and back on the Aussie–England*
>   *tour.*

There was lots more in the same vein:

> *There was FOT, FOT giving the vee a lot …*
> *There was Ross, Ross giving the port a toss …*
> *There was Cast, Cast, giving the boys a blast …*

FOT ('flipping old tart') was Dennis Lillee, Ross was Edwards, and Ray Steele was known to the team as 'Cast' or 'Castor'.

Such were their talents that the trio found themselves making two records, *Here Come the Aussies* and *Bowl a Ball, Swing a Bat*. Both records were produced by Penny Farthing Records and recorded at a dingy studio, somewhere near Marble Arch in London, in the wee hours of the morning, sustained by ample supplies of cold beer and collective cheer. While not exactly in the league of the Rolling Stones, *Here Come the Aussies* was a hit for a week in Perth.

Australia lost that first Test by 89 runs, but there were some good performances. Dennis Lillee took 2/40 and 6/66, Keith Stackpole had a splendid batting double with 53 and 67, and Rod Marsh belted a superb 91 in the Australian second innings, hitting the genial left-arm spinner Norman Gifford for four sixes. But it was a brave end to a lost cause. Ian Chappell was out for a duck, hooking at Tony Greig. He hit the ball well, only to be caught on the fine-leg boundary. English captain Ray Illingworth was delighted to have Chappell out early. 'Ian passed me at cover and I said to him, "Bloody good shot for nowt, lad," and he just laughed and continued on his way. Ian was prepared to take a risk. He attacked. I identified with that style of captaincy, because I liked to set out to win from the outset.'

'Chappelli was like me in that he treated his men like men,' Illingworth recalled in 2004. 'He gained their trust and they performed well for him. I place Ian Chappell as a top-notch captain. I played under Richie Benaud in a Commonwealth tour and found him to be brilliant. Chappelli, for me, is as good a captain as Richie Benaud. I don't think I can give higher praise than that. I remember a match at Lord's in 1972. I was leading MCC and there was a lot of swearing going on. Even John Inverarity said a few words and I burst out laughing because that wasn't his go, was it? Ian was all about trying to toughen up his men. He did that and even though the umpires made reports in that match, things settled down. But the Aussies got tougher and a whole lot better as the series wore on . . . Chappelli was a bloody good cricketer. He was a brilliant slip fieldsman, could bowl his leg breaks pretty well and was a superb batsman. I really enjoyed playing cricket against Ian Chappell's Australians. That, to me, was a great contest. In recent times, the last ten years or so, Australia has been so far on top that there has been no contest. Whoever leads them has it very easy.'

Losing that first Test at Manchester was tough on the players; they felt empty and were desperate to succeed. Chappell told them the loss was 'not the end of the world, nor the end of the tour. We have a long way to go.' In the team room, Ray Steele held up a newspaper with a banner headline, 'Aussies take loss lying down'. He removed his horn-rimmed glasses, placed them on the newspaper in front of him, looked about the room and said loudly, 'Pig's bloody arse we do!'

Ian Chappell had now led Australia in two Tests and had lost both. The team wanted to drag Australia out of its losing streak. They wanted it for themselves and they wanted it for Ian Chappell.

God chose Thomas Lord to find cricket's promised land. The first ground he made was on a patch of earth near what is now Dorset Square, and it was here in 1787 as the First Fleet was sailing towards the Great South Land that Middlesex and Essex met for the first time. In 1811, the MCC headquarters moved to a second site at North Bank finally settling upon the ground we all know and love as Lord's at St John's Wood in 1814. Lord's Pavilion was built in 1889 at a cost of £21 000, its architect, Thomas Verity, having an acute sense of humour, for the little window over the members' urinal affords the best view of the ground's Test wicket. Over the years, Australian teams have had a good record at Lord's.

In the second Test of the 1972 Ashes series, England batted first and Bob Massie, on debut, clean bowled Boycott for eleven with a late-dipping inswinger, running through Illingworth's men to take 8/84 from 32.5 overs in an England total of 272. For Australia, Stackpole and Bruce Francis fell early, but Ian Chappell steadied the ship. He played aggressively, hooking one six and dominating the partnership with brother Greg before he fell for 56 trying to hook Snow. Greg Chappell went on to bat for six-and-a-quarter hours for a majestic 131 in an innings of immaculate style and grace, a knock of near perfection that received a standing ovation. A brilliant young batsman had made his mark. Ross Edwards, also making his debut, scored a solid 28, Marsh smote with great power for 50 and David Colley hit out at everything, getting a handy 25 and giving the Australians a lead of 36.

Massie did even better in England's second innings, taking 8/53 off 27.2 overs for a match haul of 16/137. This was indeed 'Massie's match'. Lillee took the remaining four English wickets, but the Australians also enjoyed a seven-over spell of genuine pace by David Colley, which netted him the undeserved figures of 0/8. Ian Chappell said, 'We all came up a bit closer in the slips and the first ball from Colley whistled through, Bacchus taking it high and to his right. We then assumed our original places for Lillee. It was a terrific spell and allowed us to maintain pressure at the pavilion end while Massie wheeled away at the other end.' The English were skittled for 116.

Perhaps Colley's spell typified the vagaries and irony of a bowler's lot; sometimes the results don't always reflect the effort. However, Massie's great bowling will forever remain in cricket folklore. Lord's was Bob Massie's field of dreams. His performance was the best of any Test bowler on his first appearance in a Test.

There were a couple of hiccups before Australia got the required 81 runs for victory. Ian Chappell went for six and Francis fell for nine before Stackpole cut and pulled his way belligerently to an unconquered 57 when the target was finally reached. The Lord's dressing-room became a scene of wild celebration that afternoon in June 1972. After numerous beers and champagnes—anything upon which to sip and celebrate—Ray Steele called the team to order. 'Chaps,' he said with a huge grin, 'now settle down. We have just received a message from Buckingham Palace. We are to meet the Queen there for afternoon tea at 5 pm.'

The Australians didn't rush the showers—they wanted to savour Australia's first win in some eleven Tests, so there was some confusion and delay in arriving at the palace. The late arrivals were ushered into the White Room, where Ian Chappell and Ray Steele were preparing to line up the players and make the introductions. Ian escorted Her Majesty down one line and Steele took HRH the Duke of Edinburgh down the other. Stopping in front of Dennis Lillee, Ian made the introductions.

'Your Majesty, Dennis Lillee,' he said.

'G'day,' replied Dennis.

Rod Marsh was standing next to Lillee and both he and Chappell struggled to contain their mirth. When the ceremony was over Chappell sought out Ray Steele.

'You wouldn't want to know what Dennis said when I introduced him to the Queen.'

'Yes, I would,' Ray said with a broad grin. ' "G'day," exactly the same as he said to the Duke!'

Ray Steele was like Ian in that he had the unique gift of being able to be one of the boys and yet command the utter respect of all players. For him team harmony was paramount and part of that was that all the players were required to honour their commitments. On one occasion Steele asked if anybody would like to play golf the coming Sunday. Jeff 'Bomber' Hammond indicated that he wished to play, but didn't make it kerbside in time to travel to the course. Steele knew how annoying this kind of tardiness could be for those who are there on time, so he phoned Hammond from the course. 'Bomber,' he said, 'you are supposed to be on the golf course.' Hammond was only a couple of words into a limp explanation when Castor announced in no uncertain terms, 'Bomber, get your arse down here now, and the cab fare comes at your own expense.'

Steele had a heart of gold. When he smiled his whole face lit up and although he loved taking the piss out of the Poms, he always did so with a laugh and a joke. He loved England and the English way of life, but he also loved winning and he realised that a happy team was usually a winning team. A Melbourne lawyer of note and long-time cricket administrator, Steele was a Double Blue at Melbourne University, captaining both the football and cricket teams. He later led the Hawthorn–East Melbourne cricket club and he was a champion Australian Rules footballer, playing VFL for Richmond. Ian Chappell says:

Ray Steele was a terrific manager and the ideal bloke for me captaining my first overseas tour. He handled the players like you do a favourite puppy—he would let the lead out until we got too frisky and then he gave it a good solid tug. He was unlike all the other ACB guys who I had as managers in that he was extremely competitive, and yet he knew not to try and get involved with the cricket side of the tour. His speech at the Lord's dinner before the Lord's Test after our loss at Old Trafford was crucial to the tour being a success. His words were well chosen and perfectly timed. He used just the right approach—he didn't mention our play, just made sure that the level of competitive spirit was ready for such a crucial Test match. While Castor got on well with all the players he struck a chord with Dennis Lillee, and this was important, especially in the early part of the tour when Dennis was struggling with a back injury. I had great respect for Castor as a human being and a manager and it was out of this respect that I presented him with a stump following the win at The Oval.

Golf is many a cricketer's passion. When the team wasn't on the cricket field, the golf course usually beckoned. One Sunday in 1972 Castor and Ian drove 30 miles from London to the Berkshire Golf Club, where they were matched against former English captain Gubby Allen and MCC secretary Billy Griffiths. There they met Douglas Bader, the RAF pilot who lost both of his legs in an aircraft accident in the mid-1930s but went on to fly Spitfires during the Battle of Britain.

What a delight it was to meet this man . . . Gubby told me of Bader's work to inspire people who had lost limbs. He also told me later about their round of golf. Bader hooked into the rough and was thumping through the high grass trying to find the ball when he fell over. There was no cry of alarm from Douglas, but after some time Gubby went on a search for the famous airman and found him lying on his back, with his tin legs crossed. Gubby explained to me that when Bader's artificial legs became tangled in that way after a fall it was impossible for him to get back to an upright position. He needed someone to help him and Gubby offered, but Bader refused, rather bluntly. 'Fuck off Allen,' he bellowed, so Gubby told Bader to get himself up. Bader's predicament, however, was obvious. He really did need help. Both men knew it, but neither would budge. After an uncomfortable silence Bader conceded he needed Allen's assistance.

'OK, Douglas,' Gubby said, 'I'll help you but you must apologise for your intolerable behaviour.' Neither wanted to give any ground, but eventually Bader said he was sorry and Allen helped his friend back onto his feet.

After the second Test there was an obvious opportunity for someone to take over the opening batting spot from Bruce Francis.

I suspected that Invers [the third selector on tour] would offer up his services to open. Quite frankly, I was thinking how I might go about knocking back Invers's offer as diplomatically as I could when the three of us sat down that day at the Waldorf Hotel in London. But, as Invers came up with the words, 'I'd like to offer my services to open in the third Test' Stacky jumped in first:

'Invers, you aren't good enough.'

Stacky's words hit the spot. There was no more discussion about Invers opening. His only chance to play was in an all-rounder's role, batting at eight and bowling his left-arm orthodox spinners. Invers did a good job for us at Headingly and he also played well again later at The Oval.

The third Test, played at Trent Bridge, was drawn. Australia made 315 (Stackpole 114) and, thanks to Lillee (4/35) and Massie (4/43), Illingworth's team were bowled out for 189. When Francis failed again in the first innings, Ross Edwards asked Ian Chappell if he could open the batting. 'When it came time for our second innings I told Rosco that he had the job. And what a job he did. At the end of the day's play he was unconquered on 90, and he had reached 170 when I called a halt to the innings. It looked as though we had at last found the ideal partner to open with Stackpole.'

Chappell was lbw to Illingworth for 50, Greg Chappell hit a brilliant 72 and Australia declared at 4/324. But England fought ferociously to draw the game, with Brian Luckhurst scoring 96 and occupying the crease for five-and-a-half hours. The Australian bowling lacked penetration that day and it proved to be the only Test match of the series which failed to produce a result.

Although Ross Edwards, at 30, was the oldest member of the 1972 team in England, he felt he was one of the least experienced, and he learned to appreciate Ian Chappell's captaincy. He recalls: 'I was inordinately proud of wearing my "baggy green" Australian cap, but I was also overawed being among so many good players. When we played the MCC at Lord's, one of the MCC players, John Jamieson, was hitting Lillee square on the off side down the slope towards the Tavern. There weren't too many fieldsmen in front of the wicket, in fact, at cover I was the only one on the off side. I got frustrated and asked the captain why he didn't put me squarer.

"Rosco, if you think you should bloody well go squarer, go squarer," Chappelli barked. "You're the cover specialist in the team. I've got a few other things to think about other than looking after you all the time." I slunk off to cover and brooded. I felt I had no future with this team. Then it dawned on me—he had just given me free rein to go where I thought best. That opened my eyes to the possibilities and for the first time I started thinking about the game. Chappelli demonstrated complete trust in you and your capacity to perform.'

After a game against the minor counties at Stoke-on-Trent, the team boarded a coach bound for Hove. After an hour or so, the bus left the motorway and stopped in front of a large restaurant, which was soon occupied by the Australian touring party. At one of the tables team physiotherapist Dave 'Doc' McErlane held court with a collective of players. Doc loved to tell stories; while some were true, he always gave them that special touch he would call embellishment and others would call bullshit. Dave loved the touring life and caring for his Test cricketers, of whom he was extremely proud and fiercely protective. He was also a mischievous soul. In the motorway restaurant, caught a waitress's eye, winked and said: 'See that bald-headed bloke sitting over there on his own? He's got a bomb in his bag!' The waitress got Doc's meaning okay—she realised it was a joke—but, unfortunately for Dave and for the Australian team, the manager behind the counter overheard the bit about the bomb and saw nothing funny in it at all. In 1972, terrorism in the United Kingdom was rife. The IRA was setting off bombs in London almost on a daily basis. The entire United Kingdom was on high terrorist alert. Within minutes of the manager's ensuing telephone call, the place was surrounded by a squadron of armed police and army commandoes wearing flak jackets and brandishing machine guns. By the time they were satisfied the situation was under control Doc had removed his horn-rimmed glasses and was sitting quietly in the team bus. The squadron leader and the restaurant manager boarded the bus in search of the culprit.

'A grey-haired man with horn-rimmed glasses, you say?'

'Yes.'

At that, the pair stopped at the seat occupied by our team assistant manager Fred Bennett, who fitted the description perfectly. Fred was frog-marched off the bus and Ray Steele had to negotiate a deal with the squadron leader. He eventually talked him around, but not without first letting him give the team a thorough dressing-down: the words 'irresponsible' and 'night in jail' were used more than once. It was a good thing the bloke liked cricket—hundreds of autographed sheets went the way of the police and the commandoes along with a profusion of apologies.

The Australians arrived in Hove to play Sussex a much-chastened group. Chappell declared our second innings closed at 2/262 with Stackpole unbeaten on 154, and Sussex got the required runs to beat Australia for the first time since 1888.

The Australians' failure to win the Nottingham Test steeled their resolve to win at Leeds. Until then the wicket had been very much a track for the seamers, but when they arrived at Headingly there was a sward of lush green and smack in the middle was 22 yards of dead, barren turf, with not a blade of grass. It looked like a chook yard in the height of an Australian summer.

During a training session the day before the Test began, Stacky asked me to come over and have a look at the pitch. I reminded Stacky that I only looked at the pitch on the first morning of the match.

'Well,' said Stacky, 'you'd better look at this one.'

When we reached the middle, Stacky threw a ball hard into the surface of the pitch and it bounced no higher than his toe. The official reason for the large bare patch in the middle of Headingly was that the Test pitch had been infected by a fungus called *Fuserium*, which apparently thrives in temperatures above 75 degrees Fahrenheit. That in itself was very suspicious, given we are talking about the chilly confines of Headingly, Leeds.

The selection of Derek Underwood in the England team for the first time in the series added to the intrigue. And he bowled like a demon, at his deadly accurate best, providing Illingworth with an unrelenting attack upon Australia which brought him a match haul of 10/82 and England victory by nine wickets.

The Australian camp was angry about the pitch, but Steele and Chappell kept a lid on it. Steele told the players, 'We were dudded, we all know that, but we won't be whingeing about it to anyone, least of all the press. Anyone whines about the Headingly wicket and I'll come down on you like a ton of bricks.'

It was a commonsense strategy, and it made the team more determined to fight back and win at The Oval. At the team meeting before the last Test, Ray Steele gave another stirring speech. He seemed to be able to find the right words and pick the mood of the players: 'We will be remembered as a good—maybe great—side if we win this one and draw the series. But if we lose, we will become three to one losers and that will reflect badly on us, both individually as we play on and hope to retain selection and as a team which failed. Win here and we will be known as winners.'

Then Doug Walters, who had sadly been dropped after a run

of failures, piped up from the back. He had borrowed a pair of glasses and, looking over the rims in true Ray Steele style, he mimicked the team manager's words after the loss of the first Test: 'Take this lying down . . . Pig's bloody arse we will!' It brought the house down. Ian Chappell also lifted the spirits of the players at that team meeting:

'I think we are the better team, and if we go home two-all we will have been seen as the better team,' I told the boys . . . After Doug's comments there seemed to be a 'Let's do it for Dougie' attitude among the team. He was a hugely popular member of the Test squad and his actions that night helped lighten the mood. He did us proud.

England made 284 (Lillee 5/58) and Australia replied with 399 (Ian Chappell 118, Greg Chappell 113). Jeanne and Martin Chappell were there to watch the historic achievement—the first time in Test cricket that brothers each scored a century in the same innings. As usual, Illingworth's team fought hard, coming back with 356, with Lillee taking another five-wicket haul, giving him a record 31 wickets for the series. Australia needed 242, and at 4/137 looked vulnerable, but Paul Sheahan (44 not out) steadied the innings before Rod Marsh came in and smacked 43 off 51 balls to win the match and square the series. Marsh and Sheahan ran off the ground swinging their bats around their heads, dancing towards the pavilion at Kensington Oval. Richie Benaud wrote: 'The 1972 tour was one of the most significant happenings in all the time I've been in the game—from 1948/49 onwards. When Sheahan and Marsh ran off the field I almost wanted to go down and run off with them.'

Marsh jumped onto the table in the middle of the dressing-room at The Oval and gave a heart-felt rendition of the team's victory song:

Under the Southern Cross I stand,
A sprig of wattle in my hand,
A native of my native land,
Australia, you fucking beauty!

The song has now become part of the folklore of the baggy green.

It was a defining tour for Australian cricket, a drawn series that was a victory for the game because of the attitudes of the Australian and English captains. Ian Chappell learnt well from Ray Illingworth, a tough and uncompromising skipper. Looking back after the 1972 tour, Illingworth observed: 'I loved pitting my wits against Chappelli. He was always a step ahead, looking ahead of the game—the hallmark of a good captain. He didn't allow the game to meander along. He made things happen. I noticed a huge difference with the Australian side once Ian took over from Bill Lawry. Bill was a terrific cricketer and a good chap. I like Bill, but he was so defensive as a cricketer and specifically as a captain. Australia had John Gleeson, whom none of us could read, yet Lawry rarely had more than one slip and no bat-pad catchers. Ian would have made more of Gleeson at that time.'

Dennis Lillee emerged as the up-and-coming great bowler and the Chappell brothers had established themselves as world-class batsmen. Wisden's *Cricketer's Almanack* Five Cricketers of the Year included four Australians, Dennis Lillee, Greg Chappell, Bob Massie and Keith Stackpole as well as English fast bowler John Snow as the fifth. Chappell gives Keith Stackpole, his deputy on the 1972 tour, great credit for the tour success, as well as paying tribute to the selectors:

The selectors may have gambled a little when choosing the players for this tour, but I feel their decision has been proved both sound and wise. There are eight or nine automatic choices for the future, and it is a happy situation for selectors when nearly all the players they need have proved themselves in tough competition and are ready to carry on.

But Chappell conceded that Australia may well have won the Ashes in 1972 had Bill Lawry toured instead of New South Wales opener Bruce Francis. The Australian selectors were wrong to think that Lawry would not have fitted into this 1972 line-up. Lawry would have put his head down and batted as though his life depended upon it.

Chappell always made time for friends and family of the players. They were welcomed into the fold as an extension of the Australian team. Walk into the Australian dressing-room in 1972 and you might bump into Dennis Lillee's father Keith, Ross Edwards's father Eddie, former Australian table tennis star Lou Laza, Martin Chappell, Australian Rules football legend Neil Kerley, baseball star Kevin 'Crazy' Cantwell, golfers Graham Marsh and Jack Newton, actor Ed Devereaux and pop idol Mick Jagger. Chappelli created an atmosphere of trust and joy, not only for the players, but for their mates and their family. The room attendants and groundsmen were always treated with respect and courtesy. An invitation to sit down and have a beer with the players was Chappelli's way.

Mike Coward, broadcaster, author and a prominent cricket writer for News Ltd for many years, found Chappell to be: '. . . approachable, thoughtful and respectful of our jobs. He was always mindful of time difficulties, especially in the United Kingdom in 1972 and in other parts overseas. He was also an educator by the way he went about his press conferences. And if you gained his trust he would confide in you and provide background and helpful information. Chappelli understood the workings of the media and his responsibility to it. Unquestionably, Ian Chappell was the biggest influence in my career as a cricket writer. I owe him a lot. I well remember the rapport Chappelli had with manager Ray Steele and his deputy Fred Bennett, and I recall a number of occasions when players, press and officials mixed comfortably and easily, often at a sing-along. These were more uncomplicated days when trust between the parties was much greater and individuals were not pushing their own agendas. Pity there is not greater respect for the respective roles these days!'

In Wales, the Australians sang to a crowd at the Pontelodus Rugby Club. After a team rendition of *Tie Me Kangaroo Down Sport*, Chappell called in his star turn: 'We put it to the club that one of our players could really sing. Mike floored them with his voice and they didn't even question that he didn't really look like a Test cricketer; they simply appreciated his voice, so much so that he was offered £100 to sing at the Mecca Dance Hall the following Saturday night.'

Other familiar faces in the Australian media contingent included Phil Wilkins, Norm Tasker and Dick Tucker. As Mike Coward recalled, the members of the 1972 team and the media got on well. They would meet and have a drink. They knew they would be ostracised if they broke a confidence and thankfully that didn't happen. ABC radio veteran 'Voice of Australia' Alan MacGilvray was ever on hand, so too Richie Benaud, who covered the tour for both press and television.

Ray Steele died in 1993, only weeks after a reunion of the 1972 team was held in Sydney. The reunion was timely for the team members wanted to make their individual farewells to Ray, whom they all adored as a man and a manager. Everyone was aware that he was desperately ill and, although they knew he would fight like hell to beat the cancer that was attacking his body, they sensed they might never see him again.

My respect for Castor remained right through the days of World Series Cricket. While he was a strident critic of World Series Cricket, saying at one point, 'I wish them great success—in Siberia,' he always had a chat and shook me by the hand when we were in the same room . . . I remember my last phone call to him—he must have got the message that he didn't have long to live. We chatted away for a while and then he broke down and cried. It was one of the worst phone calls I have ever experienced.

Five

Ashes to Ashes

When it came to the last over of the day, to be bowled by Willis, Doug was on 93. He needed ten runs for a hundred in a session and we were all betting he'd do it. When it came to the last ball he still needed six runs, but most of us in the dressing-room thought, 'Somehow the little bastard will find a way.'

Soon after the fifth Test at The Oval, which Ian and Greg had contributed so much towards winning, their parents received a letter from Arthur Gilligan, President of the MCC and life-long friend of Jeanne's father, Vic Richardson. Gilligan was a former English captain. He and Richardson played a lot of cricket against one another and, when their playing days were over, joined forces to become a celebrated cricket commentary duo on radio, covering many Ashes contests together. Richardson's oft-repeated lines, 'And what do you think, Arthur?' and, 'That was a better ball, Arthur,' became part of the Australian vernacular. Gilligan's letter is dated 20 August 1972.

My dear Jeanne and Martin,

I thought I would write you in Australia to tell you how delighted I was at Ian and his team's great victory at The Oval. It was a very great performance, coming on top of that miserable Leeds wicket, which spoilt, to my mind, the whole tour. Anyway Ian has led his team magnificently during the whole of the 1972 tour—a very great credit to him and all the boys.

I am sure you are both very pleased to have had two sons who have achieved greatness over here, and I do congratulate you very heartily. I think Australia will regain the Ashes in 1974/75, unless some of our 'Dad's Army' are replaced by young blood.

England has benefited greatly by Ian's team and the whole game of cricket has come to life again when it looked like dying in 1971. We are all grateful to Australia for putting cricket right back on the map.

I do hope you had a good trip back to Adelaide. Meanwhile, all the very best to you both, and you will be able to wear haloes round your heads for many years to come.

Yours very sincerely,

Arthur Gilligan

The 1972 Test matches in England attracted 383 345 spectators who paid £261 283 to watch the games—then the highest sum ever received from a Test series.

The 1972 team arrived back from that epic series in time for the first Sheffield Shield matches in October, and looking forward to a home series against a talented Pakistani side that included Zaheer Abbas, Asif Iqbal, Sadiq Mohammad, Intikhab Alam and Mushtaq Mohammad.

But first the Australian captain had some unfinished business with the South Australian cricket officials. Chappell had told the

South Australian Cricket Association (SACA) that he would be unavailable to play for the state if the selectors picked Pakistani import Younis Ahmed. He had written to Les Favell from England during the Ashes tour, outlining his concerns about playing the Pakistani left-handed batsman, and Favell had tabled Ian's letter at a SACA committee meeting.

We didn't need Younis as we had a strong batting line-up and he was only an ordinary player, so we would have been better off blooding a promising home-grown batsman. He was not a pleasant individual and was less than honourable and as it was my job to ensure team harmony (which was very good without Younis) I was annoyed that the SACA hadn't asked me whether I wanted him in the side before issuing an invitation.

When he got home, Chappell met with Sir Donald Bradman, who told him that Coca-Cola Company had brought Younis to Australia and would be sponsoring him. Chappell accepted this and withdrew his threat to make himself unavailable. But he later discovered, from Greg Chappell who was working for Coca-Cola at the time, that the company had not sought the services of Younis Ahmed, nor did it bring Younis to Australia; rather, the SACA had approached Coca-Cola to sponsor their latest import. Chappell had been deceived.

In South Australia's first Sheffield Shield match, against New South Wales at Adelaide Oval, Younis made three in the first innings and batted recklessly for 28 in the second innings when South Australia was trying to consolidate. South Australia then went on a tour of the eastern states and, against Queensland this time, Younis failed again and the tour selectors reacted by dropping him for the next two matches. (On tour, the captain, vice-captain and one other picked the eleven from the twelve selected by the official state selectors.)

Having the man they imported for the summer unceremoni-
ously dumped from the South Australian team for two of the three
matches on the eastern tour did not sit well with the SACA.
Bradman was livid.

The Queensland game had seen the debut of Trevor Chappell who,
in company with his brothers, made a creditable 67 in a match
that South Australia won by an innings. The following game,
against Victoria, was drawn, Ian Chappell going in at one wicket
for nil in the second innings and eventually saving the game with
75 not out, despite having a badly cut hand after slamming a glass
on a table following his dismissal in the first innings.

Ian Chappell's form continued into the first Test, played on
his home ground in Adelaide, where he hammered the Pakistani
bowlers unmercifully for 196, more than once dispatching
deliveries from Intikhab Alam over the Victor Richardson Gates,
which stand at mid-wicket to the east of Adelaide Oval. Rod
Marsh, with a score of 118, became the first Australian wicket-
keeper to score a Test century as Australia won by an innings and
114 runs. In the second Test, at the MCG, Chappell declared with
Australia 5/441. The pitch was a cracker and the Pakistanis had
amassed 8/574 when, with its tailenders wasting time, Chappell
thought enough was enough. Dennis Lillee stormed in and
unleashed a bouncer barrage against Salim Altaf and Sarfraz
Nawaz. He thought that it might hurry captain Intikhab into
making a declaration: 'I asked Dennis to bounce those blokes,
saying, "You can keep bouncing them until they declare or the
umpire speaks to you."'

Intikhab got the message and Pakistan declared. Australia then
made 425, with big hundreds from Sheahan and John Benaud,
both of whom were dropped for the next Test. This was Jeff
Thomson's debut, as well as the first time he and Dennis Lillee

had bowled together. Thomson was below his best, but Australia still won by 114 runs, due mainly to Max Walker, who took 3/39 from 14 overs, and poor running by Pakistan, which suffered three run-outs. The *Melbourne Sun* summed it up with the headline: 'PANIKSTAN'.

There was more of the same in Sydney, where Pakistan, needing only 159 to win in its second innings, could manage only 116. Max Walker again did the main damage with six for 15 from 16 overs, including 5/3 off his last five overs. Australian cricket writer Ray Robinson wrote in *On Top Down Under*: 'Snatching the most preposterous win in modern Test annals, Chappell and his men trooped off the field like eleven Houdinis freed from a padlocked chest submerged in a river.'

The downside for Australia was that Dennis Lillee, who bowled unchanged throughout the 138 minutes of play on the final day to take 3/68 from 23 overs, suffered serious back pain. Chappell was concerned for his fast bowler, but Lillee unwisely drove himself through the pain barrier. 'Dennis offered to bowl,' Chappell says, 'and when I told him he'd done enough after taking a wicket, he said it was better to keep going because he wouldn't be able to start again.'

Ian Chappell's Australians beat the Pakistanis three–nil and now had to face an arduous few months in the Caribbean against the might of the West Indies. Key paceman Dennis Lillee was still not quite right with his nagging back injury.

He bowled 0/112 from 26 overs in the first innings of the first Test in the Caribbean and 0/20 from six overs in the second innings. It became increasingly clear he had a serious problem with his back. He was nursed through a couple of island matches then, on the eve of the second Test, in Barbados, the press watched as Lillee bowled in the nets with sustained pace and assumed he would be fit to play. But Lillee would not commit himself. He needed to see how his back felt after he had cooled down. When he returned to the nets and tried bowling again, his pace was down and he realised that he could not justify his selection in a Test match. Although he played a few more matches in the Caribbean, mostly as a batsman and fieldsman, Lillee was heading for a long term of painful rehabilitation, frustration and hard work to get back to the Test stage.

The first two Test matches—at Sabina Park, Jamaica and Kensington Oval, Barbados—were drawn. Ian Chappell sensed the West Indians had been stalling, banking on Lance Gibbs, their champion off spinner, to bowl Australia out on the spin-friendly wicket in Trinidad.

I remember saying to Rodney Marsh during the second Test in Barbados that the West Indians were playing for a draw—they were happy to draw the first two Tests. They were banking on a win in Trinidad, but the plan backfired. With Max Walker at his very best and good support from the spinners, Kerry O'Keeffe and Terry Jenner, we won a great Test match by 44 runs.

Max Walker proved the mainstay of the Australian attack. His lion-hearted efforts covered the Lillee injury and Massie's loss of form.

Max was like a machine—just wind him up and he would bowl for hours. I remember after he had bowled 37 overs in 85-degree heat one day in the Barbados Test, Max turned to me and said, 'Geez Chappelli, I used to think Barassi [Australian Rules coach Ron Barassi, who coached Walker when he played VFL] was a hard man, but he's got nothing on you.' Walker teamed with young Jeff Hammond, who made his debut in this series. The Australian selectors' decision to blood Hammond the previous year on the tour of England paid off on the West Indies tour.

The West Indies had counted on Lance Gibbs as a match winner in Trinidad, but it was Doug Walters, who had been dropped in England and failed when brought back for the third Test against Pakistan, who turned the game. Walters was in his element:

Walters is the best player of top-quality off spin that I have ever seen. His bat came at you on a bit of an angle, so the more the ball spun the more likely Walters was going to meet it bang smack in the middle of his bat. He had sparkling footwork and was a brilliant judge of length . . . Doug walked out to bat at Queens Park Oval in Trinidad and hit the first ball from off spinner Lance Gibbs through the covers for four. I believe the drive through the covers against an off spinner on a turning pitch is one of the most difficult in the game. Greg Chappell had just fallen to Gibbs a couple of balls before lunch. Doug tucked into curried goat and immediately after lunch he proceeded to take the West Indians apart. At one stage Gibbs had six men on the on side and only three on the off. Doug belted a Gibbs delivery over mid wicket, one bounce into the advertising hoardings, so Gibbs took the man from point and placed him on the mid-wicket boundary. It was now a seven–two field. The next ball landed in an identical spot to the one Doug hit over mid wicket, only this time he backed away and cut it past point to the boundary. The frustrated bowler waved the man from mid wicket back to point and the next ball was round the same spot. This time Doug hit him over mid wicket for four. Gibbs shrugged his shoulders, threw up his hands and walked away a disillusioned man. Doug went from nil to 102 in that session: the finest innings I've seen on a pitch taking a lot of turn.

Australia scored 332 batting first, with Walters (112), Redpath (66) and Greg Chappell (56) providing steel in the batting. The Windies replied with 280, an even performance, with Rohan Kanhai (56), Alvin Kallicharran (53) and Deryck Murray (40) doing the bulk of the scoring. Terry Jenner got 4/98 off 38.3 overs and Walker built the pressure with 1/55 off 30 overs. O'Keeffe played a major support role in taking 2/62 off 28 overs.

By the time Australia batted again the wicket was a shocker, but Ian Chappell played one of the great Test knocks, combating Gibbs despite a severely sprained ankle. He stayed for four hours, hitting 97. There were useful contributions from Redpath (44), Walters (32) and Walker (23 not out). The lead was 332.

By lunch on the last day the West Indians were cruising. They needed just 66 runs for victory and they had five wickets in hand. Alvin Kallicharran was on 91. Chappell had been unimpressed with the body language of his men in the field and some of the on-field talk:

I was pretty angry. I lay on a bench with my cap over my face. I used to do that, not just when I was angry, but when I needed to think. And I reckoned that it was time to have a direct talk with the team. It was not my way to give a lecture, or anything like that, but the blokes were starting to whinge out there. I got up and told the bowlers that our policy had always been to bowl line and length, no matter what.

'Some of you blokes are starting to whinge and complain about our luck and that won't help us win,' Chappell said. Then he stopped as he walked out the dressing-room door, tugged at the peak of his cap and said, 'Be a good one to win.'

After lunch Kallicharran flashed at a ball from Walker and edged it to a gleeful Rodney Marsh. O'Keeffe and Walker then wrapped up the West Indies' tail for only 21 more runs.

Australia went on to win the fourth Test in Georgetown, Guyana by ten wickets, Ian Chappell again leading the way with 109 and solid support from Walters (81) and Greg Chappell (51). With a 25-run lead the West Indians, batting a second time, were blown away for 109, Hammond (4/38) and Walker (4/45) doing most of the damage.

The fifth Test was drawn in Australia's favour, so the

Australians, without their main strike bowler, took the series two–nil, and with it the Frank Worrell Trophy. Again, much of the credit went to their captain, who consistently led from the front and inspired his team to perform at their best. All those who played under Chappell showed him immense respect, although in Doug Walters's case the respect was sometimes streaked with humour. On one occasion in the West Indies, Walters slept in and by the time he got to the game the players had been on the field for some time. Doug quickly changed and rushed into the arena, hovering around cover point until Chappell calmly indicated that he wanted Doug to field on the fence. Chappell ran Doug ragged that session; every over Walters had to move from the fence at fine leg or third man to the corresponding position at the other end of the ground. As the players congregated at the drinks break, Ian spoke to Doug: 'That won't happen again, will it Freddy?'

'I hope it doesn't Chappelli, but I can't guarantee it,' Doug replied.

By the start of the 1973/74 season, Greg Chappell and his wife Judy had settled down in their new home in Brisbane. Greg was installed as Queensland captain and in November 1973 Queensland hosted Ian Chappell's South Australian side in a Sheffield Shield match; Ian and Trevor faced brother Greg in a no-holds-barred clash. South Australia batted first and scored a paltry 224 on a good track; Trevor made 16 and Ian 70. Greg declared Queensland's innings closed at 5/400. Then, despite Ian Chappell's brilliant 126, South Australia struggled again and were all out for 247, leaving Queensland an easy task to hit off the required 72 runs for victory.

During South Australia's first innings, Ian was at the wicket when Greg was bowling to the South Australian number eleven batsman, Barry Hiern. Greg bowled him a bouncer and Ian, at the non-striker's end, scolded his younger brother.

'Listen, pal, if you are going to bowl bouncers, bowl them to me, not our number eleven.'

'Piss off, Ian. You'd be better served to concentrate on your batting.'

'If you have a look at the scoreboard, Greg, you'd notice I am concentrating on my batting.'

That night Ian rang their mother, Jeanne. 'Mum, Greg's doing well up here,' he said. 'He's settling in okay and sends his love. You'll be interested to know that we had an argument after about ten minutes.'

'What took you so long?' Jeanne asked.

As the new season wore on, Ian's attention turned towards the likely makeup of his Test attack for the coming series against New Zealand. The one dampening note from the West Indies tour was the injury to Dennis Lillee, who would miss the entire 1973/74 first-class season with stress fractures of the back (although he played the summer as a batsman for his club side in Perth). Not only would Lillee be missing, but promising medium-fast bowler Jeff Hammond was also having problems with his back and was likely to be sidelined for the season. Queensland's Tony Dell would press for selection against New Zealand, so too Victoria's Allan Hurst. And there was a string of medium-pacers including Max Walker, trump card in the Caribbean, Queensland's Geoff Dymock and New South Wales all-rounder Gary Gilmour.

There had been only one official Test between Australia and New Zealand up to that point, and that had been back in 1945/46 when Bill Brown led an Australian team including Keith Miller, Ray Lindwall, Sid Barnes, Don Tallon and Bill O'Reilly. The Kiwis were so badly mauled in that first Test at Basin Reserve, Wellington that they didn't meet again until Congdon's team played Ian Chappell's Australians at the MCG in 1973/74.

There were to be six Tests, three in Australia and then three in New Zealand. The Australians won 2–nil at home, although the New Zealanders provided stiffer competition than expected. The second Test was drawn in New Zealand's favour, with Australia left needing more than 450 to win after having lost Stackpole and Ian Chappell for 30 in the second innings.

The Wellington Test was played on a flat pitch at Basin Reserve. The brothers Chappell murdered the Kiwi attack, with Ian hitting a brilliant 145 and Greg scoring 247 not out, before Ian mercifully called a halt to the slaughter at 6/511. The New Zealanders replied with a tidy 484, with Congdon getting 132 and Brian Hastings a classy 101. Australia savaged the Kiwis in the second innings and once again it was the Chappell brothers—Ian 121 and Greg 133—who dominated. In the end though the game eventually petered out to a tame draw. It was the first time on record that two brothers had both scored a century in each innings in a Test, and only the second time it had been achieved in first-class cricket.

More history was made when New Zealand won the second Test, played at Lancaster Park, Christchurch, by five wickets, mainly due to centuries in both innings by Glenn Turner, who scored 110 and 101 not out. Turner played splendidly, although the game soured late in the piece. As the Kiwis were approaching their historic win, the tension was high. Turner was a fine opening batsman, but he had annoyed the hell out of Chappell's team, padding Max Walker away constantly as the many appeals for lbw fell upon deaf ears. The Australians felt Turner had been given more than enough leeway by the umpires, and when Umpire Bob Monteith signalled six when clearly the ball had bounced before going over the fence something had to give. As Turner lent on his bat at the non-striker's end, with his legs crossed and a hint of a smug smile, Chappell hurried across from slip to question the umpire.

'Hey Bob, where did that bloody ball bounce?' he asked.

Turner interrupted and Chappell turned towards him, giving him the full blast. 'Shut up, pal, it's none of your business. The umpires have to make the decision here, not you.'

Ian continued to pursue his line of questioning with Umpire Monteith, asking where, in Bob's opinion, the ball had bounced. But Turner kept butting in and eventually Chappell told Turner to 'Fuck off'. Turner subsequently claimed that Chappell had deliberately made the comments to unsettle and needle him.

'That's wrong,' Chappell later said of Turner's claims. 'I was angry with him because he was annoying me. He should have stayed out of it. My conversation was with Umpire Bob Monteith. Had I wanted to needle him, I would have done it a lot earlier.'

Umpire Monteith eventually apologised to Chappell and changed his signal from six to four, and the match resumed. After play, Kiwi captain Bevan Congdon came into the Australian dressing-room and told Ian that Turner demanded an apology from the Australian captain.

'Turner can sing for an apology,' Chappell replied.

Congdon accepted that. 'It's all over as far as I am concerned,' Congdon said. But the New Zealand press wouldn't let it go. Next morning Chappell's men were dubbed the 'ugly Australians'.

Losing a Test match is a draining experience. For Ian Chappell, the loss was initially a burden, but later he reflected that more can be learnt from a loss than from a win.

I always used to say to Rodney Marsh, 'Mate, when you win you drink to celebrate and when you lose you drink to drown your sorrows and after about four or five beers you are not quite sure what you are doing anyhow.'

I always thought it was very important to celebrate a victory, because you work your butt off to win, and I couldn't see any point in working so hard to win, then just coming into the dressing-room, throwing all your gear together and saying, 'Bye guys, see you next game.' To me, if you work that bloody hard, you needed to sit down together and celebrate . . . And I realised after a time that they would be sort of saying to themselves, 'Gee, this is fun when we win, we have a bit of a party, so the more times we win the more parties we have,' so that became a bit of a psychological ploy.

But the thing I say about losing is, if it doesn't hurt then I don't know what you are playing for. To me, the pain of losing makes you sit down and think about why you lost. And I always felt that I learnt—and I felt we as a team learnt—a lot more from our losses that we ever did from our wins. Why? Well it's pretty simple. If you've won you've probably played pretty well and you probably don't think too deeply about it. But if you've lost, you think, 'Okay, why did we lose?' I always felt it was a bit like when I got out in batting. For the first half hour afterwards I wasn't a sane person. And I'd probably say the same thing for the first half hour after I lost a match. You go through the range of responses, like, 'They were lucky bastards,' 'We got some shit umpiring decisions,' or, 'That prick stood on his ear and took a catch.' You go through all of that shit and after about half an hour you think, 'Hmmm . . . that wasn't a very good shot that I played,' or you say, 'We really didn't play very well in that game.' Once you come to that realisation, you are starting to get to the point of the matter. But you had to go through that range of emotions first, and to me that's what I was talking about with the four or five beers. You're getting rid of that crap from your system and then, by about the fourth or fifth beer, you start to think a bit more logically and to admit, 'We didn't play too well.'

The 'ugly Australian' tag got another outing during the next game, versus Otago at Dunedin, when, on a bitterly cold day with only eight overs to go and Otago crashing towards defeat, the umpires decided to go off for bad light, but said to Chappell, 'We may come back later.' Chappell thought there had been no deterioration in the light and felt the decision smacked of the umpires intervening to save Otago from defeat. Chappell's reply was, 'If I leave this ground, pal, I won't be coming back.' The Australians packed up and left for the team hotel, which may not have been in the best interests of public relations. They copped a lot of flak and Ian Chappell bore the brunt of it. But the bad publicity brought the team together and made them totally focused on winning the final Test of the series, to be played in Auckland.

They did not start well. Water had seeped under the covers and a large wet spot on a good length made batting difficult. Keith Stackpole was out to the first ball of the match, caught by John Parker off Richard Hadlee. Ian Chappell (37) and Rod Marsh (45) did well on the difficult track, but the star was again Doug Walters. Only Walters looked the master of an attack which included Richard and Dayle Hadlee, and big left-armer Richard Collinge. Deliveries were lifting alarmingly off a good length. Chappell was keen for his bowlers to have a crack at the Kiwis while the wicket was still dangerous: 'I was going to declare at lunch except that Walters and Marsh were still in and I knew they'd score quickly. My intention was to declare as soon as one of them got out, but by then Walters was well on his way to a century.'

Walters got 104 in a session to give Australia a decent score of 221 on a difficult wicket. At stumps that day New Zealand were 8/80, with Gary 'Gus' Gilmour getting four cheap wickets. Australia won the match and levelled the New Zealand leg one to one, giving them a three to one series victory. Ian Chappell's reputation as a leader was enhanced, and his strategy of empowering his men had once again paid off.

With the media constantly referring to the Australian team as sledgers and 'ugly Australians', the public could have been forgiven for thinking that Ian Chappell's men were something akin to the 'Dirty Dozen': a relentless, hard-working, hard-playing rabble who took no prisoners in getting the job done successfully, whatever the cost. Was Ian Chappell the king of the sledge? If there is a perception that he was, it is very much a myth.

Sledging was a word coined years ago and was originally related to swearing in mixed company—a far cry from on-field antics and gamesmanship in the heat of battle.

When a New South Wales player swore in front of a team-mate at a party, that's when the term sledging came about. Normally a few swear words at a party wouldn't be cause for concern among Australian cricketers, but at the time the team-mate happened to be accompanying a lady. The response was straight-forward: 'Mate, you're about as subtle as a sledgehammer.' From then on anyone who committed a faux pas in front of a woman was classed as a sledge—it was a term only used in relation to off-field behaviour. But a later generation of players, unaware of its origin, began to describe on-field antics as sledging and, with the help of the media, the meaning of the word has broadened.

The aggressiveness of Ian and the Australians during the 1970s often caused apprehension among the opposition, but there were no direct verbal attacks. If Chappell swore at an opponent it was in reaction to an insult directed at him. When such insults were flung his way, he gave them back, with interest.

I think a lot of the reputation came about because it used to annoy me when opposing batsmen objected to our appealing or tried to influence an umpire's decision by indicating that they had or hadn't hit the ball . . . When that happened I used to tell them to get on with their batting, leave the appealing to us and let the umpire do the umpiring—and there was usually an expletive or two tossed in. I think a lot of opponents thought I was doing it to unsettle them, but I only did it because it annoyed me and [because], in the case of trying to influence the umpire's decision, I felt it was cheating.

When I'm asked about sledging I quote the Macquarie dictionary definition: 'The practice among bowlers and fielders of heaping abuse and ridicule on the batsmen.' If we had indeed been 'heaping abuse and ridicule on batsmen', do you think respected umpires like Dickie Bird, Charlie Elliott and Douglas Sang Hue would have allowed it to continue? I was never spoken to once by any of these umpires in regard to me or any of my players swearing at opponents.

With an Ashes summer approaching, it was good news for Australia that Dennis Lillee seemed certain to make his comeback to first-class cricket. Chappell went to England in the winter of 1974 on business and was hounded by the British press, eager to find out the latest on Lillee's fitness, and whether rising star Jeff Thomson could possibly be as fast as rumours suggested. Ian sensed the press didn't believe that Lillee could recover from his serious back ailment and that Thomson was just a figment of Australia's imagination. In June 1974, Thomson went on the public record: 'Truthfully, I enjoy hitting a batsman more than getting him out. It doesn't worry me in the least to see the batsman hurt, rolling around screaming with blood on the pitch.' At that stage of proceedings many knew that Thommo was quick, but no one could have envisaged just how fast he could be. And they did not know the nature of the man. Thomson was fast—arguably the fastest bowler to have drawn breath—but he was no killer. He was dangerous in that he was so fast he could get the ball to rear alarmingly off a length but, despite what he said, he never tried to knock a batsman's block off. And, unlike Lillee, Thomson didn't bowl bouncers at the tailenders.

Lillee had become quite the psychologist and was quoted before the series as saying: 'I try to hit the batsman and thus intimidate him. I try to hit the batsman in the rib cage when I bowl a purposeful bouncer and I want it to hurt so much that the batsman doesn't want to face me any more. I want to be in complete control of the situation, and that's one way of keeping hold of the reins.' There was one saving grace: 'I don't want to hit

the batsman on the head,' Lillee said, 'because I appreciate what damage that can do.'

Such words from Australia's two fast bowlers indicated a volatile series to come. England had picked five fast bowlers in its Ashes squad: Bob Willis, Peter Lever, Mike Hendrick, Chris Old and Geoff Arnold. Amazingly, John Snow stayed at home; the emphasis was on pace, with spinner Derek Underwood selected to shore up an end. Mike Denness, the England captain, was a Scotsman, the first of his countrymen to have led an English cricket team since Douglas Jardine, who brought the bodyline scourge to Australia in 1932/33. As the tour went on, Denness would face widespread criticism for not having fought harder to have John Snow on the team, for the firepower England possessed was no match for Lillee and Thomson.

The English team played quite well in the opening matches, drawing against South Australia and Victoria, and beating New South Wales and Queensland. In the Queensland match Jeff Thomson bowled erratically and didn't cause too much concern. But the Englishmen had fallen for a bluff; Thomson revealed later that Queensland captain Greg Chappell had advised his fast bowler 'not to show them anything—save it for next week'. And Thommo had a point to prove.

'I was a man on a mission,' Thomson said. 'This was my second Test match, but it really was my first because when I played that time at the MCG I was not a hundred per cent fit. There would be no excuses this time. I was ready to go and it wouldn't have mattered who I was playing against, I was just going to give them a work over. It just happened to be the Poms. Bad luck for them.'

In addition to his revitalised fast-bowling attack, the Australian captain had a new bat. Armed with his revolutionary 'Scoop', Gray-Nicholls bat-maker John Newberry had turned up at the Gabba nets in Brisbane the day before the first Test as Chappell's men were having their final practice session. Chappell, who was contracted to use Gray-Nicholls bats, liked the feel of the Scoop and decided to use it in the Test the next day.

John Newberry wasn't keen for me to go straight into the Test using the proto-type Scoop, I assume because it was a prototype and he wanted to give it to a few other people to test. But I refused to let him have the bat back. When I decided to use it I believe he didn't come to the Test. He locked himself in his hotel room in Brisbane, worried the Scoop was going to split into a million pieces and that would be the end of it.

Newberry would have been relieved if he turned the television on and saw Ian Chappell hitting the ball sweetly. Australia scored 309, Ian Chappell top-scoring with 90, and the Scoop very much intact.

Lillee had made a successful return in the lead-up games, but was yet to perform in the Test arena. He opened the bowling, with the wind. Chappell had planned to open with Max Walker into the breeze and bring Thomson on first change after Lillee. But impulse took over. He threw the ball to Thomson, saying, 'Good luck, mate.' Thomson's first few balls were blisteringly fast. The players behind the wicket were amazed.

'I watched in awe,' Chappell recalls. 'Thomson was the fastest into-the-wind bowler I had seen. I don't think the Englishmen knew what had hit them. Rodney Marsh probably summed it up best after he leapt for a ball from Thommo which climbed off a length and thudded into Rod's gloves. "Hell that hurt," he said, "but I love it."'

A courageous century from Tony Greig, hitting out at anything wide of off stump—either smashing the ball to it off boundary or snicking it high over the expectant members of the slips cordon—helped England to a total of 265, just 44 runs behind. Thomson had taken 3/59 off 21 overs of sheer pace. Lillee bowled well in support, with 2/73 off 23 overs, and Max Walker plugged away to take the lion's share of the wickets with 4/73 off 24.5 overs. Chappell declared the second innings at 5/288 and once again let Thomson loose on the Englishmen. This time he bowled with even greater venom, firing Greig out with his famous 'sandshoe crusher' and taking 6/46 as England was blasted out for 166.

Chappell was delighted with the victory, but he was still not happy with the balance of the team, in particular with his spin attack.

The selectors didn't pick Mallett in Brisbane; they selected O'Keeffe [who was twelfth man] and Jenner. I went to [Test selector] Sam Loxton and I said, 'What's the theory behind no Mallett in the Test team?'

'Oh, he's bowling a load of rubbish—too much variation in his length.'

'Fucking hang on Sam. I'm playing in the same state side as him and that's not what I am seeing. Sam, he's the best spin bowler in Australia and the one thing I know about Rowdy [Mallet], even if he's not getting blokes out he's going to be hard to score off and he's going to help us get wickets down the other end. The other thing I know about him is that when the fucking heat's on, he'll be there. I can't say that about any other spinner in Australia.'

Loxton had been a member of Don Bradman's 1948 'Invincibles' side, a fine all-rounder for Victoria, a hard-hitting batsman and bustling medium-fast bowler in the mould of an Andy Bichel. Chappell sensed that he was getting through to him, so he went on:

'Look, Sam. We are going to Perth for the next match. Spin's not going to decide the Perth result, but the problem is if you play one of the leg spinners in Perth and they happen to get a couple of wickets and we win the game, then you won't be able to get rid of them. Then we've got Adelaide and Sydney coming up which is when we do need some spin bowling, so for fuck's sake pick Mallett in the Perth Test, then we've got him for Adelaide and Sydney, Melbourne as well—places where it is going to count.'

Ian got his way. In Perth I took 0/35 and 2/32; in Melbourne 2/37 and 4/60; in Sydney 0/8 and 4/21; and in Adelaide 3/14 and 2/36. My role, and that of Max Walker, was to support the sheer pace and aggression of Lillee and Thomson, but it was important to be able to maintain pressure from both ends all of the time.

England was struggling with injuries. Opening batsman John Edrich had a broken bone in his hand and bruised ribs, and a couple of others were in doubt. As well, the batsmen were now very much aware of what fast bowler Bob Willis had dubbed 'the nuclear explosion that is Jeff Thomson'. The team management decided they needed to fly a replacement player out—someone with lots of heart, someone to stand up to a constant barrage of pace bowling. They called up old champion Colin Cowdrey, the man they affectionately called 'Kipper', who had played his first Test match in Brisbane in 1954 and was only a few weeks shy of his 42nd birthday. Cowdrey had stood up to some of the greatest fast bowlers in history: Ray Lindwall, Keith Miller, South Africa's Neil Adcock and Peter Heine, and West Indies's Wes Hall and Charlie Griffith.

In Perth, David Lloyd opened with Brian Luckhurst for the English, and when Luckhurst fell to Walker, caught in the gully, in strolled Cowdrey. The pear-shaped veteran took guard and looked about the field. There was no sign of fear and Cowdrey got in behind the fast men, with neat footwork and the straightest of bats. Thomson struck Cowdrey a number of sickening blows to the chest and ribs, but the man of Kent didn't flinch. At the end of a particularly torrid over, Cowdrey strolled to the other end and said to David Lloyd: 'I say, David, this is all rather fun.' To which

Lloyd, who had spent over an hour ducking and weaving and was still nursing a broken finger, replied: 'Fooking fun, Kipper? I am bloody shattered!'

Cowdrey fell to Thomson for 22, losing his leg stump when he moved too far back and across. Lloyd fell for a solid 49, caught at second slip by Greg Chappell—the first of a record seven catches for the match. Alan Knott batted aggressively for 51, taking the fight to the quick men, but in the end England scored just 208. The wickets were shared between Thomson 2/45, Lillee 2/48, Walker 2/49, Doug Walters 2/13 and Ian Chappell 1/10.

Ian Redpath (41) and Wally Edwards (30) got Australia off to a fair start, and Ian Chappell chipped in with 25. Greg Chappell (62) played superbly in support of Ross Edwards (115) before falling to Willis, paving the way for Walters to come in with Australia at 4/192. Chappell recalls:

Doug was three not out at tea . . . At drinks, with Doug well into his 60s, I said to twelfth man, Terry Jenner, 'Check with the little fella and see what his chances are.'

As Terry handed Doug a drink, he asked, 'How's it going?'

'Oh, it's a bit warm,' Doug replied in his usual laconic manner.

'Not the weather,' Terry said tersely.

'Oh . . . I think I've got a chance.'

That was the extent of the conversation. At no time was there any mention of a century in the session. Nevertheless, when it came to the last over of the day, to be bowled by Willis, Doug was 93. He needed ten runs for a hundred in the session and we were all betting he'd do it. When it came to the last ball, he still needed six runs, but most of us in the dressing-room thought, 'Somehow the little bastard will find a way.'

Willis bounced him, and Doug's footwork, so swift and precise, had him in a position for a pull shot that flew over square leg with tremendous power. The ball didn't appear to get any higher off the ground than about two metres yet it cleared the boundary rope for six to give him his century and exactly 100 runs in the session.

The Australian team then hid in the back of the dressing-room at the WACA and when Walters came into the room it was empty. He had just walked through a mass of clapping people who were deliriously thankful they had witnessed one of the great innings in Test history. The door to the shower-room was slightly ajar and the team could see Doug slowly removing his cap and his gloves and, as was his routine whether he scored a duck or a hundred, reaching for a cigarette and his trusty Dunhill lighter. He lit up and wiped his brow, then looked around, a bit nonplussed at the total absence of anyone in the room. He was hanging out for a beer, but sat there for a moment, rooted to the bench, before the rest of the team finally burst into the room. There were hand-shakes and cheers and beers all round.

Chappell was always a fan of Doug's, not just for his extraor-dinary ability, his calm temperament and the fact that he had the constitution of an ox. 'It is a pity they broke the mould when they made Kevin Douglas Walters,' Chappell says, 'because everybody should have the pleasure of playing with a Doug Walters type—they tend to keep the game in perspective.'

Walters was out without adding to his overnight score, but there was a flurry of hitting from Rod Marsh (41) and Australia got to 481. When England batted a second time, Umpire Tom Brooks approached Ian and reminded him that one of the English opening batsmen had a serious hand injury. Even before the game had begun, Brooks, a former New South Wales fast bowler, informed Ian Chappell that there was to be no short stuff bowled at Brian Luckhurst for this reason. 'I told Tom I didn't agree with him,' Chappell says, 'but he was in charge and so there wouldn't be any bouncers bowled at Luckhurst.'

In the English second innings, David Lloyd was forced to retire injured after he and Luckhurst had weathered the storm. England was 0/52 when Lloyd (then on 17) was hit in the groin by a ball from Thomson. Lloyd, who was wearing one of the old, pink plastic protectors, recalls: 'Everything that should have been inside the box had found its way through the holes and was trapped on the outside. I heard this announcement: "Is there a doctor at the ground?" We needed a welder, not a doctor, to get this box and its contents pulled apart. You know, I tend to lose my voice every December, and I put that down to Jeff Thomson.'

Lloyd returned and took his score from 17 to 35; Luckhurst fell to Lillee for 23; Cowdrey again batted bravely, this time scoring 41 runs and two hundred bruises; and there were some runs from the lower order with Fred Titmus (61) and Chris Old (43) batting well. But in the end England managed only 293 on a flat, hard and bouncy pitch. It seemed that the faster Thomson bowled, the quicker Lillee tried to bowl, which made things very uncomfortable for the English batsmen. During that innings Thomson bowled a ball which cleared Marsh by some distance and hit the bottom of the sightscreen on the full. How would the next man in be feeling? And this was before the days when batsmen wore helmets!

A drawn match in Melbourne brought the fourth Test in Sydney. Rick McCosker replaced Wally Edwards at the top of the order to open with Ian Redpath, and he batted boldly, hitting a brilliant 80. Ian Chappell (53), Greg Chappell (84) and some lower-order big hitting by Marsh (30), Walker (30), Mallett (31) and Thomson (24) got Australia to a total of 405. John Edrich led the English side in the wake of Denness—he had dropped himself—but, despite a great performance from Knott (82), England scored only 295 in the first innings.

Redpath (105) and Greg Chappell (144) scored so quickly in the second innings that Ian was able to declare at 4/289. With the English score at 2/70, the first ball Edrich faced from Lillee hit him in the ribs and he was forced to retire injured.

Umpires Brooks and Bailhache were sensitive to the media's protestations about a so-called bouncer war, and the Sydney Test saw some hot words exchanged during the match when a couple of Australian tailenders were struck with nasty blows to the hand. But Lillee and Thomson bowled no more bouncers than their English counterparts—they just bowled them a whole lot faster and more accurately.

With just six overs left to complete the last day's play, Greg Chappell caught Geoff Arnold, the England number eleven, at short leg to give me my fourth wicket and an end to the English innings. Ian Chappell's Australians had regained the Ashes. There is a photograph showing Greg Chappell throwing the ball aloft and Rod Marsh leaping high and turning in mid-air to see Ian's reaction. Marsh knew how much that win meant to Chappell. There were a few beers downed that night in the Australian room.

The political and sports cartoonist, Paul Rigby, drew a superb picture depicting the English lion, swathed in bandages from head to foot, being carried in a coffin by pallbearers in mourning attire, complete with top hats. The caption was: 'Ashes to Ashes, dust to dust. If Thommo don't get yer, Lillee must.'

Winning back the Ashes in 1974/75 was a sweet reward for Ian Chappell. At that time he was doing all manner of promotional work for travel companies and airlines under the banner of Ian Chappell Enterprises, which he had formed in 1973 after leaving WD & HO Wills. His media work had continued: he wrote for newspapers and Australian cricket magazines, appeared on Channel Seven's *Sunday* sports program in Adelaide, and since

1971 had been doing cricket segments with radio stations 5AA, 5DN and 5AD.

The 1974/75 series is memorable for more than the Australian team's total dominance and the barrage of short-pitched bowling. It attracted bumper crowds and, after the series had been won, an article appeared on the pages of a major news-paper under the headline 'Lillee blasts board'. Lillee, apparently, had been chatting to a stranger in the Australian dressing-room and had commented that members of the Australian cricket team should be on a contract of at least $25 000 a year. This got out to the press. Members of the board were not amused. They sent Ray Steele, a mate of Lillee's, to Perth to have a one-on-one conver-sation with him. Steele admonished Lillee as sweetly as possible, saying that in future he should keep such opinions to himself, adding that this was all for his own good.

It was Lillee's turn not to be impressed; the board seemed more intent on counting dollars than looking after the people who made them. But Lillee wasn't going away. He was echoing in his columns what all the Australian players thought—that they were being paid a pittance for playing Test cricket and bringing in big crowds and huge profits to the board.

The board approached Ian Chappell in an attempt to put a stop to Lillee's supposedly provocative comments over money:

Board Chairman Tim Caldwell came to me and said, 'You better tell your fast bowler to back off a bit in his columns, you know, because we are starting to get a bit pissed off with it. In his contract, you know, we are being lenient allowing him to write.' And I said, 'Tim, why don't you tell him yourself, because I happen to agree with what he is writing.'

Lillee kept at it, pointing out that the champion Australian crick-eters didn't get paid any more than a lowly office clerk. Other players, including Chappell, also wrote columns bemoaning the lack of financial security in playing the game at the highest level. Such insecurity had driven players such as Bob Cowper and Paul Sheahan out of Test cricket before they had reached the age of 28.

The start of the Sydney Test match had seen an off-field confrontation between players and administrators. The ACB secretary Alan Barnes, a Bradman disciple, was quoted in *The Australian* of 4 January 1975 as saying, 'There are 500 000 cricketers who would love to play for Australia for nothing.' Ian Chappell read the piece and fumed:

I had come back from the nets fairly early that first morning of the fourth Test. I had to get changed for the toss and I was back early because I wanted to catch Barnes, and if I did I would have throttled him . . . And when I walked back from the toss, I walked in and there's Redder [Ian Redpath]. He's got Barnesy by the throat—he'd grabbed his shirt and tie—and he's got him up against the wall and he's saying, 'You bloody idiot, of course 500 000 people would play for nothing, but how bloody good would they be.' And I thought to myself, 'I don't have to give Barnesy a burst, Redder has done it for us.'

There is no doubt that Chappell's agitation for better pay and conditions for his players led to the ACB making some concessions. Ian had met with the board just before the Adelaide Test against England in 1975 and, while Sir Donald Bradman proved an immediate and seemingly impenetrable stumbling block, Chappell won a small battle in what was to become an all-out fight for survival. A pay dispute was subsequently averted during the Test when the ACB rewarded players with a bonus and a credit to their two-year-old provident fund. This fund meant a small lump-sum payment for retirees according to their Test experience. The money could be claimed after the player had retired for a period of not less than two years.

Meanwhile, there were reports that the ACB coffers were filled to overflowing by the takings from the 900 000 people who went to the six Tests including the 251 721 who attended the tense, drawn third Test in Melbourne. Television had brought the game into the lounge-room of the average cricket follower, with the television audience in Sydney and Melbourne topping 800 000 on one occasion.

The television era of cricket had arrived. Colour telecasts officially began in Australia on 1 March 1975, but in the lead up to that date colour telecasting for restricted hours was already in full swing. The Australian Broadcasting Commission (ABC) showed ball-by-ball cricket in colour. Lillee and Jeff Thomson, Ian and Greg Chappell, and Ian Redpath and Rodney Marsh became heroes to the masses. Television had already transformed the entertainment business and, likewise, cricket was soon to reap vast financial rewards. The players probably did not realise at that time the financial heights those rewards would reach, but they did feel the need to agitate for a decent share.

Six

A year to remember

If I say, 'Yeah we are going to play', and suddenly Underwood pitches in
this fucking oil and the ball's jumping all over the place and we get pissed
out in half an hour, the rest of Australia is going to look at me and say,
'What sort of a fucking idiot are you to put your team in that position?'

Ian Chappell's men turned their thoughts to the coming tour of
England: the inaugural One-Day International (ODI) World Cup,
followed by a four-Test series in defence of the Ashes.

Australia's first outing in the World Cup was at Headingly,
where it defeated Pakistan by 73 runs, Ross Edwards scoring 80
and Dennis Lillee taking 5/34. Against Sri Lanka at The Oval, Rick
McCosker (73) and Alan Turner (101) had an opening stand of
182, enabling Australia to get 328. The Sri Lankans batted well on
a plumb wicket, with Jeff Thomson in a fiery mood. With the
opening batsman, Wettimuny, playing well, Chappell suggested
to his fast bowlers that he had seen enough of the Sri Lankans

playing forward and that he would like to see how they played off the back foot. Thomson first hit Wettimuny in the midriff, and the next ball was a Thomson special—the sandshoe crusher—which struck Wettimuny a fearful blow on his right big toe. He retired injured and was taken by ambulance to nearby St Thomas's Hospital. Diminutive Mendis, batting number four, had played some good drives and used his feet well to all the bowlers. Enter Thomson; his first ball hit Mendis between the eyes and the little bloke fell over backwards.

I thought we'd killed the guy! Our public image hadn't been that good and Thomson had copped a lot of criticism over his 'Wanting-to-see-blood-on-the-pitch' comment. Bad image or not, our concern was for the little fellow lying on the wicket.

'Are you all right, pal?' I said, glad to see that his eyes were open and he was still alive.

He looked up at me and a big tear started rolling down his cheek and he said, 'I going now.'

He too retired hurt and Australia won by 52. In the semi-final England was bowled out for a paltry 93, Gilmour taking 6/14 off twelve overs. The gifted left-arm medium-pacer swung the ball disconcertingly to run through England, but the conditions were perfect for swing bowling and Australia struggled to get the runs. Gilmour (28 not out) and Doug Walters (20 not out) saw Australia through to a four-wicket victory.

Then at Lord's on 21 June 1975, in what was the 33rd official one-day international match, Clive Lloyd hit a marvellous 102 in the West Indies total of 291, Australia managing only 274 in reply. Ian Chappell top-scored with 62 before becoming the first of five run-outs, three of which were taken by the brilliant young Viv Richards. The Australians watched West Indian captain Clive Lloyd holding the first World Cup trophy aloft, with MCC president HRH Duke of Edinburgh standing nearby. Some 26 000 spectators attended the game and the paying crowd produced receipts of £66 950, a record for a one-day match in England.

The first Test match proved a disaster for England, and for captain Mike Denness especially. On a cold, grey July day in Birmingham, Denness won the toss and sent Australia in to bat. Rick McCosker (59), Alan Turner (37), Ian Chappell (52), Ross Edwards (56), Rod Marsh (61) and Jeff Thomson (49) gave an even batting performance and Australia reached 359. John Edrich and Denis Amiss had just begun the English first innings when a thunderstorm struck and the ground became saturated. (In 1975 the quaint English tradition of covers for each end while leaving the wicket exposed was still in force.)

In the wake of the storm England made 101, Dennis Lillee taking 3/13 and Max Walker 4/35. Following on, England fared only slightly better and was soon all out for 173, with Thomson taking 5/38. Australia won by an innings and 85 runs.

For the Lord's Test, the genial Scotsman Mike Denness was replaced as captain by tough South African Tony Greig. Born in Queenstown, South Africa, Greig qualified to play for England through British parentage. He had toured Australia with the World XI team in 1971/72, remarkably so in that he was selected for that tour before he had played a single Test. Playing alongside the likes of Garry Sobers, Graeme Pollock and Sunil Gavaskar in Australia— seeing from close range the cricket greats doing their stuff—had given Greig great confidence. A tall, right-handed all-rounder, he was big and brash, with an awkward-looking, pigeon-toed gait. There was a certain amount of bluff and bluster with Tony Greig, but he was highly competitive and had a penchant to attack—with bat, ball and mouth. And he certainly made the most of his abilities.

Apart from the sacking of Denness, England's most notable change for the Lord's Test was to include the bespectacled David Steele, a dogged right-hander from Northamptonshire. Steele looked anything but an athlete, but he proved himself, getting onto the front foot to Dennis Lillee on a dead Lord's wicket, which produced a predictable draw after John Edrich took nine hours to make 175 in England's second innings.

At Leeds, England made 288 (Gilmour 6/85) then Phil Edmonds (5/28) wrecked the Australian middle order and it made only 135. England followed with 291, leaving a target for Australia of 445, with plenty of time to make the runs. The bookies were laying odds of nine to one against Australia, but when at stumps on the fourth day Australia was 3/220, the odds had halved to nine to two. Rick McCosker was batting beautifully with 95 and Doug Walters had cruised to 25. Ian Chappell had shown the Australians' intent, opening the batting with Rod Marsh. Chappell's 62 included eleven fours and a six high over mid-wicket off Tony Greig. He was given out lbw off Chris Old, a decision that displeased him. He stormed off, slammed the dressing-room door and took a long shower. But his anger soon dissipated.

I had a premonition that Walters was going to get a century. Rick McCosker was batting well and just before I got given out I was just starting to think that if Rick and I are here at stumps we'll win this match.

And then I got the decision and when I got in the dressing-room . . . I'm swearing and throwing the soap at the wall, and I suddenly thought, 'Shit, hang on Ian, there's a Test match going on and it's a Test match we can win.'

Suddenly, I thought that if Doug gets in before the new ball is due and has ten or twelve overs, he can make a hundred on this pitch easily. I went straight out on to the balcony, draped in a towel, dripping wet. Greg was in and Rosco was padded up to go in next and I quietly said to Dougie, 'Go and put the pads on, Doug.'

'Chappelli, I'm not in next.'

'Doug, go and put the fucking pads on.' And I followed him into the room, 'Doug, I'm going to bat you next. You go in next and get a bit of a hit against the old ball. You get a good start—I've seen you get hundreds on much worse pitches than this one. It's a fucking good pitch.' And when he got padded up I went to Rosco and said, 'Take 'em off, mate, Dougie's going in next.'

Greg Chappell was out soon after and Walters looked comfortable, stroking four boundaries before stumps. Australia needed 225 on the final day with seven wickets in hand, on the ground where Bradman's Invincibles had made 404 in less than a day to win the fourth Test in 1948. The match was nicely poised, but on the morning of the last day Chappell had an early call from team manager Fred Bennett. During the night, vandals had dug holes in the pitch near the popping crease and poured a gallon or more of oil in the region where a good length ball would have landed.

It was pretty early and I said to him, 'I'll just have a shower.'

'No, Ian, you haven't got time to have a shower. Get into your clothes quickly, we've got to get going.' That's why in the photograph, Tony Greig's all dressed up with his jacket and tie and I just threw on what I had on the night before—and I couldn't find my shoes so I put on a pair of slip-ons. We arrived at the ground and the umpires—Arthur Fagg and David Constant—said that the pitch had definitely changed in nature and, according to the laws of cricket, if a pitch was changed in nature, or whatever the wording is, the game can be called off . . . [but] we could, they said, take a punt on playing.

When I saw the dug up pitch and the oil, I thought, 'What do I do?' If I say, 'Yeah we are going to play,' and suddenly Underwood pitches in this fucking oil and the ball's jumping all over the place and we get pissed out in half an hour, the rest of Australia is going to look at me and say, 'What sort of a fucking idiot are you to put your team in that position?' I was a bit reluctant to play, mainly because of the oil. But I didn't utter those words, because Tony Greig stepped forward and said, 'Well I agree with you [the umpires], the pitch is not fit for play and I think we'll have to call the game off.'

And I thought to myself, 'Well, Greigy could have made it very difficult for me because obviously England thought they had a good chance of winning, but he could have left me in the lurch. I shook Greig's hand and said, 'Thanks very much for that, mate, I appreciate that.'

The Headingly pitch had been sabotaged by four people (one of whom was named Peter Chappell) who were campaigning to free a London East Ender serving 17 years for armed robbery. English cricket lost more than face: some £8000 in revenue on the last day from gate receipts and scorecard sales.

The fourth and final Test match was played at The Oval. Ian Chappell batted brilliantly to hit his highest score in England— 192, made in 442 minutes with 17 boundaries. McCosker scored 127 and Walters 65. Chappell declared at 9/532 and England crashed for 191, Thomson (4/50) and Walker (4/63) doing the lion's share of the damage. When England followed on Woolmer scored 149, his century taking 396 minutes—the slowest hundred on record made by an Englishman against Australia. And so on another lifeless, dull wicket, the match petered out to a tame draw.

After the excitement of the World Cup, the wickets had turned the series into a drab affair. Still, Australia had retained the Ashes and Ian Chappell and Rick McCosker were among Wisden's Crick-eter's *Almanack* Five Cricketers of the Year. But Ian Chappell had already begun to think about his future in the game.

I became increasingly conscious that the captaincy was getting me down during the 1975 England tour, particularly off the field. I still enjoyed the job on the field, although the last three Tests, which were all drawn, took the edge off my enthusiasm in that direction. That fourth Test at The Oval was the most boring, uninteresting Test match I have ever played. If ever there was a chance I would decide to go on with the captaincy, it disappeared during that long, hot, drawn-out exercise in run-getting.

Chappell was not keen to go into another tough series with the West Indies in the frame of mind he was in during the final Test against England. Had there been a break of six months he might have continued as leader, but the hounding of the press over the South African issue and the repeated references to Jeff Thomson's 'blood on the pitch' and the 'ugly Australians' tag all took their toll, and Ian eventually bowed to the pressure. He was mentally exhausted. 'I felt I would not be thinking as aggressively as I should in a hard, six-Test series. Even in England in 1975, I found myself adopting a more defensive outlook than previously. So I reasoned that it was time for fresh, new leadership.'

Ian Chappell reckons a Test captain has roughly 25 to 30 games in him as a leader. As he points out, nowadays Test captains are surrounded by support staff and are not faced with the volume of off-field pressures which were once the sole responsibility of the man at the helm. Chappell led Australia 30 times, for 15 wins, five losses and ten draws. Writing in the 1976 edition of Wisden's *Cricketer's Almanack*, Richie Benaud said Ian Chappell left 'a legacy of a very good cricket team with a wonderful team spirit and a burning ambition to stay on top in world cricket. He did more than that, however, for his players. He has had more brushes with officialdom than any other player since Keith Miller and Sid Barnes just after the end of the war, and most of those brushes have been because of his unwillingness to compromise'.

In 1976, Tony Greig wrote in *Cricket: The Men and the Game*:

The Chappell magic was never better underlined than in the West Indies in 1973 when, without Dennis Lillee and Ashley

Mallett who would have thrived on those turning wickets, Chappell led Australia to victory. His front-line speed men were Max Walker, a proven work-horse, and Jeff Hammond, who blossomed under the Chappell mantle. It takes a great captain to bring off a victory like that.

But it's Chappell's non-conformity that has caused the problems which hastened his retirement as Test captain. There would have been times when it would have been a lot easier on himself to agree with any Board decisions, but the first thing he asked himself was, 'How would that affect the players.' If the answer was, 'Not in their best interests,' then Chappell would fight to the death. His method gained Aussie Test players a one-hundred per cent Test match increase, from $200 to $400, and I'd venture to say that wouldn't have come about unless Chappell had stuck to his guns. I also believe Chappell liked the Australian image, and wanted John Citizen to recognise him as an Australian cricket captain he could associate with.

When we went out to toss at Lord's in my first game as England's Test captain, I wore my England blazer, for I believe that's the right thing to do. Chappell didn't and on the way out he said, 'Hey Greigy, what are you trying to do, show me up?' When I replied that what I did was my own business, he said, 'That's right, mate.'

Even at Headingly, when the wicket was hacked about so much that play was abandoned on the last day with the game in a cliffhanger situation, Chappell came to the ground wearing casual clothes and thongs. That was the way Ian Chappell wanted to dress and that was that. More often than not you'd see him in a tracksuit or tee-shirt and his players followed suit. So many people were incensed at his attitude, but that could never take away the umpteen credits Chappell gained on the field. Ray Illingworth and Ian Chappell were surely the two best captains of my time.

Paul Sheahan was an outstanding young Victorian batsman whose cricket career was cut short when he decided an academic career would be more secure and fulfilling. An upright, stylish batsman who drove with elegance and power, Sheahan played 31 Tests, scoring 1594 runs at 33.91 with two centuries. He was 27 when he quit big cricket. He fondly remembers playing under Chappell.

'Ian Chappell, both as a captain and as a person, has probably come under more scrutiny and endured more adverse comment than any cricketer I know. Why? You would be tempted to say "Because he liked it that way"; if you did, you might not be far from the truth. I had the good fortune to play under Ian Chappell in the early part of his captaincy and, entering a period of turbulence between players and administrators that was to continue into the eventual emergence of World Series Cricket in 1977, it was reassuring, funnily enough, to play for a man who was so emphatically a players' advocate.

'Those who were not close to the action will not appreciate Ian Chappell's role in restoring the players' dignity and wresting them from the master–servant relationship they had with the administration. But there is no doubt that he was a man for the times and, with essentially a young team behind him that went on to sweep all before them, it was an exciting period in which to be involved . . . The two things that distinguished Ian as a captain for me were, first, his supreme confidence in his own judgment and, secondly, an unswerving belief in his players.

'Any successful captain would have to admit that at least part of their success was attributable to the quality of the players in their charge . . . but, equally, if players are committed to their captain, they will frequently produce super-human efforts . . . He didn't give a fig for what the press thought or, for that matter, for convention. He knew what he had to do; he tried to convince his players that was what they should do, too; and he got on with it! It was as simple as that . . . History should judge him fairly, rather than fixate on him as captain through an era when our Test team was dubbed the "ugly Australians". He gave a sureness of style and a toughness to Australian cricket that endures today.'

Chappell's closest mate in his cricket playing days was Rodney Marsh, the tough little Australian wicket-keeper/batsman. 'Chappelli made it clear from the outset that he would never ask us to do anything that he would not do . . . When the going was toughest Ian was the man for the situation. Not only did he lead by example—and I believe his best innings were scored under duress—but he was an ace guy, too. He'd come up with a funny remark which would manage to turn our despondency into determination. I don't think I've ever known a leader who could generate team spirit as Chappelli could.'

Chappell had led Australia to the top of the mountain and then shed the captaincy. There was press speculation about who might take over the reins as captain, some arguing for Victoria's Ian Redpath, but Greg Chappell was, to most observers, the obvious heir apparent, and he got the job.

While Ian Chappell had been happy with the way the Test team was travelling, he was far from impressed with the South Australian state team and wanted to get it back into winning mode. Now that he was no longer Test captain, he could put all of his energy into the state team.

Before the season got under way, Ian sounded out each of the South Australian players, telling them they had to take more responsibility and start playing positive, attractive cricket. Finishing last was simply not acceptable. He wanted the other states to respect South Australia, just as his revitalised Aussies were respected by all and sundry in world cricket. There's little doubt that South Australia needed to develop a hardness and a will to succeed that was absent in the previous two summers. Ian mulled over what he might say to his men at a team meeting at the start of the season:

The day before the first game, in the 1975/76 season against New South Wales at Adelaide Oval, I remember walking back from practice at the Adelaide Oval, up those stairs and thinking, 'I need to say something to the blokes.' We came last the previous two years. I needed to say something. And I thought, 'If we really play well, we can come third here.'

And I got to the top of the stairs and I said to myself, 'What are you talking about, Ian? If we work really hard and play really well and come third . . . what's the difference between coming third and winning it? No point in aiming for three. Let's aim to win it.' And I remember saying to the guys, 'We've got some young blokes coming in. That will add a bit of enthusiasm and also give us some young legs in the field. We've got some older guys here who have played some decent cricket and we can get you through the tough times when the heat's on because we've got the experience. But if you [young] guys can contribute you'll help us because you'll bring enthusiasm to the side and give us a new lease of life'. You had Rick Darling and David Hookes, who were bloody good in the field, and then when it got a bit tight blokes like Mallett, Jenner, Woodcock and myself were able to keep our heads and get the young blokes through those situations.

Against the strong New South Wales side at Adelaide Oval, Ian declared the South Australian innings closed at 8/325, with Drewer (68), Chappell (86) and Cosier (76) the main scorers. New South Wales passed South Australia's total and was cruising along at 8/367 when Ian began to get frustrated. He had expected Walters to declare:

New South Wales was 6/357 overnight and had batted on for a few overs after the new ball was taken. I had declared just before the second new ball because you couldn't get any bonus points once the second new ball was taken. Doug [New South Wales captain] and I were interviewed at Channel Seven on the Sunday morning and he said he was going to bat on. I didn't say anything on-air, but in the car driving to the Oval I told him I was going to do something in protest. That is when I bowled two overs of full tosses to the wicket-keeper. I was only going to bowl one over to protest the lack of protection for the team batting second but Prior took his second wicket of the morning after my first over and I figured it had gone from being a protest to a tactic.

New South Wales batsman Kerry O'Keeffe found himself ducking and diving to avoid a series of beamers. He glared down the pitch at Chappell, but it had no effect at all; Chappell simply glared straight back. They exchanged a few comments, mostly good-natured, although the umpires didn't see it that way. Walters eventually declared at 9/372 and Ashley Woodcock (82) and Ian Chappell (97) put on 158 for the second wicket, in a total of 311, a lead of 264.

There was great feeling in this match, with South Australia determined not to be the whipping boys for anyone. New South Wales began well with Turner and McCosker putting on a 51-run opening stand. Gary Gilmour hit 74 and Peter Toohey 65, but it was Walter's wicket that turned the match. Prior had gone to Chappell saying he wanted to bounce Walters. At first Ian told him that Doug was a good hooker and he would be better served to keep the ball well up, but when Prior was persistent Ian agreed that he should 'Give him one.' Prior's bouncer took Walters by surprise, it came on quicker than he had expected, but his miss-hit pull-shot ballooned and fell safely. Prior stood mid-pitch, arms folded and said, 'Hey mate, thought you were supposed to be a great hooker.' Doug Walters needed only a reasonable score to ensure an easy New South Wales victory. He got to five when Prior decided to bounce him again. Doug went back and across his stumps and got into perfect position to pull, but as he swivelled with the shot his sprigs stuck in the turf and there was an awful crack as his knee gave way. As he fell his bat hit his wicket and he was out for five, and unfortunately that was the end of Doug Walters's season.

It was also the end of New South Wales resistance. Prior took 5/80, including a hat trick, and New South Wales were all out for 243, just 21 runs short. Although that New South Wales game revealed—as his performance in the Caribbean with the Test side in 1972/73 had also done—that Ian Chappell knew how to galvanise a depleted side, a number of the team, including Chappell, were hauled before a SACA judiciary committee and given a dressing-down for allegedly sledging in the New South Wales game. It had been mainly gamesmanship, good fun and banter, but that's not how it was perceived by the administrators. Slaps on the wrists all round.

A few days day later South Australia faced Queensland. In a low-scoring match, South Australia needed only 170 in the second innings to win. Ian Chappell opened the batting and took most of Jeff Thomsons's bowling, hooking, cutting and driving his way to 89 not out and a seven-wicket victory. South Australia had another significant win against Victoria at the MCG. (In 13 years Ian Chappell had never played in a South Australian side that had won outright at the MCG.) Chappell failed twice (nine and six) and Victoria needed only 181 to win in the fourth innings of the match. Victorian captain Ian Redpath went for nil, I took four wickets, Prior and Attenborough took three each, and Victoria fell seven runs short.

In January 1976, South Australia went to Perth, where traditionally they rarely won. Going in at one for one after Dennis Lillee had dismissed Rick Drewer for a duck, Chappell strode to the crease and belted the hell out of Dennis Lillee, Wayne Clarke, Terry Alderman, Bob Paulsen and Ian Brayhaw—a pretty good attack in any company—for 117 in 208 minutes, and South Australia declared at seven for 330. Western Australia fell for only 161 in its first innings and 268 in the second innings after Chappell made them follow on. Batting to knock off the required 102 runs for victory, South Australia lost Drewer (nil) and Woodcock (retired injured, hit on the elbow by Lillee) before Chappell again launched himself at the Western Australian attack, hitting 67 in blistering time as South Australia cruised to an eight-wicket win.

By this time Australia, under its new captain, had played three Tests against the visiting West Indies, winning by eight wickets in Brisbane, the same margin in Melbourne, and by seven wickets in Sydney. The West Indies had won the second Test, played in Perth, where Roy Fredericks and Clive Lloyd made big hundreds and Andy Roberts ran through Australia in the second innings, taking seven for 54 from 14 overs. Greg Chappell, with innings of 123 and 109 in the first Test and 182 in the fourth, had reached his full potential and, except in Perth, Lillee, Thomson, Gilmour, Walker and I had generally kept the West Indian's considerable talents in check. The remaining two Tests provided more of the same; Australia won by 190 runs and 165 runs for a five to one series margin. Ian Chappell made his second century of the series (109 not out) at the MCG in the sixth Test, and he was then able to put all his talent and energy into securing the Sheffield Shield for South Australia.

Perhaps the South Australian team's most critical match of that summer was against Victoria at Adelaide Oval. The match was notable for the debut of former Victorian Rodney Hogg on the South Australian side. Hogg had found it tough to make his mark in Melbourne, so had moved to Adelaide. His opening spell was fast, furious and rather untidy. He fell flat on his face once and bowled five no-balls, but he nevertheless picked up three wickets. I finished with 4/38 and Terry Jenner took 3/69. Victoria made 247 in the first innings, then Max Walker demolished South Australia with 6/49 in a total of only 146. Batting a second time, Victoria made 262, Hogg 4/57 and Mallett 4/71. South Australia needed 364 to win. A big hundred was needed, and it was duly delivered by Ian Chappell. He batted for just over seven hours for 171, an innings which *The Australian* newspaper said 'will be recalled as long as there is an Adelaide Oval'. Chappell had good support from Barry Curtin (52) and Rick Darling (41), but when I joined him with the score at 6/225, South Australia still had a long way to go. Chappell by then was completely in control and he made the lion's share of our 63-run partnership. I couldn't hook and when Alan Hurst, the Victorian pace man, tried to unsettle me with a series of bouncers, Chappell intervened.

'Listen pal,' he said to Hurst, 'if you are going to bounce a batsman, bounce me, not our tailenders. You haven't the guts to play bouncers yourself.'

Hurst soon bounced me again and I snicked it into my midriff, from where it went gently to short leg. Umpire Tony Crafter said, 'Not out.' Hurst stood and glared, then Crafter cautioned him for the number of short-pitched deliveries, at which Hurst threw the ball down in disgust. At that point Chappell stepped in at the non-striker's end; lining the ball up as if he was about to play a golf shot, he hit it way back past Hurst's bowling mark at the River End of Adelaide Oval.

'The umpire said, "Not out, pal," he said to Hurst. "Now piss off back to your mark."'

I went at 288, but Yagmich played another valuable support-
ing role as Ian batted on. The score stood at 358, six runs short of
victory, when Chappell was dismissed:

Higgsy [Jim Higgs] bowled me a flipper. It was real desperation time for him as
he never bowled that ball to me normally. It was very wide and I let go of the bat.
But I actually hit the ball and it would have gone for four, well, for three at least,
but it was so wide to reach it I had to let go of the bat with my right hand. I had
to swing so hard to reach the ball that the momentum took the bat onto the
stumps. I couldn't believe it. Hit-wicket bowled Higgs. Shit.

Despite Ian's fall, Yagmich and Attenborough saw South
Australia through to a critical win. However, more drama was to
unfold after stumps. Before the summer began, Ian had been
given an assurance by the state selectors that he would be
consulted on team selection. While he had been out in the middle
guiding South Australia to victory, the selectors met and decided
to drop Rick Drewer from the twelve in favour of Bob Blewett, a
tough all-rounder from Prospect. Chappell thought it would have
been more logical to keep Rick Drewer in the twelve, a player who
had done so much towards the team's position, rather than intro-
duce a bloke who had not played before and was unlikely to play
in the side anyway. And he was angry that the selectors had failed
to consult with him over the team, regardless. He felt that they
could have waited until the end of the match. When confronted
by Ian, Phil Ridings offered a feeble excuse: 'How could we
consult with you, Ian? You were out batting in the middle of
Adelaide Oval when we picked the team.'

'Out there batting? That's my bloody job, Pancho—scoring
runs.'

Chappell then told the players that because he had not been
consulted by the selectors, he would pull out of the tour to

Sydney and Brisbane. The team was on the verge of winning the Sheffield Shield and the man most responsible for its success was going to jump ship! There was, of course, a principle involved and Chappell wasn't in the mood to compromise. Terry Jenner took over as self-appointed facilitator, arguing for the players to show solidarity: either all in, or all out.

Chappell, with Rick Drewer, myself and Terry Jenner, who was an employee of Coca-Cola, a key sponsor of the SACA, abstained from voting. Six supported Chappell and said they would not tour. Gary Cosier and Rick Darling voted 'No'—they wanted to play and not do anything that might preclude them from future selection for South Australia and higher honours. Rodney Hogg said, with a cheeky smile, 'I've waited a decade to go on a Shield tour and you've just blown it for me,' but nevertheless he voted 'Yes' to the ban. Jenner went through it again and took it to another vote. It was nine–nil in favour of the ban. Jenner went to the three selectors—Ridings, Les Favell and Geff Noblett—and told them the players were in total support of Chappell. The selectors gave an ultimatum: the players had until midday the following day to agree to go, otherwise an entirely new side would be picked. After hearing what the selectors had proposed, Ian urged the players to relent and go on tour: 'Splinter [Ashley Woodcock] rang me. He was dealing with the younger blokes a bit and I just said, "You tell Hookesy and Rick, Cosier and Hogg, whatever they do they have to go in the team. They are new in the side and it is their future."'

As expected, the South Australian state players' strike caused a huge commotion in Adelaide, and it was a phone call from Bob Blewett, the man picked to replace Rick Drewer, that finally persuaded Chappell to relent and make himself available: 'Bob rang and offered to stand down. I told him that was not necessary, but the phone call from Bob was the thing which made me decide to play. I had lost all respect for the SACA, and I told them I was playing for the players only.'

Chappell's South Australian team left Adelaide for the eastern states tour with a complement of thirteen players. Good performances against New South Wales in Sydney and Queensland in Brisbane would ensure South Australia won the Sheffield Shield. In Sydney an early wicket fell. As Ian strode to the wicket a wag on the SCG Hill yelled: 'I thought it was one out, all out for your mob, Chappelli'.

Chappell went on to score 119, but rain ruined any chance of a result. Rain also ruined the last match against Queensland, however, South Australia had gathered enough bonus points to win the Sheffield Shield. The following summer, Chappell left South Australia to play for North Melbourne, never expecting to play for his home state again. He'd had a gutful of the SACA. In March 1976 Chappelli toured South Africa with the International Wanderers, a team managed by Richie Benaud. Three unofficial Tests were played and Benaud stipulated that the South African Eleven must include three non-white players. Other players in the squad included Dennis Lillee, Martin Kent and Ashley Mallett, New Zealand's Glenn Turner and John Morrison, and England's Derek Underwood, Bob Taylor and Denis Amiss. Apartheid, however, ensured South Africa remained largely ostracised from the world stage until the 1990s.

In 1976, Richie Benaud wrote in the foreword to Chappell's autobiography, *Chappelli: Ian Chappell's Life Story*:

> It is as a captain and a militant leader and as a person that he interests me most . . . Chappelli took over when Bill Lawry was guillotined by the selectors and his team was in tatters— Australia had just gone through an extraordinarily long

period of not winning a Test match: Chappelli had it all to do. After losing that first Test match, he didn't lose a series against any other country, and he retired from the captaincy just in time. What kind of captain was he? Well, he was a player's man for a start and a great blender of team spirit in a side. Tactically he was very good and he rode his hunches; he was a brave captain and he had one aim in life, to put Australia back at the top of world cricket.

He added another dimension to captaincy that was out of my reach when I was in the same position. He was a militant leader of his men, not quite a union leader, but along those lines. He took on officialdom and still does if he considers they are doing the wrong thing. Sometimes he does it sensibly, sometimes stupidly, sometimes with an inbuilt knowledge of just how far he can go. His men would do anything for him because it was not just a matter of them believing in him, they knew he believed in them.

Sometimes it is difficult to believe he has any common-sense at all, such as when there was a strike of South Australian players because of certain moves by the South Australian selectors for the eastern tour of Australian in 1976. He has clashed with umpires and has been reported to the Australian Cricket Board for bad language, and many Australian administrators have added a few grey hairs in the time he was captain of his country. But it would be a mistake to underestimate the tremendous effect Ian Chappell had on the game of cricket in Australia.

Seven

Duelling with Bradman and Botham

At the end of it I walked out of his office and thought to myself, 'Ian, did you just ask Bradman to fill your wallet with money?'

As a player, Don Bradman had always been peeved over the Australian Board of Control for International Cricket's attitude to the players during his playing days. Yet when he became an administrator of enormous influence and power, Bradman appeared, like many of his colleagues on the board, to carry on as though the money was his own.

After his honeymoon trip to the United States and Canada in 1932, Bradman returned to Australia keen to secure his financial future. His three-year deal with bat-maker Mick Simmons was about to expire. In 1988 Bradman told ABC Radio, 'While I did not want to lead a life that was totally dependent on sport, it was a very difficult time. I didn't have any qualifications and I had been offered a very lucrative contract to play Lancashire League cricket in England with the Accrington Club.' Bradman's fame was such that the nation would never allow him to accept the English offer if counter offers could be found within Australia. Rich offers came from three separate sources: Sydney menswear outfitter FJ Palmer & Sons, Radio 2UE and Associated Newspapers, which published the *Sydney Sun*. Bradman accepted a three-year contract with Associated Newspapers worth £1500 a year, and wrote a letter to the board, 'as a mere formality', requesting permission to play Test cricket and write for the newspapers.

The board took a dim view of players writing for the press while still a member of the Test team, their resistance stemming from earlier in the century when some players publicly criticised their peers. The rules provided an exception for those whose sole occupation was journalism, but this was not the case with Bradman. The permission he requested was denied, upon which Bradman said that he would honour his contract with Associated Newspapers, even if it meant his retirement from cricket.

One of Bradman's employers under his three-way deal was Kerry Packer's grandfather, Robert Clyde Packer, the editorial head of Associated Newspapers. The board, stunned at the weight of public opinion against its stand in the Bradman case, asked Johnny Moyes, then sports editor of the *Sydney Sun*, to set up a meeting with Mr Packer in a bid to persuade the publisher to release Bradman from his contract. Packer told Bradman that he must play for his country, to which Bradman said steadfastly, 'You can force me to write, but there's nothing in the contract which allows you to force me to play cricket.' Packer, however, was persuasive and Bradman eventually relented.

While Bradman was officially banned by the board from writing newspapers articles, he was allowed to talk about the Tests on Radio 2UE. Bradman felt it was unfair that the board should be able to limit a player's income in this way and wrote at the time: 'I must emphatically protest against the Board of Control being allowed to interfere with the permanent occupation of any player. The difference between journalism and radio work is so small as to make any distinction appear ridiculous.'

From his early days in cricket, Bradman had a reputation for being tight-fisted. After his brilliant 334 at Headingly in 1930, Australian-born soap manufacturer Arthur Whitelaw sent a telegram to the Australian team management saying, 'Kindly convey my congratulations to Don Bradman and tell him I wish him to accept £1000 as a token of my admiration of his wonderful performance'. In 1930, £1000 was enough to buy two substantial houses in Sydney. Bradman was never one to breast the bar with the rest of the team, but his team-mates were incensed that the Don didn't even offer to buy anyone a drink from his newfound wealth; he pocketed the lot.

Years later, after Bradman's playing career had ended, Adelaide Oval head groundsman Arthur Lance recalled approaching Bradman, who was then SACA president, asking for a rise in pay.

'Why do you need more money, Arthur?' Bradman asked.

'Edna [Lance's wife] and I are getting on a bit and we are feeling the summer heat more these days. We need an airconditioner and the only way I can see clear to get one is to have a pay rise.'

'No, Arthur, we can't do that. What SACA can do is buy you an airconditioner and have it installed at no cost to you.'

The exchange gives an insight into Bradman's thinking; a one-off payment was just that, but a pay rise was ongoing and, in the long run, far costlier. As a player, Bradman had expressed his concern about payments to players and the financial plight of the

Test cricketer. But when he held the board's purse strings during the Chappell years, his attitude had changed markedly.

Outsiders might assume that Ian Chappell's attitude towards Bradman had been coloured by all the talk in the family home.

Some people believed my opinion of Bradman as a person was prejudiced because my grandfather, former Australian captain Vic Richardson, had clashed with him in their playing days. This was not the case. When asked about Bradman the only thing I ever heard Vic say was, 'He was a great batsman.' That was all he ever said and I assumed Vic wanted me to make up my own mind about Bradman, which is exactly what happened.

However . . . the fact that I grew up in a cricketing family probably meant I began my career knowing more about the history of the game than most players . . . Jack Fingleton and Bill O'Reilly, two of Vic's great mates when he captained Australia on the 1935/36 tour of South Africa, took an interest in me when I was a young player and often talked about cricket in their era. I heard how Bradman had crossed swords with the board over money when he was a player. I also knew he'd accepted £1000 from an admirer when he scored 300 in a day at Headingly in 1930, and when he didn't share the money it was a source of great annoyance to his team-mates.

Soon after Ian Chappell became captain, he led South Australia against Ray Illingworth's MCC team at the Adelaide Oval in the summer of 1970/71. Thanks to big scores by Geoff Boycott and Colin Cowdrey, the Englishmen hit up a huge total. Then it was South Australia's turn. Barry Richards smashed a brilliant 224 and tea was taken on day three with South Australia 8/649. In a chance meeting outside the South Australian dressing-room Bradman said to Chappell, 'I trust you intend batting on, Ian?'

Chappelli declared straight away.

Chappell traces the deterioration of his relationship with Bradman from the time he became captain of Australia. Until then

Glenelg Schoolboys Cricket Team 1954

Phillip Johns, Personnel Officer at Edwardstown looking through his treasured relics, came across this photo and sought its inclusion in the Herald. It is not everyone that gets a chance to play among the "Greats," although at the time of going to press South Australia would probably prefer Phillip to be playing, rather than the lad bottom right of the picture, "Ian Chappel." Phillip is third from the left back row and Bob Bastian, ex H.O. and Courier Sydney is 6th from the left back row.

Chappelli started his long cricket career playing with Glenelg as a schoolboy. (Courtesy the Chappell family)

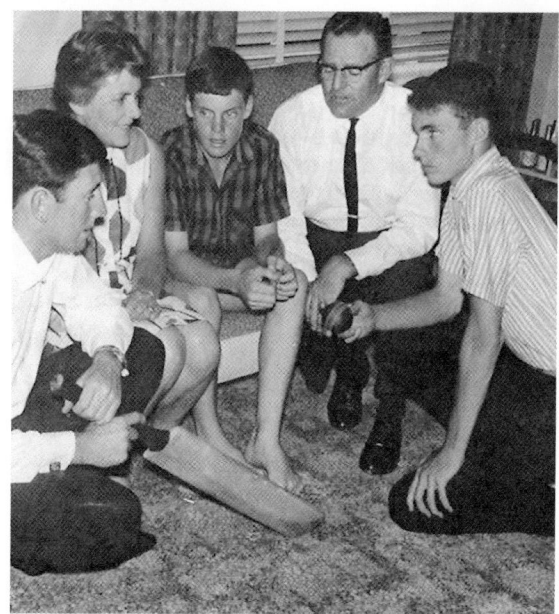

The Chappell family lived cricket. From left to right: Ian, Jeanne, Trevor, Martin and Greg. (Courtesy the Chappell family)

Like his father Martin, Ian (left) played baseball when he wasn't on the cricket pitch. (Courtesy the Chappell family)

From left to right: Trevor (aged 14), Martin, Ian (aged 19) and Greg (aged 14) practising their shots at home on the front lawn. (Courtesy the Chappell family)

Ian with fellow South Australian Barry Jarman. (Courtesy the Chappell family)

In 1963, at the end of his first successful Shield summer, Chappell headed off to the United Kingdom to play in the tough Lancashire League. (Courtesy the Chappell family)

Out! (Courtesy the Chappell family)

Ian (centre) was 21 when first selected to play for Australia in 1964. His brothers were immensely proud of his achievement. (Courtesy the Chappell family)

Ian has always enjoyed a game of golf, despite the formal attire required during this game in the United Kingdom. (Courtesy the Chappell family)

During the Australian tour to South Africa in 1966–67, Australian manager Bill 'Fagin' Jacobs sent this photo to Australian Cricket Board secretary Alan Barnes claiming it was the official tour photograph. (Courtesy of the Chappell family)

Barry Knight caught Chappell. (Courtesy the Chappell family)

The 1972 Ashes tour began with Chappell leading his team onto the pitch at Arundel Castle.
(Courtesy Getty Images)

Between them, Chappelli, Thomson and Lillee took Australian cricket to a new level.
(Courtesy Newspix)

(Left) A very dapper Ian Chappell with Doug Walters in February 1974 just before flying out to New
Zealand for the second leg of the Test series. (Courtesy Newspix). (Right) Chappelli swings Joel
Garner away for a four as Australia takes on the Rest of the World in Sydney on 14 January 1978.
(Courtesy Newspix)

Retirement from playing cricket did not mean retirement from the game. Here Chappelli the commentator interviews Steve Waugh. (Courtesy Getty Images)

During the 2004 Boxing Day Test, Australian cricket finally recognised the contribution of the first Australian sporting team to tour England, the 1868 Aboriginal cricket team.
(Courtesy Getty Images)

the occasional conversations they had together involved Bradman imparting information on batting and Ian following Bradman's advice. After he became captain, prior to the 1972/73 first-class season, Chappell requested a meeting with Bradman. Greg Chappell was at that time working with a large insurance company and Ian wanted to put to Bradman a plan for a provident fund to help retain experienced players in the South Australian side.

The meeting was held in Bradman's Pirie Street sharebroker's office; if you had been visiting Mars for the past 50 years and didn't know the man behind the desk was a cricketer you'd never have guessed it from the decor. I was apprehensive as I entered the office—nervous in the way you are when waiting to go into bat or about to make a sales pitch—and Bradman wasn't the sort of person whose manner eased tensions. As I recall it, there was no small talk and it was straight to the point.

'Would you, Sir Donald, agree to a meeting with Greg's boss so he could explain how the SACA would be able to set up a players' provident fund at an affordable cost?' I don't recall the bulk of the reply but it started with, 'No son, we can't do that.' At the end of it I walked out of his office and thought to myself, 'Ian, did you just ask Bradman to fill your wallet with money?'

Bradman's harangue confirmed my suspicions that the players were going to have a hard time extracting more money from the ACB—and that I should look for a job that didn't involve selling.

After the 1972 England tour, Ian Chappell met with the board to put the players' views on various matters.

I couldn't help noticing Sir Donald Bradman's reaction. He was then board chairman. He sat back for the first couple of points but was very attentive when it came to two points I made on finance and, in his distinctive voice, said, in no uncertain terms, 'No son, we can't do that. The board will not entertain such ideas.' Then, with no more finance to be spoken about, Bradman sat back in his chair and made no further comment.

Because of Bradman's history as a player I expected a little sympathy for our cause. However, when it came time to act as a spokesman for the players in tackling the ACB on the question of better pay and conditions, every time I mentioned player payments to the board, Bradman was the first and only member to speak. He always prefaced his comments with: 'No son, we can't do that.'

The ACB did eventually make one minor concession; they granted the players a $200 bonus per match, effectively doubling our payments from $1200 to $2400 for the 1974/75 series. Nevertheless, this gesture only increased the match payments to a total of only $4800 for the twelve Australian players in the MCG Test, when the gate takings were a record $250 000.

Bradman did have enormous respect for Chappell as a batsman and a captain, and occasionally he seemed to be trying to break the ice. Chappell was amazed on one occasion at a cricket function when Bradman sidled up to him and said, 'You know, Ian, I could never do what you do; walk round the room and mix easily with the guests, whoever they are, a beer in my hand, and making easy communication. I cannot do it.' Bradman stopped short of actually saying that he wished he could have done exactly that, but that was his way. Another time, Bradman surprised Chappell when he approached him soon after Vic Richardson died and asked: 'Did Vic ever tell you the story of how he got to be captain on a tour to South Africa? The selectors came to me and said, "If you are fit, Don, you will captain the side to South Africa."'

'I asked them if I did not report fit who would lead the side. They said, "Vic Richardson."'

'And if I am fit will Vic tour?'

'No,' was the reply.

'Then I am not fit for the tour.'

Chappell says, 'I reckon that he was trying to convey how magnanimous he was; that his not being available to make the tour would give Vic a tour.' But this exchange sits oddly with an exchange between Vic Richardson and Bradman which Ian Chappell overheard in the early 1960s:

I saw Pop [Vic Richardson] leaving the function so I rushed after him. I just wanted to say goodnight. When I was a few paces away from him I noticed he was chatting to Sir Donald Bradman. Broadcaster Alan MacGilvray was a step or two behind. Bradman said to Vic: 'Nice to see your old mate [Arthur Gilligan] get the job as MCC president.'

'Good thing they don't work on the Australian system,' Vic replied.

'Why's that, Vic?'

'In England the president is picked by his friends. If they had that system in Australia you'd never get a vote, you little cunt.'

Chappell believes Bradman's meanness over player payments and his reluctance to help drive a move to improve conditions in the 1970s was the catalyst for the big cricket rebellion which became known as World Series Cricket.

Bradman, to me, had as much to do with the starting of World Series Cricket as anybody else, because I got the feeling that Bradman treated the board's money as though it was almost his own. I first advanced this opinion in the book *The Cutting Edge* I wrote in 1992 when Bradman was still alive. I repeated the claims in the television documentary [*Cricket in the 70s*, ABC TV] because it was an important period in cricket history that needed to be on record and I didn't think the ACB presented the situation fairly when, at the time World Series Cricket was formed, they claimed, 'We've been stabbed in the back by the players'. Bradman was a member of that board, and there are two sides to every story.

Ian Chappell's clashes with Bradman were always verbal and never very heated. His relationship with Ian Botham was something entirely different. Ian Botham and Ian Chappell never quite hit it off. There are two versions of the clash the pair had at the MCG bar back in the summer of 1976/77. Chappell had quit South Australia to play club cricket for North Melbourne. That same summer Ian Botham was in Australia on a Whitbread scholarship and was contracted for the season with the University Club. Botham has not wavered from his version of events, as told to Peter Hayter in *Botham: My autobiography*:

> One night I was drinking in a bar with players from both sides when I overheard Chappell giving it the typical Aussie verbals and rubbishing England. In fact, he was getting so full of himself that it would have been impossible for me not to overhear him. I didn't like what he was saying and I told him in so many words, warning him that if he carried on there would be trouble. I don't know if Chappell was aware of my reputation for thinking with my fists or whether he was intentionally goading me, but in any case he went on and on. Three times I warned him and three times he ignored me. Finally, I could take no more so I threw a punch at him. The impact sent him flying over a table into a group of Aussie Rules footballers, whose drink was scattered to all parts.

Botham further alleges that Chappell fled and that he followed in pursuit, hurdling the bonnet of a car in his mad chase, but fell away at the sight of a police car. Botham denies having gone after Chappell with a bottle or an empty glass.

Ian Chappell remembers the night. By the time he got to the MCG bar, Chappell says:

Botham had obviously had a few beers and he was having a lot to say in a very loud voice. He made a couple of comments and I can't remember exactly what they were, but Botham said something about an Australian player to which I responded: 'Yeah, you're a typical county player, you're the sort of player who thinks that if an Australian hasn't been to England and played county cricket he can't play. You think the only guy who can play in the Australian side is Greg Chappell because he played two years for Somerset.'

'That's right,' he said.

'Well, you blokes wouldn't know shit from a bull's foot.'

And he said to me, 'The reason you're not going to England next year is because too many blokes are looking to knock your block off.'

'Oh yeah? Who are all those fast bowlers in England who are going to knock my block off? You've got a lot of fast bowlers, haven't you?'

So it degenerated to that extent . . . The following Friday night, I was leaning back in my chair [at the MCG bar] and I had my feet up on the underneath part of the table. He must have been sitting really close to me and I was getting really annoyed by him, so I started to say a few things. I wasn't making personal comments, it was really more about county cricket. At some stage he said, 'Everyone's looking for you in county cricket, because you're a prick. You abused me when Australia played Somerset. I came in at number eleven and I can take a bit of abuse, but you kept at me and at me, and in the end when you said to me, "Does your mother fuck?"—that's when I got really angry'.

Ian Chappell knew that he had not played against Botham at Somerset and a long argument followed, but Botham could not be persuaded. Eventually he lost his temper completely, grabbed an empty beer glass and pressed it up against Chappell's cheek.

'I'll fucking cut you from ear to ear,' Botham said.

I said, 'Son, that won't fucking impress me very much. In fact, I would say that would be an act of cowardice. I'll tell you what would impress me—if you cut me with a cricket ball. And you'll get every chance tomorrow because I'll make sure I bat for as long as I can and give you every fucking chance. But I'll just give you one tip. You better do it with a ball that bounces. If you try doing it with a beamer, you had better make it a fucking good one because if I can get up I'll get down the other end and I'll hit you over the head with the fucking bat.'

Then he pushed me backwards off the chair and got hysterically angry.

'C'mon, let's fight,' he yelled.

'Look, I don't fight. Fighting is stupidity. If you lose the fight you go to hospital and if you win the fight you go to jail. And I have no intention of going to either of those two places over a cunt like you.'

And it was about that stage when the pub was closing up . . . He said he chased me through the carpark, and it is crap. We were in a bar—a narrow two-storey building. There is no carpark. You have the Hilton Hotel at the back of this bar and the [front] door leads straight out onto the main road. I've never been out the back of this bar. There is no carpark as far as I am aware. We went out the front door, onto the main road. By the time we got out onto the footpath Botham's going berserk—he's fucking off his tree and he's yelling crazy things, and I'd had enough of this shit . . . He starts coming behind me and Ian Callen grabbed him from behind and told him to settle down. I can't remember who I went with, but I disappeared because the situation threatened to deteriorate even further.

Botham continued to tell his version of the story. Chappell says:

As far as I was concerned it was par for the course. I have actually called Botham an 'habitual liar' on radio, and he hasn't done anything about that. I was in the States at the Masters Golf Tournament in Augusta in 1995. I can't even remember why the BBC man was interviewing me about it, but he asked me about Botham. I said, 'Look mate, I'm sick of talking about Botham, he is an habitual liar.' I was looking right at this bloke and I could see the look on his face when I called Botham an 'habitual liar'. I had called Botham a liar before, but I had never called him an habitual liar, which is pretty serious. Anyhow, when we finished the interview I said to the guy from the BBC, and I knew him from cricket, 'You've got a bit of a problem, haven't you?'

'Mmmm, yes I have, yeah.'

'You've got a decision to make. I'll meet you here tomorrow, because I'll be really interested to hear what your decision is.' Next day he comes up and I ask him, 'Well, what decision did you make?'

'Well, I played it.'

In 1996, Ian Botham and former England team-mate Alan Lamb sued former Pakistani star Test all-rounder Imran Khan for alleged libel. Botham and Lamb lost the case. Eight years on there was a subsequent High Court challenge over costs. During a recent trip to Pakistan Chappelli spoke with Imran about the trial.

Somebody sent me [Chappell] a clipping from one of the English newspapers covering the trial and [in it] Imran's QC said, 'that was a lie.' Botham backed off a bit, then the QC said, 'well, you have a history of lying don't you, Mr Botham?'

Botham and Chappell have hardly spoken since the MCG bar altercation, although their careers as commentators bring them together from time to time. They were once interviewed for *A Current Affair* by Ray Martin on Channel Nine and the bad blood between them was brought out.

At the end of it, I'll never forget, Ray said to Botham, 'Oh well, you'll still have a drink at the end of a day's play.'

And Botham replied, 'Yeah, that's cricket mate. You sit down and have a beer, or wine.'

Ray turned to me and said, 'You'll be having a drink with him after the commentary is over?'

And I said, 'No, Ray. I can find plenty of decent people to have a drink with. I won't be drinking with him.'

Eight

World Series Cricket

I got to Sydney and went to Australian Consolidated Press in Park Street, walked in the door, and there was Kerry sitting behind a desk, his shoes off and feet on the desk. There was no, 'hello, how are you, I'm Kerry Packer.' Packer's first words were: 'What are you, a fucking cowboy?' followed by, 'Well, who do you want in this fucking team of yours?'

The Australian Cricket Board recorded a profit of $78 000 from the 1975 England tour as well as bumper receipts from the 1975/76 West Indies tour of Australia. In contrast, the players were paid a measly $2734 each on the 1975 tour (or a mere $182 a week for the 105 days away) and $400 per Test match against the West Indies. The groundswell of discontent among the Australian Test cricketers was gaining momentum. In order to survive, Test players held down jobs outside cricket—some were paid while they were away on Test duty, others were not.

Chappell worked for himself as a director of Ian Chappell Enterprises; admittedly, playing cricket at the highest level was good for business. During this period Rick McCosker was a bank officer with the Rural Bank of New South Wales, Max Walker worked as an architect, Rod Marsh was a promotions officer with Perth's Swan Brewery, Ian Redpath worked as a wool classer before becoming an antiques dealer, Jeff Thomson was sponsored by a radio station in Brisbane, and Dennis Lillee ran an office-cleaning business while continuing his call for more substantial annual contracts for the players. Chappell, who had agitated for so long to win a better deal for the players, claimed they were getting nothing more than 'fish and chips money'.

The board talked about cricket being an amateur sport and said the game could not afford to pay the players a professional fee for services. Alan Barnes's ludicrous statement that 500 000 other cricketers in Australia would love to take their place reflected the board's hard-line and unrealistic attitude. In *Cricketer Annual*, editor Eric Beecher urged cricket to find a mediating force between the players and the administrators, commenting, 'The gap, which has probably always existed, has been widened by players' requests for more money'.

A perfect environment had emerged for an entrepreneur to run a professional cricket tournament in direct competition with the Test-playing nations. After all, Jack Kramer did it for tennis and, after much disruption and agony, open tennis eventually evolved.

While he was Australian Test captain, Ian Chappell was approached on three separate occasions to play professional cricket. 'Each time I advised the entrepreneurs to meet with the appropriate cricket board because they controlled the grounds,' Chappell recalls, 'and, every time, the administrators sent the entrepreneurs packing, and it quickly became clear they weren't interested in a better deal for the players.' One entrepreneur who approached Chappell spoke of running a professional cricket tour in Australia in a different time slot to the regular scheduling, so as not to directly compete with Test cricket. 'If the board had any sense they would have gone along with it because it would have taken the pressure off them to pay us because these guys were going to pay us quite well.' Ian said he was interested in the concept but, as usual, he advised the entrepreneur to speak with the board and the proposal was subsequently rejected.

Chappell goes on, 'Another group talked to me about the same thing. The third approach came from an international group, during the World Cup in England in 1975.' For a few days the players of all the competing nations stayed at the Kensington Close Hotel in London—a perfect opportunity for any entrepreneur wanting to network and to meet with a lot of high-profile Test cricketers.

Bishan Bedi said there were some Indian businessmen who wanted to start a professional troupe.

'Are you interested?'

'I am definitely interested, Bishan,' I said, 'but I don't think I will last very long as Australian captain. I'm just about at the end of my tether. Is it okay if I bring Greg Chappell along? He's the vice-captain and he's probably going to take over the captaincy.'

Once again, Chappell advised the group that it should go to the boards because they controlled the grounds. But unfortunately the attitude of cricket boards around the world was similar to that of the ACB: the players were to be seen and not heard.

For three years in the early 1970s Ian and Greg Chappell played in South Africa in the Datsun Double Wicket competition.

Major sponsor Datsun was so pleased with the competition in 1972 that the company wanted to offer the players a bigger financial deal.

In 1973 a guy by the name of Robin Binckes, who was the liaison man between Datsun and the players, called a meeting before the second tournament.

'Look guys, I'm sorry the money is the same because the sponsors were really happy with the way the tournament went last year. The sponsors wanted to pay you a lot more money and they spoke to the South African Cricket Association about it. The association said they would get back to Datsun after they had spoken to the other boards.'

The boards' response was along the lines of, 'Oh for Christ's sake don't pay 'em more money because then they'll expect more money when they play Test cricket.' And that's why I was so pissed off when World Series Cricket was announced and the board came out and said, 'We've been stabbed in the back by the players. There's no way they were stabbed in the back—on each occasion a group had suggested a professional cricket troupe to me I said they needed to speak to the board in question to get the major grounds.

I said the same thing to John Cornell and Austin Robertson when they came knocking over World Series Cricket and their answer was, 'Fuck that, we'll get the grounds. We are not going to the board.' Then I thought, 'Oh well, you're in trouble. It won't work,' and that shows you how bloody smart I was, because going to the board was not the way to go. Bullshit the board was stabbed in the back; they had numerous chances to do something about it. And it was only by kicking and screaming that they [the board] gave us an extra $200 a Test in 1974/75.

On 5 October 1975, an Ian Chappell XI met a Tony Greig XI in a charity match at Drummoyne Oval, organised by the Sydney Spastic Centre. After I had bowled Tony Greig and Ian Redpath out, the familiar figure of ACTU President, Bob Hawke, came to the wicket. Chappell sidled up to me and said, 'Now Rowd, go easy on this bloke. It would be nice to see him get a few runs.' A strange request indeed from a captain who was hard as nails.

Hawke top-scored for the Greig XI with 30 odd. Unbeknown to me, Ian and Greg Chappell and Bob Cowper wanted Hawke to drive an envisaged Australian Players' Union. Later, at the Melbourne Hilton Hotel, just a couple of Keith Miller drives from the MCG, Hawke had a dinner conversation with the Chappell brothers, Rodney Marsh, Cowper and Rick McCosker (McCosker was the Test team's unofficial treasurer). Hawke told the group that they had been 'raped for years' by the board, but strongly suggested that they refrain from calling their collective a 'union'—'association' would be a better choice. Later, when World Series Cricket started, an Australian Players' Association was established with Rick McCosker as secretary and Ross Edwards, an accountant, as treasurer. But that was after the revolution.

A casual conversation between Dennis Lillee, John Cornell, Cornell's wife Delvene, Austin Robertson and Paul Hogan in Perth in 1976 was the genesis for the modern sporting phenomenon known as World Series Cricket (WSC). Cornell and Robertson were Lillee's managers and Lillee, as with most first-class cricketers, was struggling to make a decent living. He came up with the idea of playing a few international matches in addition to Tests so that the players could get better financially rewarded. He did not intend to interfere with the game as it was currently structured; these would be extra fixtures, never clashing with official ACB matches. Cornell asked Lillee if he had ever heard of Kerry Packer. He hadn't, but he was soon to learn that Packer wanted exclusive rights to televise Test cricket. No one person can claim to have started World Series Cricket, but Lillee's association with Cornell and Robertson was certainly the spark that set it going.

Austin Robertson was a former champion footballer with Subiaco and South Melbourne and had worked alongside John Cornell as a journalist at Perth's *Daily News* before Cornell moved to Sydney, where he eventually became Paul Hogan's manager. Cornell had first met Paul Hogan in 1971 when they worked together on *A Current Affair*. Hogan's take-home pay was a lowly $50 a week, so Cornell got Hogan out of his contract with Mike Willesee and in 1973 the pair established JP Productions which produced *The Paul Hogan Show* on ATV–7.

Robertson and Cornell were aghast that the greatest fast bowler in the world could be playing top-level cricket for peanuts, while the ACB was reaping millions of dollars in revenue. Asking the question, 'Why doesn't someone do something about it?', they set up JP Sport to contract the players and establish their own series.

Cornell and Robertson (through JP Sport) contacted Bob Cowper, and in October 1976 Cowper wrote to Chappell advising the ex-Test skipper that Packer was seeking support for private cricket sponsorship. 'You might reflect on the thought of twelve-week contracts ranging between $20 000–$30 000 and let me know your reaction', Cowper wrote. In his final summer of playing for Australia, Chappell had earned $5000 from the game, so the envisaged Packer sponsorship was worth thinking about. His reply to Cowper was a simple 'Thanks'.

I'm portrayed as one of the instigators of World Series Cricket. I think that is too high praise really, because there are three other people who had more to do with it: John Cornell, Austin Robertson and Dennis Lillee. It was Lillee's unhappiness with pay and conditions that made Cornell and Robertson decide to do something about it. Paul Hogan is also in the mix, so in all there were four people who were the main players. Then, at some point, Ross Edwards, an accountant as well as a cricketer, read the contract. He noted that JP Sport, the company with whom we signed initially, was a two-dollar company.

Edwards asked the question: 'Well, if everything falls over, who's going to pay our money?' So it was at that point that Cornell and Paul Hogan went off and got Kerry Packer involved. They realised they had to have someone with financial clout to back them. Packer was the perfect guy because, not only did he have the financial wherewithal, he had the power of the media, television and print. And that power was probably as important, if not more important, than the actual financial clout.

When Ian Chappell was first asked to sign a contract, he said to Austin Robertson:

'Mate, count me in, but I can't sign a contract yet, because I've got this three-year contract with North Melbourne. I'm not going to feel comfortable signing another contract while I have [an existing] contract. Leave it to me. I'll have to pick the right time and I'll have to think about how I am going to do this so I don't alert the administrators to what I am doing. I'll have to speak to Len Maddocks, because it was through Len that it all happened with North Melbourne. I want to talk to him because I like Len and I don't want to betray his trust, but leave it to me to do it in such a way that I won't tell him that World Series Cricket is starting.'

Then, during the Centenary Test match in March 1977, Chappell had another meeting with Austin Robertson, this time with John Cornell present.

We met on one of the Test-day mornings, I think Cornell just wanted to confirm that I was 'in', and I said then that it was vital to get the major grounds. At that point I sort of thought it was like all the other approaches—if it happens it happens . . . I first started to think it might actually work when I saw John Maley [WSC head groundsman] making the pitches in the cement slabs which they were going to drop in the grounds and I thought, 'Shit, this might be pretty serious.' I can't remember when I actually signed but I went to Len [Maddocks] and asked if we might 'rejig' the North Melbourne contract because I wanted to play a higher level of cricket again. I was sort of couching my terms and he said: 'Yeah, yeah, that will be no problem, that's terrific. That's good news for Victoria.'

I didn't say, 'Mate, it's not going to be with Victoria,' and Len was only too happy to rejig the contract or cancel it or whatever we did, and the interesting thing is we never fell out over that. It never affected our relationship—even now we always have a beer and a chat and laugh about the North Melbourne days. I think he realised that I was being as honest as I could have been with him at that time.

Having settled the contract issue with North Melbourne, Ian continued to play for the club while in constant communication with Austin Robertson, who was keen for Chappell to meet the boss of World Series Cricket, Kerry Packer.

I got a message from Ocker [Austin Robertson] to fly to Sydney. I used to fly to Melbourne on Friday nights, play with North Melbourne on the Saturday and fly home to Adelaide on the Sunday. So I used to leave all my cricket gear and stuff in Melbourne. I would fly very light and stayed at the Old Melbourne Inn. I had just arrived in Melbourne when Robertson got in touch: 'Go back to the airport, jump on a plane and fly to Sydney for a meeting with Kerry Packer.'

And all I had was casual gear, you know, jeans and a country-and-western shirt and a denim jacket. I got to Sydney and went to Australian Consolidated Press in Park Street, walked in the door, and there was Kerry sitting behind a desk, his shoes off and feet on the desk. There was no, 'hello, how are you, I'm Kerry Packer,' or any introduction. Packer's first words were: 'What are you, a fucking cowboy?' followed by, 'Well, who do you want in this fucking team of yours?'

'Hang on Kerry, I'm not the Australian captain. Greg Chappell is the captain of Australia, so I don't think it is really down to me as to who is in the side.'

'What do you think this is, son, a fucking democracy? You're the fucking captain.'

'Okay,' I said, 'I know what you are saying, but I don't want a family falling-out over this. Would you mind letting me ring Greg to sort it out before you announce it?'

'Yeah, sure,' Kerry said, 'that's fine.'

I'll never forget it, I rang Greg and explained the situation and he said, 'Go for your life mate. I've had two years of the captaincy and I've had a gutful of it. It's all yours mate. I'm happy to shed the bloody thing.'

. . . Mostly my role was one of encouragement. However, there were a couple of occasions when someone was unsure about signing. I was asked, probably because I had been his captain, to speak with David Hookes, and I explained to Hookesy: 'Look mate, my career is over, yours is just starting. You have a tough decision to make.' I then explained why he should join WSC, but I did understand the turmoil he must have felt. I went to Alan Hurst, the Victorian pace bowler. He said 'No,' because, as he explained, he had been playing in the shadow of Lillee and Thomson and was only likely to play in the event of one of them being injured. Now, suddenly he's got the chance to lead the new ball attack for the Test side. I understood his position. And I also realised how bad a salesman I was because if someone said 'No,' they meant 'No,' as far as I was concerned.

The South African all-rounder Eddie Barlow—one of the champion Springbok cricketers who had missed years of Test cricket because of South Africa's political and sporting isolation over apartheid—jumped at the chance to sign. Austin Robertson went to see him in London on the Easter weekend of 1977. When they met Austin began the usual introductions: 'Hi, I'm Austin Robertson from World Series Cricket,' to which Eddie replied, 'Where do I sign?'

Getting blokes like Eddie to sign up was pretty easy. I was retired from first-class and international cricket, playing grade cricket for North Melbourne, plus some commentary. It was easy for me to sign, I wasn't really risking anything . . . The real tough decisions were made by the young guys, the likes of David Hookes, Ray Bright and Ian Davis. These sorts of guys were just starting out in their Test careers. And I'm sure they probably signed thinking they would never get the chance to play Test cricket again. So to sign for World Series Cricket under those circumstances would have taken a great deal of courage. For the likes of Eddie Barlow, Greg [Chappell], Rodney [Marsh] and myself it was easy. We had played a lot of Test cricket. And if we never played again, well, that was fine.

Austin Robertson said it was vital to the success of World Series Cricket to swiftly sign up the stars of Australia, England and the West Indies. Kerry Packer himself signed Tony Greig, then Greig signed Clive Lloyd. Austin Robertson targeted David Hookes, the fresh, new face of Australian cricket. Hookes had become the darling of the Australian cricket public after his swashbuckling innings at the Centenary Test, when he hit five successive boundaries off England captain Tony Greig in a Test debut innings of 56. Hookes had missed a few of the early matches for South Australia in 1976/77 while he was completing his studies, but then returned to the South Australian team and made five centuries in six innings. Hookes wasn't one to grind out the runs—he blitzed attacks in a frenzy of stroke-play.

David Hookes signed up with World Series Cricket after much heartache. Austin Roberston said the signing of Hookes was vitally important: 'There was no doubt we brought back to cricket some older players who had retired from Test cricket. Hookes was a huge, bright star on the horizon.' There were frantic attempts by Test selector Phil Ridings and others in South Australia to lure him back to the establishment. Money, a job and the state captaincy were offered, in a package which was nearly three times the amount for which he signed with World Series Cricket. Hookes recalled in his autobiography, *Hookesy*:

John Cornell rang from London and spoke to me for two hours—I was at my mother's place—about why I shouldn't pull out of World Series. Then an Adelaide accountant and I flew to Sydney to see Kerry Packer, at his invitation and expense. We went into his office and he said:

'What's your problem, son?' I said I was under pressure from the ACB and would like to pull out of my World Series Cricket contract. He said, 'You'd better come with me,' and we went down to a video room where he had an operator screen all the Channel Nine commercials for World Series Cricket. I seemed to be in most of them, either featuring up-front or merely in the background, presumably because I was the youngest player and World Series Cricket needed young players. Packer looked at me, looked at the accountant and said:

'If David pulls out, I'll sue the board for inducing breach of contract and David will spend the rest of his life paying me back what I sue him for. You've got two minutes to think about it.' And he walked out of the room. The accountant turned to me and said,

'You're going to enjoy playing World Series Cricket.'

When I first heard news of World Series Cricket in North Terrace, Adelaide, where I was working for *The News*, I immediately thought of a return to the game. Here was a chance to actually earn some money from playing the game I loved. By that time I was an ex-cricketer, having retired from all forms of the game. But I didn't waste a moment getting on the phone to Ian Chappell.

'Any chance of getting a place on your team?' I asked.

Unbeknown to me, Ian had already asked Kerry Packer to include a few recently retired players—Ian Redpath, Ross Edwards and me. Redpath and Edwards were fine with Packer, but when Chappell had put my name forward, Packer had said, 'I'm not paying money to that fucking straight-breaker. No, fuck it.'

Ian told me he would get back to me. A few days later he rang: 'Kerry is happy to give you a World Series contract, on the condition that he will fly you to Sydney and you bowl an over to him. If you can get him out in the over, you've got a contract.'

'Tell Mr Packer to get fucked,' I said. Ian said he would relay my message.

A few days after that, I had a phone call from Sir Donald Bradman. There was, as usual, no room for small talk with him: 'Don Bradman here, Ashley. As you know, Bob Simpson has been asked to lead Australia, a huge task given he has been out of Test cricket for ten years. We are getting names together and as most of the good people have defected we need to build a decent team. Australia wants you back and I have been asked by the Test selectors to offer you a place in the Test team.'

'Does that mean, Sir Donald, that I would be guaranteed a place in all five Tests, same as Simpson?'

'No. You'd sink or swim on performance, just as you have always done. There can be no guarantees. Simpson is a different appointment. We need stability and Simpson will provide that for Australia. You will appreciate how difficult a task Simpson faces.'

'Yes, I see all of that, Sir Donald, but what if World Series Cricket offers me a guaranteed sum. Will the ACB match it?'

'No, we can't do that Ashley. That would be going against the way Australia has always picked its Test team.'

'And Bob Simpson is different?'

'Yes. These are extraordinary times.'

'Well, Sir Donald, I will have to have a long, hard think about your offer. My main reason for retiring was the lack of security. All of my Test cricketing life I have had to juggle work with playing. Mostly I played Test cricket by taking time off work without pay. I will give it serious thought and will get back to you.'

'I appreciate that, son.'

Two days after Bradman's call, I was offered a contract from World Series Cricket: $20 000 for one year with an option on a second. I was on the lower rung of contract amounts, but to me that was a huge sum. I didn't phone Bradman back. It was discourteous on my part, but I somehow reasoned that Bradman would soon know anyway. He would also have realised that we were coming from opposite corners in what wasn't quite a war, but was certainly a significant battle.

Nor had Ian relayed my exact message to Kerry Packer: 'No, Rowd, I didn't relay the exact words. I didn't think your telling him that would have served your best interests.'

Packer offered the top players a three-year deal worth $75 000, and planned drop-in wickets on unfamiliar grounds, including VFL Park in Melbourne, Football Park in Adelaide (then owned by the South Australian National Football League), Perth's Gloucester Park and the Sydney Showground. The intention was to attract a whole new audience, including women and teenagers, with US-style razzamatazz. Magazine editor Eric Beecher canvassed the top twelve cricketers in five Sheffield Shield sides for his December 1975 issue of *Cricketer*. He asked the players whether they thought they were being offered 'sufficient financial rewards' for playing top cricket. Only two out of sixty were happy with their financial lot and only three were against professional promoters being brought into the game.

By early in the Australian winter of 1977, Ian Chappell and Kerry Packer were in the United Kingdom trying to resolve a looming threat. David Lord, Jeff Thomson's manager, had managed to persuade Thommo to pull out of his World Series Cricket contract. Lord boasted of a mass exodus of Packer players. Chappell says, 'Packer went to England, I think, to sue anyone who threatened to pull out of their contract.'

Another threat came from the International Cricket Conference, which announced that World Series Cricket players would be banned from Test cricket. Packer's Australian Consolidated Press (ACP) backed Tony Greig, John Snow and Mike Proctor in a High Court challenge to the ICC's ban. It was high drama, a bonanza for the press, and eventually the High Court ruled that the ban represented a restraint of trade and the ICC was left with a legal bill of hundreds of thousands of dollars.

In the first season of World Series Cricket Dennis Lillee had, by his own standards, a poor summer. He had taken 21 wickets at 36.42 in the Supertests and felt his career was at the crossroads. A subdued Lillee spoke to Ian Chappell at an end-of-season party at the Old Melbourne Inn, telling Ian that he was seriously considering giving the game away. As he was leaving, Dennis extended his right hand. Chappell refused to shake Lillee's hand, saying, 'I only shake hands with fast bowlers.'

'Well, fuck you. We'll see next season,' said Lillee.

Lillee came back better than ever in 1978/79, the second year of World Series Cricket. Austin Robertson's father, Austin Robertson Senior, approached Lillee at about that time offering to help the fast bowler with his running. Robertson Senior had been the world professional sprint champion in 1933, defeating the likes of Eddie Tolan, the American sprinter who in 1929 was the first person to break 9.5 seconds for the 100-yard dash, and had won three gold medals in the 1932 Olympic Games. According to Austin Robertson, Lillee made rapid progress: 'My father was so impressed with Dennis's ability as a runner that he wanted to enter him in the Stawell Gift. This never happened, but after his first winter of athletics coaching with my dad, I was sitting in the commentary box with Richie Benaud when Dennis came in to bowl his first delivery. Dennis ran in as smooth as silk, but he looked to me as though he was doing a half- to three-quarter pace run through, rather than bowling a ball in a Test match. I turned to Richie and said, "Christ, what has my old man done? He looks like a sprinter to me, not a great fast bowler." Richie turned to me and, with a wry smile and a twinkle in his eye, he said, "Ock, just sit and watch."

'I think I could glean what Richie was saying. There was a new smoothness about the Lillee run up, which he retained until the end. Dennis admired the way Michael Holding glided to the wicket and never wasted energy.'

What a lesson for any elite sportsman. Lillee, arguably the greatest fast bowler of all time, was nearing the end of his career, yet he was determined to improve his bowling action. Greater rhythm in his approach to the wicket was the key factor, and it took an old athletics champion, whose fame was at its height in the Bradman era, to give Lillee the technique and the confidence to do it. But it was Ian Chappell's psychological ploy that night at the Old Melbourne Inn that fired up the great fast bowler.

Nine

Caribbean crisis

'Jesus Christ, you're a cantankerous bastard. I knew you'd be angry and
I thought long and hard about what I was going to say to you,
and I thought, "That can't offend him. What I am going to say cannot
possibly offend him." And you still told me to fuck off.'

The early signs were not good for Kerry Packer's ambitious venture. The first official World Series Cricket fixture was played at VFL Park in Melbourne in December 1977. The Australians went down to the West Indies in a tight, low-scoring Supertest. The Supertest series—Australia vs the West Indies, and Australia against a World XI—was followed by a triangular one-day series. Despite good cricket, the crowds at the non-traditional cricket grounds were disappointing—as Ian Chappell had been saying, 'If you haven't got the main grounds, you're buggered.' Kerry Packer's losses were estimated at $3–4 million.

World Series had applied for the use of the SCG, at a fee of

$20 000 a day, but had been refused by the SCG Trust. After more legal action, the New South Wales Government stripped the Trust of its right to priority over the ground and agreed to the construction of light towers for night cricket. The real World Series Cricket finally arrived on Tuesday, 28 November 1978 when, after 44 377 people came through the turnstiles, the gates were thrown open and a crowd of more than 50 000 saw Australia defeat the West Indies under the lights.

The balance of power in Australian cricket had changed. There were also some changes in relationships between the players in the early days of the new regime. When they first met, Ian Chappell had admired Tony Greig's attacking flair and his fairness in conceding that the vandalised Leeds pitch in 1975 was unplayable. But after the World XI had won a winner-take-all Supertest purse of $100 000 over Chappell's Australians, Chappell refused to shake Greig's hand.

Greig knew that he was gone as a player, but he was still taking his place in a team that he didn't deserve to be in . . . If I don't respect somebody I have a huge problem even being civil to them, never mind shaking hands with them. And the main reason I lost respect for him was not so much the fact that his ability had diminished—everybody's ability diminishes with time—but because while his team was out there training he was off making extra money doing advertisements with Waltons and Nutri-Grain, and that really pissed me off. I didn't have a problem with Tony making extra money through doing advertisements, but his team were getting pissed off. As far as I was concerned, you can't be off doing things to make extra money when your team's practising. That's where I lost respect for him. Then we had a few run-ins—the big one was in Perth at Gloucester Park.

This was during a Supertest in January 1978, with Greig bowling to Chappell in Australia's first innings.

There was an exchange between the two and Umpire Gary Duperouzel—an excellent umpire who appeared to enjoy the verbal jousting between players in the heat of battle—managed to cool them down when it threatened to reach boiling point. Later, Lillee struck Greig smack on the helmet as he backed away from a ball which rose sharply from just short of a length. Lillee had then mockingly pointed to his own head, a gesture which seemed to affect Greig's composure, for he soon drove at a full-length ball from Lillee and the ball spooned to Ross Edwards at cover. Greig then asked the injured Gordon Greenidge to resume his innings, and Greig came out as his runner. Chappell brought a smile to Umpire Duperouzel's face when he demanded that Greig wear his full batting kit, including his prototype helmet, which looked identical to those worn by the motorcycle police.

After retirement from World Series Cricket, Chappell and Greig found themselves together in the commentary box. Ian had not changed his attitude towards Greig; it wasn't hard to detect a certain coolness between the pair. Chappell says, 'When we began commentating together I sort of continued it a bit . . . I was a bit off-hand towards him for a while, and I must say it was from my side, not from Greig's. And at some stage I sort of thought to myself, "Shit, we are going to have to work together, that was cricket and that's gone. It's time to move on . . . Now we get on fine."'

As the 1978/79 Australian season was drawing to a close, Ian Chappell's World Series Australians were preparing for the challenge of taking on Clive Lloyd's men in the Caribbean. Jeff Thomson, who hadn't joined World Series, indicated that he could be persuaded to change his mind, saying he wanted to 'play with my mates and the blokes who can catch'. Chappell was in Sydney at the time.

Ocker said to me, 'C'mon, we've got to go out to Bankstown to Thommo's place to get him signed up.'

'You can do that, Ocker. You don't need me, I've got a lot of work to do.'

'No, Chappelli, come on, we don't want anything to fall over at the last minute.'

We went to Thommo's place and Thommo never appeared. All bloody day out at Bankstown with Thommo's mum and dad, but it was very interesting. I noticed an old pianola there and all these rolls of music and I recalled that Thommo always knew the words at the sing-alongs we'd have, and I realised why that day. On the team bus he used to play Status Quo at four thousand decibels . . .

Next time I saw him, I said, 'Thommo, you are an irresponsible bastard,' and—this is typical Thommo—'Yeah,' he said, 'you're right mate, I am,' which is totally disarming.

And I said, 'Christ, why didn't you turn up?'

'My solicitor told me not to.'

'Well, you could have rung me and told me.'

And he replied, 'Yeah, sorry mate.'

The day before the World Series Australians were due to fly to the West Indies, Chappell was called in to ACP headquarters in Park Street, Sydney, with Austin Robertson, Lynton Taylor (one of Packer's executives), and John Kitto from the legal firm Allen, Allen & Hemsley. Packer asked if everything was sorted out and it emerged that a couple of the players had raised the fact that, for the coming eight-week West Indies tour, they would be paid a fixed sum of $16 000, which was less than the daily rate stipulated under their World Series Cricket contract.

Kerry turned to his executive Lynton Taylor and said, 'Lynton, aren't we paying according to the contract?'

Taylor said, 'No, Kerry, but Ian's sorted it out with the players. It's all fixed.'

Kerry reaffirmed, 'Aren't we paying according to the contract?'

Lynton replied, 'No.'

And Kerry said, 'Well, fucking pay 'em according to the contract.'

I said, 'Kerry, this is ridiculous.'

'Lynton, how much more is it?'

'Well, Kerry, the extra amount works out to be $340 000.'

'Well, pay 'em according to the contract.'

And I said, 'Kerry, it's ridiculous. You are not going to make any money out of the Caribbean.'

'Son, I'll tell you something—$340 000 is about the price of a B-grade movie for my TV station. That's not going to break me. What will fucking break me is not sticking to the word of my contracts. Lynton, pay 'em.'

Packer's insistence that the players be paid according to the very letter of the contract meant that the players would receive around double the original $16 000 for the tour. Packer moved on:

'Okay son, are you happy with the side you've got for the West Indies? You've got some quick bowlers to fire back at the West Indies with, Lillee and Thomson and Pascoe. Thommo's signed isn't he?'

'Kerry, I don't know. I went out to his place . . .' I told him what happened that day at Thommo's Bankstown home. I said, 'He's in, he wants to play.'

Kerry turned to Austin and said, 'Is Thomson signed?'

And Ocker said, 'Oh, well, he's agreed to play.'

'Is he fucking signed?'

'The last time I saw him Lynton was going to see him and get it all fixed up.'

Then Kerry turned to Lynton Taylor and said, 'Is Thomson fucking signed?'

Lynton said, 'Oh, well, you know, when I spoke to Thommo he's verbally agreed to play. He's booked on the plane . . .'

'Has he actually signed the fucking contract?'

'Well, we had the contract. It's all drawn up and he said he left it with Kitto of Allens.'

'Has Thomson actually signed the contract?'

And Kitto said, 'Well, I am not actually dealing with that, Jim Thynne's dealing with that . . .'

'Where's fucking Thynne?'

And John Kitto said, 'He's on holidays.'

'Where's he on holidays?'

'On the Gold Coast somewhere, Mr Packer.'

'Well,' said Kerry, 'we'll fuck that holiday up . . .'

Thomson was signed pretty smartly after that meeting and the tour got under way. Ian Chappell knew his men were facing a huge challenge in the Caribbean.

Our first Test was at Sabina Park, Kingston, Jamaica. We bowled them out for 188, first day. The track was a bit up and down. I remember saying to the guys, 'If we get a lead here, a big lead in the first innings, we can win this.' So we promptly got bowled out for 132 and Lloydy came out and absolutely smashed us all over Sabina Park. There was a huge cement wall at each end of the ground, which acted as a sightboard. Lloydy was smashing the ball down the ground and the ball would rebound off the wall. The ball was like a sock. Gus Gilmour copped a fair pasting. Much of the time Gus would get back to his mark to find the ball sitting there after it had rebounded off the sightscreen wall. Later someone asked Gus, 'How do you bowl to Clive Lloyd?' and Gus replied, 'With a helmet on.'

Ian was annoyed at the Australian bowling performance. By lunch, Lloyd was unconquered on 150. Ian didn't go into the Australian dressing-room, he walked straight up to lunch at the Kingston Cricket Club dining-room, sat down and began to eat.

Halfway through the meal I heard 'boom, boom, boom'. It's either Kerry Packer or an elephant thundering across the floor. He's coming from behind me, so I couldn't see him. I get this big thump on the shoulder and he said, 'Tough day out there, son,' and I didn't even look around. I said, 'Fuck off!'

There was a pause, then I heard the sound of the big man retreating, 'boom, boom, boom', across the floor and down the stairs. Greg looked up at me from the other side of the table, 'Judging by the look on Kerry's face, he hasn't been told that many times.'

That night we were having drinks by the pool at the hotel and Kerry comes up to me and says, 'Jesus Christ, you're a cantankerous bastard. I knew you'd be angry and I thought long and hard about what I was going to say to you, and I thought, "That can't offend him. What I am going to say cannot possibly offend him." And you still told me to fuck off.'

The Jamaica Supertest was lost, but the World Series Australians played well to level the series in Trinidad. The group was in good spirits when the plane touched down in Guyana, although these were dampened somewhat when they realised it was raining heavily and had been for days. Everything was sodden. Chappell played golf with Garry Sobers on the scheduled first day of the Guyana match. When he got back to the hotel that night he spoke to Richie Robinson, the Australian team manager, who had been down to the ground with Greg Chappell. Richie told him the ground was still under water so when Ian Chappell woke the next day he assumed it would still be too wet for play.

I was lolling about, not thinking about cricket. I got the morning paper and stared at the back page headline: 'Play will start on time, if no more rain'. Fuck, what's happening here? I rang Bookshelf [Richie Robinson] and said, 'Bookshelf, you told me we couldn't play.'

'We can't mate. The ground's under water.'

'Well, have you seen the paper.'

'No.'

'Well, you'd better have a bloody look . . . Ring around and get the guys together. We better get on the bus and get down to the ground, because we don't want to lose on a forfeit.'

We raced down to the ground. The sun was shining. It was hot; the first sunny day we'd seen . . . We went out onto the ground and Bookshelf and Greg were right. The pitch was fine, it had been covered, but the ground—not just the outfield, but the whole ground—was a quagmire . . .

So I went to Lloydy and I said, 'What are your feelings?'

And he replied, 'Well, I don't think we can play. Get the fast bowlers running in on that and someone will do a hamstring and be out for the rest of the series.'

I said, 'Well, that's fine. So long as we are thinking along the same lines, let's go and have a chat to the umpires and see how they are thinking. I don't want to suddenly find that we've got to play just to please some silly bastard.' We went to see the umpires, Douglas Sang Hue and Ralph Gosein. 'Lloydy and I have had a chat. We are not that keen on playing . . . the fast bowlers are likely to pull muscles. There's no way we can play.'

And I shall never forget what Douglas Sang Hue said: 'We told the ground staff, the people running the game, not to open the gates until we say that play is possible. We got here very early—before 6 am—and we found the gates already open and the people streaming in.'

The Australians later discovered the officials had opened the gates because the back of each ticket stated very clearly that there would be no refunds once the gates were opened.

I had enormous sympathy for the crowd. They've paid all their money, they are standing out in the hot sun, they can't get a refund. They look out to the middle, the pitch looks fine. We had a Channel Nine television crew at the ground. A microphone was left 'live' with no one attending it and this guy from the crowd, a typical Caribbean, strolled up to it. He tapped it to see if it was 'live'—to his delight he found it was—and said: 'I have inspected the pitch and it is fit for play.' . . .

Shortly after, we get a call to come up to the office for a meeting. There were gathered a whole lot of administrators, including a fella called Neil McLean, who was on the organising committee and who also happened to be the chief of police in Georgetown. It was about 2 pm Neil McLean said: 'If there is no play today, I am afraid to tell you that I can no longer guarantee your safety at the ground.'

I looked at Lloydy and we all said, 'Fuck, that's not the news we want to hear.'

I think it is important to link Neil McLean's connection here. He was on the organising committee and he was the chief of police. I reckon they were starting to think, 'We had better get the players out there and at least get in a bit of cricket so we can justify not giving a refund.' They indicated to us that there had to be some play that day.

I said, 'Shit, I'm not too happy about that. Neither captain wants to play, the umpires have agreed that it is not fit for play. This is bullshit. You are holding a gun at our head here.'

Then McLean said, 'Well, that is the situation. If there's no play today, I cannot guarantee your safety.'

I told him that I was prepared to go along with him so long as there wasn't too much play on the day. I said, 'I'd hate to see the Test match won or lost on the amount of play that happens today. As long as you guarantee that we are not going to play for a long time, I'll agree to it.'

At that time of year in Guyana, stumps were drawn at 5 pm. We agreed to a 4 pm start. I went back downstairs with Bookshelf, walked into the dressing-room and told the guys that we had been held over a barrel and that we would start play at 4 pm. I think I said, 'If we are bowling we'll bowl about eight overs in the hour,' because it was just ridiculous—if they wanted to make a mockery of the game, we could do it too.

I had no sooner finished talking to the guys when we heard an announcement, 'Play will start at 3 pm.' That's one hour earlier than we had agreed. I was pretty angry. I rushed out of the dressing-room and raced up the stairs. Bookshelf was after me, trying to hold me back. I burst into the committee room where we had just held the meeting and there is this guy in a black-and-white striped shirt putting down the microphone after just having made the PA announcement.

'What's your fucking name, mate?'

'Vic Insanally.'

'Just you fucking remember, if there's a fucking riot at this ground, you started it—not us. If you think we are going out there to play you can get fucked. We are not playing.' I slammed the door and went back downstairs. But they had left it too late. Even after the announcement. The fences were already being pushed over. Bottles were being thrown. Suddenly the fence breaks and the hordes come in.

Only minutes earlier, the great West Indian fast bowler Wes Hall said to World Series Cricket's Bruce McDonald as they stood high in the Members' Stand, 'It's gonna blow man, it's gonna blow.' Spectators had been in the ground since the early hours. From about 6 am onwards they'd been standing about in the sun, drinking rum. While players strolled in the sunshine, prodded the pitch for a few minutes then wandered off, the steel band continued to play and the crowd became more and more restless. It was indeed 'gonna blow'.

The Australians gathered at the dressing-room windows to watch chairs, rocks and bottles fly. The fences were crushed under the weight of an angry mob. For a while, there was a certain amount of frivolity—Dennis Lillee walked about banging a pair of wooden thongs to simulate gunfire. Then the mood turned ugly and there did not seem to be much security. An armed sergeant burst into the room, shaking with fear, then in walked the two umpires, Douglas Sang Hue and Ralph Gosein. Jeff Thomson shut and bolted the door. Cricket bags were heaped up against the door to keep the mob out and some players donned helmets with visors to help prevent eye injury should glass start flying.

Austin Robertson will never forget that day: 'It was terribly frightening; bottles and half house-bricks were being hurled at us. Crouching beside me under an overturned table was Wes Hall—

the former great fast bowler was scared to death, which didn't help my frame of mind. To be frank, the experience was quite an ordeal. While the dressing-room was only a matter of metres away, it was too dangerous to make a dash for it. In any case, I was told the door had been bolted from inside and the players were all together with their helmets on and bats at the ready.'

Inside the dressing-room the players felt real fear, and they armed themselves for what seemed like an inevitable hand-to-hand combat with the angry mob. Chappelli recalls:

Eventually the riot police arrived and cleared them off . . . We then went down to the West Indies dressing-room. A few of their guys got injured—a couple receiving stitches for gashes to the body from things being chucked through the dressing-room window. It was interesting talking to Deryck Murray, the Windies keeper and vice-captain. I said to him, 'What was all that about, Deryck?'

'Mate, there's been tension in the place for ages. They are not happy with the president, the place has been run down, there's so many things that they are angry about that this gave them the opportunity . . . They looked at the pavilion and saw that wrecking it was a way to have a crack at the establishment. They wouldn't have hurt the players.'

'Hang on Deryck, some of your guys did get hurt.'

'That was accidental. If the mob had have got into the dressing-rooms and actually come face-to-face with the players they wouldn't have harmed them.'

The Australian team management called a meeting of all the players. Ian asked his men what they wanted to do and he found there were about eight members of the side who wanted to quit the Caribbean right then and there and go home. A few players wanted to skip Guyana and go to the next island, Antigua, where the final match was scheduled. Chappell said: 'I don't think we can do either. We had a riot in Barbados when the crowd thought we had a chance of winning. Then they looked like stopping the match in Trinidad. I left the field and went to Clive Lloyd and said, "Mate, can you go out and get on the PA and appeal to the crowd, tell them to settle down because we've got a good game of cricket—both sides have a chance of winning. Let's get it finished."'

Clive Lloyd had refused to use his influence, but eventually his deputy Deryck Murray, whose run-out had sparked the crowd's anger, told the crowd, 'Look, I was out. I was given out. We have a very good game of cricket going on here. Both sides can win it. Let's not spoil a good game of cricket. Settle down.' Chappell remembers:

So there was this build up of crowd behaviour. I felt that if we kept backing down to the crowd, no one was ever going to win another game in the Caribbean apart from the West Indies, because every time the opposition looked like they might win, the crowd would start throwing bottles. So we had to stand up. I explained all this to the guys. 'I think we've got to come back and play.' Bacchus [Rod Marsh] and Greg supported that opinion. However, few of the others were keen to play on.

Chappell told the players he would go to the Bourda Ground in Guyana early the next morning and check security. If he was completely satisfied with security he would phone his men to inform them that their safety was not in doubt and that all was well for them to come on down. This duly happened and Chappell was delighted that his men all turned up at the bus that morning. When they had settled down, he figured, they too would have seen that there was no way the team could bow down to mob rule.

So there we all were, in the bus, en route to the Bourda Ground. I was sitting across the aisle from Ray Bright and he showed me the headline on the back page of the paper, 'Australians responsible for riot at Bourda Ground', written by a bloke named Quenton Jones. I was really pissed off about this . . . I was fucking fuming and I said to Bright, and I don't know what made me say it, 'If I don't punch someone today, it won't be my fault.' I have no idea why I said that because I'd never punched anyone in my life. By the time we got to the ground I was steaming. I rushed into the dressing-room, dumped my watch and wallet in the valuables bag and then took off, heading towards the press box to find this bloody Quenton Jones.

Quenton Jones wrote that we were responsible for the riot because we didn't want to play while the West Indies wanted to. As I marched down the stairs I saw Bruce ['Ronnie'] McDonald at the top of the stairs, and with him is Vic Insanally, I recognised him with his black-and-white striped shirt. McDonald was taking a photo of Insanally with the pavilion in the background. I said: 'That's a bloody good idea, Ronnie, you take a photo of that cunt who started that fucking riot here yesterday.'

Insanally said something which made me turn about and come back to him. I said: 'Mate, you just remember who fucking lied about the starting time. You fucking started the riot, not us.' And with that I hit him with the back of my hand in his stomach. I went to the press box. There was Phil Wilkins and a few others and I said: 'Where's fucking Quenton Jones? Wilko, if you see Quenton Jones could you tell him to get over to our dressing-room? I want to see him.'

'Yeah, right-oh, Chappelli,' Phil said.

I walked back towards our dressing-room and I saw Vic Insanally talking with a police officer who had a lot of fruit salad on his shoulder. As I walked past the pair I heard the words 'abuse and assault', and when I got to the dressing-room I said to Bookshelf, 'Mate, I think we've got a bit of a problem. And I think I am the cause of it.' Bookshelf and the Doc, who apparently had played a bit of badminton with Neil McLean, went to see the police chief and tried to smooth things over. Clive Lloyd tried also, but he said, 'It's gone too far. Right to the top. Apparently the reason is that Forbes Burnham [the president of Guyana] said you abused him in 1972/73 and he hasn't forgotten it, and he's going to get you back.'

I said, 'Well, that's bullshit. I didn't abuse him, but I think I know what the incident is all about.'

I went to Greg [Chappell] and asked him if he had abused Burnham and he said 'No.' Then when I returned to Australia I checked with Fagin [Bill Jacobs], our team manager in 1972/73. He said he had an argument with Burnham during the tour. He said he didn't abuse him, but that they had traded strong words in his home.

Ian Chappell was summoned to court to answer a charge of assault. Austin Robertson, who accompanied him to court, remembers the event: 'He was wearing sandals and a pair of shorts with an open-neck shirt, which seemed a little underdressed for a court appearance. An official of the court told Ian that he would need a pair of long trousers. He wore mine, which were several sizes too big for him. When, standing in the dock, he had to keep hoisting them up, it was a lighter moment I suppose. But I don't think Ian enjoyed the court appearance very much.' Chappell recalls:

The solicitor said, 'If you write a letter of apology it will all be forgotten.' So I wrote, 'I apologise for abusing Vic Insanally and I apologise for hitting him. I should never have done that,' and that was the end of my apology. They were the only things I was going to apologise for; I wasn't going to apologise for what I said because that was true.

The solicitor said, 'No, that's not good enough, I'll write an apology and you can sign it.' I wish I had never accepted—he wrote this shit-eating apology and the worst part is he read it out in court and I still got charged anyhow, so the apology wasn't worth a pinch of poop. The upshot is that I've got a charge against me in Guyana for US$25 for assault and US$25 for abusive language.

Fortunately, the 1978/79 Guyana Supertest ended peacefully and the final Test, played in Antigua, focused on the cricket, rather than the crowd. Phil Wilkins wrote in *The Australian*:

Later that morning the Supertest proceeded as if nothing had occurred. Miraculously, the ground was cleared of the mountain of broken glass and debris and the game was played out as a draw, with Greg Chappell confirming his status as the outstanding batsman of the series with a century which drew rapturous applause from the generous Guyanese ... The tour ended in Antigua with Greg Chappell and Rodney Marsh scoring centuries to frustrate the West Indies ... bringing to close a tour never tougher or more memorable, or a one-all series never more deserved.

Chappell had one final problem before he left Guyana. He was carrying a wad of cash in Australian dollars, which he had brought with him to fund a trip to the United States he had planned to take at the end of the tour.

When we were on the plane this blue form comes around, the usual immigration questions, and one of the questions was, 'Do you have more than US$150 in cash?' So I ticked 'No', and I thought nothing about it.

We were at the airport about to leave Guyana—I couldn't have been happier about leaving—when suddenly I got a tap on the shoulder: 'Ian Chappell?'

'Yeah?'

'Come with me.'

Fortunately for me, Phil Wilkins was next to me in the queue. Phil followed, one step behind me. We went into this building. The official tried to close the door and Phil put a foot out to prevent the door from closing. By this stage Phil had his notebook out and his pen in his hand.

'I want to come in. I am a reporter from Australia and I want to come in.' He was refused. 'Okay, I'll tell you what. I won't demand that I come in but I am going to stand right here, and as soon as this meeting is over I want full details of everything that has gone on in that meeting to report back to Australia.'

Phil was very smart. He realised that they were sensitive to publicity. It was only about three months after the Jonestown massacre, so they were very touchy about negative publicity. I think Phil was right on to that . . . I had this big envelope and there were quite a few $50 bills there. He picked up a stack and stared folding back the 50s. I don't know whether the bloke who brought me to the fellow behind the desk spoke quietly to him or not about the journalist standing outside the door, but the guy counting the money suddenly stopped folding back the 50s. He put all the money back in the envelope and said, 'On your way.'

Phil Wilkins, covering the tour for *The Australian*, was the only Australian newspaper journalist in the West Indies to report on the World Series; the Fairfax Group appeared to be in the Australian cricket establishment's camp. Wilkins, a senior and respected journalist, wrote a long report on the 1978/79 World Series tour which, while it recounted the many incidents on the tour, was full of praise for Chappell's handling of a very difficult series.

'Day in, day out,' Wilkins later recalled, 'it was Ian Chappell whose volatile temperament was strained to breaking point. The gruelling 1979 tour of the West Indies, against the finest team in the world, armed with the most brutal assault force in the game, and the riots which accompanied it were enough to drive any captain to distraction.

'Chappell had never experienced such humiliation as at Sabina Park [in the first Test] with his team overwhelmed by the four-pronged fast attack of Michael Holding, Andy Roberts, Colin Croft and Wayne Daniel. He sat alone beside the swimming pool at the team's hotel, almost unapproachable in his anger. He told me, the only Australian journalist on the tour, where to deposit my typewriter and it was only at the professional intervention of Richie Benaud that Chappell realised his responsibility to discuss the team's dire situation. But, ever the fighter and ever the strategist,

Chappell continued wrestling with ways in deciding how best to overcome the West Indian fast men. Typically, Chappell decided to attack the West Indians head-on.'

Wilkins described the riot at the Bourda Ground during the third Test as 'an outbreak of violence as dangerous as any Australian sporting team has known'. Chappell had to deal with 'a series of match-disrupting, injury-threatening, bottle-throwing incidents throughout the tour, the practice of which had spread like a plague through the Caribbean, maniacally and without provocation by either team, wherever the Australians travelled . . .' In the time of crisis, Chappell's courage and leadership qualities came to the fore again, characteristics which made him one of Australia's great cricket captains.

Ten

Last hurrah

It was the second time the board had sat to consider a report against
me and they couldn't have gotten away with not giving me a suspension.
Mind you, I told Umpire Bob Marshall he was an officious
Pommie bastard, so I got three weeks for telling the truth.

A negotiated peace between World Series Cricket and the cricket
establishment was settled in June 1979. Ian Chappell returned to
South Australia to play for the state. Some within the World Series
Cricket management were afraid that a few of the 'returning
rebels' such as David Hookes and Ray Bright would not be given
a fair deal at the selection table. World Series saw Chappell as the
champion of its players now about to return to the traditional
stage. If Chappell could become Test captain, even better. He had
stood up successfully for player payments and player rights
before; he could do so again. But no one could foresee the storm
about to erupt.

I had one more year to run on my World Series Cricket contract: I had signed
for three years, played for two. Consequently, as they [the nucleus of the WSC
Australians] wanted me to captain Australia, I had to play first-class matches

to qualify. I lived in Adelaide at the time so that is why I returned to play for South Australia. When they found out I was going to play, a number of the players met with me before the season started and said they wanted me to captain the side.

The first Sheffield Shield match after World Series Cricket and the cricket establishment officially shook hands and 'normal' cricket resumed saw Ian Chappell's South Australia take on Tasmania at the Formby Recreation Ground in Devonport. It was 3 November 1979. Everything had gone along swimmingly, although Chappell was concerned that one of the umpires, ex-Yorkshire policeman Bob Marshall, had a reputation for being rather officious.

There was no trouble until David Boon, playing in one of his first big matches, played forward to Geoff Attenborough, South Australia's left-arm medium-pacer. The ball just flipped his front pad and carried through to the keeper, Trevor Robertson, who appealed. Umpire Jim Stevens said 'Not out,' and Boon turned to the slips cordon, touched his pad and mouthed something to the effect that he believed the ball had nicked his pad.

Batsmen who did what young Boon had done got up Chappell's nose. He considered the batsman was there to bat and the umpire to umpire.

'Listen, pal. You get on with your fucking batting and we'll do the appealing. You leave the umpiring to the umpire.' I repeated my advice to Boon at the end of the over. I said it on the move as I was walking towards slip at the other end. This Marshall bloke was walking into position from square leg to take up his spot at the bowler's end for the new over. He had heard my words to Boon and he bellowed: 'Coom on now, get on wi' the cricket.' It was nothing, but I was on a knife's edge already and I just snapped.

'Why don't you fuck off,' I said, and just kept on walking. As I said it I thought to myself, 'Here's a bit of a problem.' The next thing I know I hear this booming voice: 'Coom 'ere, skipper!'

By the time I got to first slip the umpire was just behind me. He said, 'The game won't continue until you coom 'ere.'

I was on fire and replied, 'Why don't you fuck off, you officious Pommie bastard!'

I think that was about the end of the conversation. I was reported by Umpire Marshall and at the after-play press conference one of the Tasmanian journalists asked me an absolutely ridiculous question, and I simply cracked again. I gave him a gigantic blast and told him to get out of the room and to never come back.

In the sober confines of his hotel room that evening, Ian Chappell contemplated his future. He knew then that he was in no state of mind to captain Australia. He rang Richie Benaud and told him the story and his concerns.

World Series Cricket and the cricket establishment had got together in time for the 1979/80 season, but there was still a good deal of bitterness, especially from the traditional body towards the players who dared to 'defect'. World Series Cricket management wanted Ian Chappell to make himself available to captain Australia again, even just for an interim period. Their concern was for the likes of David Hookes and Ray Bright, who had gone to World Series Cricket and might subsequently be discriminated against in selection.

Coming back to play that season is really one of the few regrets I have in my life. I made the decision for the wrong reasons. Originally when I retired I made the decision for the right reason because I was gone as a captain. I was fatigued and I wasn't thinking aggressively. When I retired from the captaincy at The Oval [in August 1975] I knew we were playing the West Indies straight after that and I was not in the right frame of mind . . . When Lynton [Taylor] spoke to me about coming back in 1979/80, I agreed for the wrong reasons. I agreed to it because of what they said: 'Blokes like Hookesy and Ray Bright will need someone fighting for them.'

But as soon as the game in Devonport happened, and the blow-up there, I knew I had come back for the wrong reasons. I was trying to please someone else. As far as I am concerned with retirement, you only have to please one person and that's yourself. There is no way in the world I should have played that last season.

When I rang Richie I said: 'I don't know who is involved in trying to get me the captaincy but for Christ's sake, if you know who is involved could you abort the thing? Anyway, I don't think I am going to have much choice, because I'm going to get reported.' I was never in any doubt that they timed my suspension so I would not be available for the first Test. My suspension is still the longest in Australian cricket . . . It was the second time the board had sat to consider a report against me and they couldn't have gotten away with not giving me a suspension. Mind you, I told Umpire Bob Marshall he was an officious Pommie bastard, so I got three weeks for telling the truth.

Umpire Marshall's report on Ian's behaviour became the subject of a detailed inquiry by Tasmanian Cricket Board Chairman Bob Ingamells, who then passed all relevant information on to the Australian Cricket Board. Initially, Ian met with Ingamells along with Marshall and the young batsman, David Boon.

Ingamells said to Boonie, 'What did Ian say to you?' Boonie watered it down a bit, trying to help me. And Bob said to me, 'Now, is that what you said to David?' and I replied: 'No, Bob, I actually said, "You get on with your fucking batting and we'll do the appealing. You leave the umpiring to the umpires."'

I said to Boonie afterwards, 'I appreciate your saying what you did in there and that you were trying to help me, but my father always taught me to tell the bloody truth. You won't get into any trouble for telling the truth.' Martin wasn't quite right on that occasion. But, anyhow, I deserved to get reported for swearing at an umpire.

Ian apologised for letting his backers down. The sad thing about the entire episode was that a good umpire with only a modicum of commonsense would have diffused the situation rapidly. Unfortunately, there didn't seem to be one in sight that day. The board suspended Chappell from all levels of cricket for three weeks, which importantly meant that he would not be available for the season's first Test against the West Indies. Chappell says, 'They probably felt if they got me out of the first one, that would be it, I wouldn't get back in.' That suspension remains the most severe for any player to that time or since.

Chappell's first game back after the suspension was for South Australia against MCC, and resulted in another clash with Ian Botham and another argument with an umpire—in this case Graham McLeod, who was standing his debut first-class game. Former New Zealand Test cricketer Jeff Crowe, who was playing for South Australia that season, recalls: 'I sympathised with Ian for the umpire in his debut match would not allow a leg bye when Ian ducked in an attempt to avoid a bouncer which hit him on the shoulder. It was Botham bowling around the wicket, stepping miles outside the return crease and getting away with a frightening angle because the rookie umpire didn't know to watch his back foot cutting the line. So Ian, despite a dramatic protest involving dropping his bat, was made to return to the striker's end to receive another wickedly angled bumper, which he attempted to hook and gloved to the 'keeper. He walked off to a chorus of boos from the members, who thought that he was simply stirring again. They didn't stop to consider that Chappelli was right.'

'Botham was operating from wider than the sightscreen.' They were building scaffolding for the TV cameras for the coming Test match and they miscalculated at the River End, so Botham was cribbing from well outside the end of the sightscreen. Anyway, I tried to hit him into next week, gloved it and was out. Botham told me to fuck off and as I was out for nil, I thought there's not much point in arguing.

After his duck against MCC, Chappell hit 82 and 26 against Victoria, then a brilliant 154 for South Australia against the strong Western Australian team. He was back in top form and the Australian selectors, no matter how biased, could ill-afford not to pick him.

Around that time I remember I got really pissed off because they [the Australian side] didn't have a number three . . . and I recall saying to Greg at the time, 'When are these fucking idiots going to pick a proper number three in the Test side?'

Greg said: 'If you get some runs they'll pick you.'

'If you haven't fucking noticed I am getting some runs and they are not picking me.'

And then they picked me in the bloody one-day side. That was fucking ridiculous. In my opinion I should have been picked in the Test side. However, I couldn't believe it when they picked me in the one-day side . . .

We get to the ground [the SCG, for a match against England] and Greg won the toss and we are batting. He said, 'You're batting three if we lose an early wicket. If we get a start you're number six.'

'Be fucked I am, Greg. I'm either three or six. I am not going in early to protect these pricks.'

'Fuck you then, Ian. You're six.'

Greg made a few and I was on 40 odd when they brought back Botham for the finishing overs. He pitched the first up and I hit him down the ground, hitting the sightscreen on the full. The next one I hit one bounce over mid-off for four. And the next ball he bowled a bouncer. It's a no-ball. He didn't come through the crease to bowl it. It was just a normal over-stepping the crease, but it was good enough for me. I said: 'Listen, you fucker, if you are going to come through the crease and bowl no-balls you'd better make sure that it's a good one and it hits me, because if it doesn't I'm going to come down there and whack you with the bat, you gutless cunt.'

I was about 60 not out at the end of the innings and when I get back in all our guys had gone upstairs to dinner. Greg was the only one in the dressing-room and he was on the phone, and I hear him saying something about an apology. I don't hear my name, but I've worked out fairly quickly that I'm involved.

'Greg, put the phone down,' I said to him, 'I've got a feeling that telephone conversation involved me. What's it all about?'

'Mind your own business.'

'Greg, don't do anything fucking stupid. Don't apologise on behalf of the family. If you do I'll refute it, because I am not apologising. What's the problem?'

'Oh, it was Mike Brearley [England captain] on the phone. He said Botham wants an apology for what you said to him out there.' . . .

Later on Botham came to the wicket, FOT [Dennis Lillee] was bowling from the MA Noble Stand end . . . I went straight over to Dennis. 'Whatever you do don't bounce Botham first ball. Right in the block hole, first ball. This cunt's going to have his bat over his shoulder, waiting for the short one. So straight in the block hole. You'll knock him arse over tit or lbw.'

Botham did hit the first ball for six and got out lbw next ball, but the bowler was Rodney Hogg, not Dennis Lillee.

Chappell later reflected on World Series Cricket—the intrigue, the drama, the cricket revolution that turned cricket as we knew it on its head—and whether it was worth being involved.

Yes, very much so. World Series Cricket was good for the game. Apart from the fact that the players got a far better deal, night cricket evolved. I guess at some stage the penny would have dropped and the administrators would have gone to night cricket, but how long would that have taken? Perhaps we would have only been playing night cricket for the past couple of years. The marketing and the promotion has definitely been terrific for the game—a direct plus from World Series Cricket.

You can see the great difference between what has happened in England compared with Australia. In England the BBC had a terrific audience watching cricket, but it was a dying audience because they were getting older and the game was not attracting the young kids. In England it's a tougher job than in other cricket-playing nations because of the impact of soccer, which has a huge following.

English cricket has woken up and is now seeking to attract the youngsters. What I found with World Series Cricket is that it suddenly opened up the game to a broader audience. Wherever I went people would approach me. In the supermarket women would come up to me and start talking cricket. I'd ask, 'How did you get interested in the game?' and they would talk about listening to Richie Benaud talking about leg spin bowling, and often they'd identify with that because their son was a budding leggie. It's not the sole factor, but because World Series paved the way in opening up the game to a wider audience, I have no doubt that this has contributed to Australia being well ahead of England all these years.

It was a fascinating time, World Series Cricket. I guess when you are involved in something new right from the start, it is exciting. There is a fraternity among Test cricketers anyhow, an empathy among the players. You go overseas and you meet a bloke you played with or against and you are on common ground. There is a bond, particularly so with the guys you have a lot of respect for as opponents . . . But I always think there is a special bond with the guys who played World Series Cricket, a bit stronger even than the normal cricket fraternity. I guess that is because we put our careers, our necks, on the line.

The season of 1979/80 was Ian Chappell's last hurrah. After the suspension he won his way back into the Test side and led South Australia to near Sheffield Shield glory. As he did in the

Shield-winning year of 1975/76, Ian won the coveted Benson & Hedges Cricketer of the Year trophy.

In twelve matches he scored 890 runs at 40.45, with a highest score of 158. Chappell made a courageous 112 in his last Shield match, in what was virtually a Shield final against Victoria, then announced his retirement from first-class cricket. The SACA not only bestowed upon him Life Membership, but also commissioned the painting of his portrait, which now hangs alongside a painting of Sir Donald Bradman.

Chappell rates leading the 1975/76 Sheffield Shield side high on the scale of his best captaincy, along with his effort with the World Series team in the West Indies in 1979. His performance with the South Australian side in 1979/80 is up there too, although marred perhaps by an unwise decision to bait Lennie Pascoe in a critical game against New South Wales near the end of the season. New South Wales batted first and declared at 4/304. Then South Australia went in and Chappell got stuck into Lennie Pascoe with the bat and the mouth. He baited Lennie and the big fast bowler obliged, charging in like a mad man trying to knock Ian's head off. Chappell finished with a glorious 158, most of his runs coming from Pascoe's bowling. New South Wales, batting again, were dismissed for 248 and South Australia needed only 168 runs for victory. The wicket was still pretty good and New South Wales didn't have a top-class spinner, but South Australia didn't figure on Pascoe running amok. He got Ian out hooking, caught by Bob Holland in the deep for a duck, then stormed through the South Australian middle order. South Australia was blasted out for 69, with Pascoe taking 7/18.

After the match there were no recriminations; Chappell grabbed a bottle of beer and made the trek through the bar at the SCG to the New South Wales room at the other end. He poked his head into the New South Wales dressing-room and said: 'Well done fellas, too good. Well bowled, Lennie.' But Pascoe was in no mood for congratulations from any of the opposition players, least of all Chappell. He leapt from his position on the bench, grabbed Chappell by the throat and pinned him against the wall. Pascoe's rage was due to his belief that Chappell had not shown him respect. But as Chappell pointed out, the reverse was true.

'I said to him, "Len, have you ever thought that I might have been trying to annoy you because you're the best bowler in the side?"'

Chappell's last Test match was against Brearley's England side at the MCG, where he scored 75 and 26 not out in a game Australia won by eight wickets to give them a three–nil series win; although, unusually, the Ashes were not at stake in this series.

Ian Chappell first began commentating when he was little more than a toddler playing in the backyard at Leak Avenue, throwing the ball up against a wall and hitting it on the rebound.

Favell facing the fury of Miller . . . Benaud to May . . . I remember one day I was on my own—Martin and Jeanne were out—and there I was throwing the ball up against a wall, hitting the rebound. I must have got to a thousand—it must have been the team total, not an individual's—and I went in to the next-door neighbours, Mrs Mason, and asked her, 'What comes after 999?'

Chappell's grandfather Vic Richardson had been involved in cricket commentary from its earliest days, including the synthetic broadcasts with Alan McGilvray of cricket in England in the 1930s, which were produced in Sydney from cables, using the end of a pencil to simulate the sound of the bat hitting the ball. In the 1950s, when Chappell was growing up, Richardson was a well-known and respected journalist and broadcaster. 'So I guess, subconsciously, I was exposed to Vic's commentary and came to like that work,' Chappell says. 'He used to write in the newspapers, work on radio: it's amazing the similarities.'

In the early 1970s, Chappell was watching an English television program called *What Makes a Champion?* when he heard a question put to Herb Elliott that made him realise there would come a time in his life when he needed to stop and think about the future:

I must have been about 28. I was the Test captain. [David] Frost asked [Herb] Elliott a question which really got me thinking: 'Herb, you were never beaten from the time you were 14 years of age until you retired. You know, you got a gold medal at the Olympics, you broke the world record, you did everything and you retired at 22. How did you stop the rest of your life being an anti-climax?'

I don't remember Herb's reply, but the question came as a bolt from the blue and I thought, 'They say we get three score and ten years on this earth. Gee, if I stop playing at 35, I'm only halfway there. I needed to find something as interesting as my cricketing life for the second half.'

Chappell first became involved with the media after he became captain of South Australia and Australia. He worked on a Sunday TV sports show with Les Favell on Channel Seven in Adelaide and on a Saturday morning radio cricket show on 5AD. He had gained some commentary experience after he left Adelaide in 1976 to play for North Melbourne.

My deal with North Melbourne in 1976/77 was $36 000 over three years. Now, North Melbourne didn't have much money, so most of it came from the O–10 [Channel 10] Network for commentary and a first-class trip with Singapore Airlines for my wife Kay and me, wherever we wanted to go. I think for the commentary I got $200 a day and I remember thinking, 'I am earning the same for one day's commentary as what I got for playing a Test match.' We did all the Tests, plus a lot of Sheffield Shield games. Then, when I went to England in 1977 to write for *The Age*, I told Richie and he said, 'I'll get you some work with the BBC.' Richie lined it up and I worked on three Test matches with the BBC. That was really the first time I did it. It wasn't part of any grand plan to become a commentator, because there wasn't really enough work available—you had to do something else apart from being a commentator. Then in World Series when I broke my finger, Hilly [Channel Nine producer David Hill] got me to do some commentary for a couple of weeks.

Since 1980/81, Ian has commentated for Channel Nine in Australia. For eight years he co-hosted Channel Nine's *Wide World of Sports* with Mike Gibson and he had a further five years as co-host of *Sports Sunday* with Gibson for the most part, and for six months with Max Walker.

Commentary has its dangers, particularly if, like Ian Chappell, your habit is to speak your mind. One Saturday morning on *Wide World of Sports*, Chappell and Gibson had to fill in for a couple of minutes after a number of technical problems, commentating on some football footage that had no sound.

There was another cock-up when the footage came up and we threw to it. So I said: 'Jesus fucking Christ, how many mistakes are we going to make today?' It was a silly mistake. Stewie [producer Stewie Richmond] came rushing out of the control room and said, 'That went to air.' Then he came rushing out again and said, 'Gibbo, you've got to apologise for the language.' Gibbo was pissed off because he had to say, 'Mr Chappell,' complaining that he'd never called me Mr Chappell in his life.

The switchboard at the Channel Nine studio in Willoughby lit up like a Christmas tree. Chappell was suspended from duty for three weeks and was called in to see Kerry Packer:

From the moment I walked into his office, I was never in any doubt that this was a totally different type of meeting from all the ones we had had on cricket. In those meetings, because we were talking cricket, I always felt like we were on equal terms. But this time I figured it was best to sit there and shut up and cop whatever was coming my way.

Kerry said: 'The only reason I am not sacking you is that you didn't do it deliberately. Graham Kennedy did it deliberately so I sacked him. You are a time bomb waiting to go off, you are. It might sound hypocritical for me to say it because I swear a lot, but I am not on television. You are, so you are going to have to come to grips with it.'

After another similar incident, Chappell decided that if he wanted to keep his job, he would have to stop swearing altogether.

And I did achieve that for about six months . . . Then I ran into Sobey [Garry Sobers], who was in Australia for something, and he said: 'Ian, somebody told me you are not swearing.'

'Yeah, that's right, Garry.'

'Man, I'm going to have to do all the talking!'

Then in 1993 Chappell found himself out on the balcony at Old Trafford. It was the first Test, the game Shane Warne bowled Mike Gatting with that brilliant leg break in the first ball of his superb England campaign. As it happened, Ian's second wife, Barbara-Ann, was sitting up in bed, watching television. Barbara-Ann didn't generally watch a lot of cricket, but she couldn't sleep, and the moment she saw Ian she knew he was unaware that he was on camera. As Ian tells it:

During the tea break there were parachutists landing at the ground and there was a guy on the PA describing the action. The speaker was right next to where we were doing our on-camera stuff. In the tea break we would fill from England:

highlights, classic catches, whatever. Gary Shaw was our unit manager, but was filling in as a floor manager on this occasion. I had my earpiece in, but there was so much noise that I couldn't hear the director, Brian Morelli, who was yelling, 'We're on, we're on.'

Gary was only a few feet away and he said, 'Did you hear that?'

I replied: 'I can't hear a fucking thing.'

After the 1996 World Cup there was an explosion of television in India with the introduction of cable and pay TV. Suddenly, TV commentary work was available everywhere, and commentators found themselves rejecting work offers, rather than seeking more. Then Channel Nine won the contract to produce TV cricket in India. Chappell enjoyed working in India in those years, especially in association with media magnate Mark Mascarenhas.

I used to really enjoy working for Mark. It was just hard to say 'No' to Mark, and when I did say it he never took any notice. He'd say, 'C'mon mate, you enjoy it, it will be good and we'll have a good time.' He was dead right and that was the problem—I knew I was going to have a good time. I just couldn't say no to Mark and he had a lot of cricket in those days.

I was travelling a helluva lot. Then one day I said to myself, 'Jesus Ian, you live in a really nice area and you're never home to take advantage of it.' Then, sadly, Mark was killed in a car accident, and I think the Fox thing happened around the same time. And 9/11 happened about then too, so there wasn't any real incentive to travel much after that. Those things combined made it a lot easier for me to stay at home. I pretty well had two or three winters at home where I didn't do any commentary. I like the work, it's just that I don't like to be away from home for long periods. So I've hit upon a compromise: a couple of two- to three-week stints, plus the Australian season, that's about right for me.

Chappell greatly appreciates the advice and support he gets from his wife Barbara-Ann, particularly in regard to his writing.

Barb's always helped with my writing. She edits all the stuff I do. It's important to have someone who knows your style and your method. She's been a terrific help and will always improve a column that I write.

In terms of my commentary, Barb is always at me to speak properly . . . even when I am around the house and I start dropping my 'Hs' and 'Gs' she's always on my case. It can be a bit annoying at times when you are feeling a bit tired and you don't feel like concentrating too much, but I can see that it must help to get into the habit of speaking properly at all times. And if I balls-up my English at all she will always pick me up on it.

Barb was at the newspaper in Perth when John Cornell was there [and] Ron Saw, Paul Rigby, Mike Willesee, Austin Robertson; so there were a lot of good journalists there at that time. And she does a lot of reading. It was Barb who said to me, 'If you want to be a good writer, the best thing to do is to read good writing. At least then you will understand and recognise good writing.' It was pretty good advice. I went out and got a lot of sports books, by good writers, especially baseball books.

Chappell read the works of the world's great cricket writers, including Neville Cardus, John Arlott and Ray Robinson. Author and cricket scorer Irving Rosenwater urged Ian to read all that he could of R.C. Robertson-Glasgow, a brilliant wordsmith; he opens his tribute to Don Bradman in the 1949 edition of Wisden's *Cricket's Almanack* thus: 'Don Bradman will bat no more against England, and two contrary feelings dispute within us: relief, that our bowlers will no longer be oppressed by this phenomenon; regret, that a miracle has been removed from among us. So must ancient Italy have felt when she heard of the death of Hannibal.'

Barbara-Ann has made Ian Chappell more aware of life generally. With a Bachelor of Science already under her belt she is currently studying to be a herbalist, and her interests include music, nutrition, marine biology and animal behaviour.

Barb encouraged me to accompany her to the Superdome at Homebush to see the orchestra. They played the classics. It was terrific. If you had asked me 30 years ago to come and listen to that stuff I would have said, 'Bullshit, there's drinking to be done.'

Eleven

Tampa and the 1868 Australians

I was yelling at the TV as the SAS boarded the *Tampa*. After a while
Barb made the comment, 'Bad things happen when good people
do nothing.' It made me think. Those words sort of got me off my
backside. I guess I thought to myself, 'Yes, Barb's right, I can't just rail
at the television set and do nothing. I am in a position where I have
a public voice. Maybe I can do something here.'

To ignore the evil that men do is to support that evil by our
silence. Thousands of thinking Australians were outraged over the
Howard Government's handling of the *Tampa* crisis. But few
people, even people of good intention, had the will to do
anything about it. The *Tampa* affair made Chappell's blood boil. As
he watched the drama unfold on his television screen, he grew

increasingly angry. Eventually, Barbara-Ann said to him, 'Bad
things happen when good people do nothing.'

Those words were first uttered by the 18th-century British
statesman and political philosopher Edmund Burke. The Howard
Government's refusal to allow the Norwegian vessel *Tampa*,
carrying more than 400 asylum seekers rescued from a sinking
boat, to dock at Christmas Island in August 2001 is chillingly
reminiscent of the voyage of the *St Louis*, which sailed from
Hamburg in 1939 with more than 900 passengers, mostly
German refugees, and was refused permission to land in Cuba,
the United States, and several other countries in the Americas. The
refugees were shipped back to Europe where many came under
Nazi rule and some were subsequently sent to Nazi death camps.

What was to happen to the Afghan refugees aboard the *Tampa*?
If their efforts to find asylum in Australia failed, were they to be
forced to return to Afghanistan, to potential terror and fear? Like
many Jews of the Holocaust fleeing persecution and hatred
in their native land, they had no papers. They were exhausted, in
many cases penniless and spent. The *Tampa* was ordered out of
Australian waters. Was this the act of a caring nation? Ian Chappell
is no political animal, but he saw red over *Tampa*.

I was yelling at the TV as the SAS boarded the *Tampa*. After a while Barb made
the comment. It made me think. Those words sort of got me off my backside. I
guess I thought to myself, 'Yes, Barb's right, I can't just rail at the television set
and do nothing. I am in a position where I have a public voice. Maybe I can do
something here.'

The *Tampa* crisis and the treatment of the refugees brought Ian
Chappell to the stark realisation that what our government was
doing to the refugees was forcing good people to make apologies
for their own nation. Ian was indignant about *Tampa*, but he

continued to lead a quiet, comfortable life until one day when he got a phone call out of the blue. Stuart MacGill left a message for him to call. 'Strange,' he thought. 'Why would Stuart MacGill ring me? I don't know a hell of a lot about leg spin bowling. Maybe he wants me to help him with his batting.'

But the Stuart MacGill who left the message was not the New South Wales and Australian leg-spin bowler. This Stuart MacGill was in advertising, and he was gathering support from prominent people to sign a letter to help raise money for the Afghan refugees. MacGill's phone call and the *Tampa* affair got Chappell thinking. Barb's well-timed words echoed in his conscience: 'Bad things happen when good men do nothing.'

Ian rang MacGill, the advertising man, and said he would be glad to help. He joined the United Nations High Commission for Refugees (UNHCR) and is now a special representative for that body. Shortly after, Naomi Steer from the Australian UNHCR contacted Ian and gave him more information about their work in the field, and Chappell put his name to a letter calling for donations to raise money for the Afghan refugees. When Naomi told him there had been a positive response to the letter, Chappell indicated he would like to contribute more to the cause than merely putting his name to a fund-raising letter. Late in 2001 Naomi rang him again, and said the organisation had received some funding that was to be used to redevelop a playing field and to build a gymnasium in East Timor.

Naomi said, 'We are going up there as a delegation for the opening of the gymnasium and the soccer field and a few other things. Would you like to come with us and be part of the opening presentation?' I didn't see many refugees there, but I got an insight into a situation which had created many refugees . . . I saw houses that had been burnt to the ground and were just a pile of rubble. There was a string of these devastated towns, particularly as we headed out of East

Timor and towards Baucau. Naomi said in many cases the families who actually lived in these houses either burnt them or knocked them down themselves because they didn't want to leave them for the rebels coming in. I found it very disturbing, to think that you would be so desperate as to destroy your own house.

In Baucau, a town some two hours' drive from Dili, Chappell saw two committed young Australians, Nicolas Mortimer and Fiona Hamilton, running a 'coach the coaches' program, their way of spreading the gospel of sport in that war-ravaged land. The UNHCR provided the much-needed sports equipment for Nicolas and Fiona's program, which aimed to convince refugees that there is a safe and viable future for East Timor.

Mortimer played volleyball for the Australian Institute of Sport and Australia. He has travelled extensively throughout Asia, often seeing how the poor struggle to cope. Hamilton played and coached netball and worked for World Vision, and says her work in East Timor helped 'combine her sporting interest with satisfying an urge to help people in other countries' . . . One time Nicolas and Fiona took a Baucau women's volleyball team on an eleven-hour drive to Kupang, on the western tip of Timor. This proved a great success for reconcil- iation and a vindication of lateral thinking. The trip was the brainchild of Boonshan Sangfai, a Thai UNHCR officer. Those two games in Kupang had little to do with winning and losing. Boonshan suggested a women's team rather than a men's so there was 'less likelihood of aggression' . . . The women from East Timor interacted with the refugees. They spoke to them about the fact that good things were happening in East Timor and maybe it was time to start thinking about coming back.

The courage and humility shown by Nicolas and Fiona in East Timor has left a lasting impression on Ian Chappell. 'I saw how happy they were,' Chappell says, 'these people who do very good things for so many and for so little in return. People such as

Nicolas and Fiona, they love what they are doing and it shows. And they are doing such a good job. The whole experience gave me an insight into the good side of human nature.'

Soon after his return from East Timor Ian got a call from journalist Mike Coward, who covered the 1972 Australian Cricket Tour of England, Ian's first English tour as Australian captain. But Mike and Ian had known each other well before then, their association going back to the early days in Adelaide when Mike was a journalist covering both Australian Rules football and cricket. Coward is an articulate, humane and committed individual who has always demonstrated a caring attitude towards other people.

Mike rang me and said he was involved with a group which is now called 'A Just Australia', and he said the group was trying to do something for the refugees and asked would I be interested in becoming a patron.

He read through the impressive list of names they had already in place as patrons. I told Mike I was interested, but couldn't give him a definitive answer until I checked with Naomi Steer, because I did not wish to cut across what I was doing with Australia for UNHCR. I got the okay from them, so I rang Mike and agreed to become a patron. My experience with this organisation has also broadened my educational lot. It has probably made me even angrier about what I think is the unjust treatment of refugees.

Other prominent supporters of A Just Australia include ex-prime minister Malcom Fraser, former Labor Party president Barry Jones, three-time Wimbledon tennis champion John Newcombe, the Reverend Tim Costello, Aboriginal activist Lowitja O'Donoghue and well-known columnist Philip Adams.

The aim is to achieve just and compassionate treatment of asylum seekers, consistent with the human rights standards that Australia has developed and endorsed while advancing the country's international and national interests. There are some 2500 Afghan refugees living in Australia whose temporary protection visas [TPVs] are due to expire. The major concern is that many of these people will be returned to an unsafe environment. Most of the Afghan refugees on TPVs in Australia are from the Hazara tribe and the Taliban has a history of killing these people . . . At an AJA rally in Parramatta an Australian man told how he and his wife adopted a young Hazara lad and how he had grown to 'love him as a son'. He spoke of the anxiety the family now experiences as the boy's TPV comes close to expiring.

In March 2003, Ian was part of a delegation that met Immigration Minister Philip Ruddock, calling for urgent changes to the treatment of asylum seekers being kept in long-term detention throughout Australia. He became involved in lobbying political leaders in Canberra, and he visited the Baxter Detention Centre, near Port Augusta, a relatively isolated region of South Australia.

At the Baxter Detention Centre I queried something and the guard said to me, 'These are the rules.' The inmate said, 'No, they're not rules, you people just make them up. The rules change all the bloody time.' It is much worse than a jail. The real problem is the long-term internment and then, even when you get out, the temporary visa is quite a stressful thing because they can't really get on with their lives. There were kids, or younger people there, who want to study. One guy I met wants to be a dentist. He was studying like buggery to become a dentist but he knew that it could all end in an instant if his temporary protection visa ran out and he wouldn't be able to finish his studies.

To have kids behind barbed wire is a disgrace to our country . . . They have committed no crime, yet the impact of being interned behind barbed wire for a long period of time is going to have a huge mental effect on them . . . They are no different from us in that they strive to make their lives as good as possible. They are so hungry that they work like buggery, they study like buggery. As soon as you meet one of these kids and talk to them for a little while, you think to yourself, 'Here's somebody who has got a lot of talent. We should be utilising this talent, not punishing the kid.'

All I do when I speak to groups is put forward those sorts of ideas . . . It is really quite humbling, because people come up to me after I've spoken at a group function and say, 'Thank you so much for what you are doing,' and I say, 'But I'm not doing anything much at all. It is you people who are doing the good work. You're meeting the refugees and you are going to Baxter and other detention centres, you visit the people there regularly.'

Probably the biggest discovery I've made is that if you really want something changed, it's only people power which can achieve it. The politicians won't change anything unless there is a demand from the people to change it. I've used the analogy with Nazi Germany and, while it may seem a bit extreme at first, I have [met] people who know a lot about the Nazi atrocities and the history who say to me, 'No, it is not a distorted analogy.' Once you allow a government to get away with some of the crap they've been getting away with, where does it stop?

Ian Chappell was inducted into the Sport Australia Hall of Fame in 1986, the International Hall of Fame in 2000 and, at the annual Allan Border Medal presentations in Melbourne in 2003, the Australian Cricket Hall of Fame. He gave a moving speech at the 2003 medal presentations, not on captaincy or his career, but on the need to recognise Australia's pioneering cricket team—the 1868 Australians, the first Australian cricket team to tour England.

Thirteen of the 1868 team were Aboriginals, most of whom hailed from the Western District of Victoria and had nicknames such as Dick-a-Dick, Mullagh, Cuzens, Sundown, King Cole, Tiger, Redcap, Bullocky, Mosquito, and Twopenny. They were led by an Englishman, Charles Lawrence, who in 1861 sailed to Australia with the first English team and stayed in the colony to play and coach cricket. The Central Board for Protection of Aborigines lobbied the Victorian Government to stop the tour, but Lawrence took his men to Queenscliffe Beach where they used long boats to board the *Rangatira*, which was bound for Sydney. From Sydney, the team sailed for England on the wool clipper *Parramatta*.

In Australia, Aboriginals were treated like second-class citizens. They had no legal or voting rights and around the time of the 1868 tour moves were afoot to separate whole family groups. This was the policy that resulted in the Stolen Generations. Following Federation, the White Australia Policy ensured no Aboriginal, let alone a black cricketer, would be recognised as an Australian citizen. Even after they gained the vote in 1967, Aboriginal Australians continued to be marginalised.

Chappell went in to bat for the Aboriginal cricketers and his persistence paid off. He drove a campaign to have the 1868 team officially recognised and be allotted a special players' number, in the tradition of presenting player numbers to Australian debutantes in Test and one-day international cricket. 'To actually get to England in those days was a remarkable act of endurance,' Chappell says. 'I am not suggesting for a moment that if they hadn't gone in 1868 Australian cricket wouldn't have had tours of England, but in my opinion there is no doubt that they paved the way for what followed. On that basis alone they deserve to be recognised as Australian cricketers.'

Charles Lawrence was the only non-Aboriginal in the 1868 side. In their first match at The Oval, batsman Johnny Mullagh revealed his wonderful talent, scoring 73 in the second innings after a first dig of 33. He was given a standing ovation by the crowd of 8000. Mullagh, a wristy, attractive batsman who occasionally dropped on one knee against fast bowling and cut the ball over the wicket-keeper's head, scored 1698 runs on tour at 23.65, with a top score of 94, and took 245 wickets at ten runs apiece. Johnny Cuzens, who had a high bowling action and could run like the wind, hit 1358 runs at 19.9 and took 114 wickets at 11.3.

Redcap played all 47 matches, scoring 630 runs at 8.46 and taking 54 wickets at 10.7.

During breaks in play, Dick-a-Dick would challenge people for a shilling a throw to try to hit him with a cricket ball thrown from ten paces. In one hand he held a parrying shield about four-feet long and as wide as a cricket bat, and in the other a boomerang, which he used to deflect the missiles. He was only hit once during the tour. Peter and Mosquito gave stock-whip demonstrations while Charles Dumas enthralled the crowds with his boomerang throwing.

After his speech in Melbourne, Chappell embarked on a series of lengthy discussions with the board and the Australian Cricketers' Association to have the achievements of the 1868 Australians officially recognised. Chappell met with Ian Healy, president of the Australian Cricketers' Association, and with Bob Merriman, chairman of Cricket Australia. In addition, he suggested that they make up 14 shirts of the kind used by current Test teams, with the allotted players' numbers on them, and that Cricket Australia should pick 14 of the best Aboriginal cricketers from the Impaja Cup tournament and present them with the shirts.

It can be a ceremonial presentation: 'Here's the shirt for Dick-a-Dick and it goes to . . .'

Then you could do up a memorabilia kit, with a quote which encapsulates the 1868 tour. Funds can then be channelled back to Aboriginal cricket. Heals said they can use some of the ACA funds for a needy cause such as Eddie Gilbert's last resting place. [Gilbert was the great Aboriginal fast bowler of the 1930s.] He was buried in a pauper's grave, so funds could be used to give Eddie a decent headstone.

The other thing is, I want to write to MCC Chief Executive Officer Peter French at the Hall of Fame, and propose that they put Johnny Mullagh in the

202 **chappelli speaks out**

Hall of Fame—even if they establish a separate category, one that acknowl-edges special cases, be they players or administrators. Johnny Mullagh's inclusion in the Hall of Fame is deserved acknowledgement of his skill and, equally importantly, it will set in the minds of current indigenous people and sportsmen that there is a history of Aboriginal cricketers playing decent cricket.

At the moment they have got a lot of footballers playing league, union and Australian Rules. There is a tradition of Aboriginal footballers, men who have trod the path before, but there's not much there in the way of cricket. If anything, there is an anti-tradition: 'Why should I put myself through the crap that Eddie Gilbert went through?'

During the tea break of the Boxing Day Test against Pakistan in December 2004, the 1868 Aboriginal Cricketers were formally honoured by Cricket Australia at a ceremony at the MCG. Those attending included: Faith Thomas, Australia's first female Abor-iginal to be selected in a national Australian side; Len Clarke, a descendant of 1868 all-rounder Johnny Cuzens; and Cricket Australia chairman Bob Merriman. Two framed replica shirts, similar to those worn by the 1868 team, were presented. One will be housed in the Australian Sport Hall of Fame and the other will be displayed at the Johnny Mullagh Cricket Centre in Harrow, Western Victoria. (Johnny Mullagh was the star turn of the 1868 team, which played 47 matches in England, winning 14, losing 14 and having the best of most of the 19 drawn matches.)

'Australian cricket had been seeking for some time to recog-nise the contribution of the 1868 team in the most appropriate manner,' Merriman told the MCG crowd. 'This matter was drawn to our attention by Ian Chappell, who has a strong interest in the history of the 1868 team, and we thank him for his contribution. Allocating these special player numbers to the 14 tour members, with the prefix AUS, is formal recognition of the team's place in history as the first cricketers to represent Australia. We are very

proud of the achievements of the 1868 team and of the continued involvement of indigenous players in Australian cricket.'

Thanks to Ian Chappell every player who toured England in
1868 has now been given an official Australian player number. It
was decided that the special numbers for the 1868 players would
bear the prefix AUS, so that Charles Bannerman—the man who
opened the batting for Australia in the first official Test match,
scored Test cricket's first century and was given Number One
from the time the numbers system began—could retain the
Number One.

Chappell's interest in the Aboriginal cricketers reflected that of
his grandfather, Victor Richardson, who in 1951 was asked to
unveil the monument dedicated to the 1868 team at Edenhope in
Victoria, the area where the Aboriginal players trained. In 2002
Ian Chappell was invited to go to Edenhope and rededicate the
monument. 'I took that to be a great honour,' Chappell says.

The 1868 team's recognition is now complete. They can thank
Ian Chappell for that; his determination and drive to have these
cricketers honoured and acknowledged as bona fide Australian
cricketers is another noteworthy contribution by him to the
national game.

Twelve

Heroes have heroes too

On my first tour of England as captain of Australia, we were at the British Sportsman's Club in Tottenham Court Road, when Keith came rushing up to me, shook hands and said, 'I'm glad they made you captain. Good luck, and by the way, Chappelli, don't take any notice of anything I write about you.'

Ian Chappell was a curious mixture: on the one hand he was the captain who took no prisoners, fighting in the Test arena like a gladiator in ancient Rome; on the other hand, he is a man of compassion. The asylum seekers and the descendants of the 1868 Aboriginal team can attest to that; so too those close to him.

A cricket hero to thousands, Ian has his own set of heroes. Among them his boyhood idol, the irrepressible Keith Miller, charismatic all-rounder of the late Bradman era. A magnificent athlete, Miller oozed natural talent. He was, arguably, the greatest Test all-rounder of them all, except for Garfield Sobers. Keith

Miller was right out of *Boys' Own Annual*. He was a real life hero: Test cricketer, VFL footballer, war hero, film-star looks, Miller had it all.

I was seven years old when Dad took me to Adelaide Oval to watch Australia play England. Despite Arthur Morris getting a double century and Len Hutton carrying his bat for 156, the thing I remember most about the game was Keith Miller hurdling his bat. Miller was sliding his bat towards the crease to avoid being run out, when the toe of his bat dug into the turf and stopped abruptly. Miller actually jumped over his bat. If Keith hadn't reacted so quickly and athletically he could well have been skewered by his own bat.

There is good reason why I remember Miller. He was my idol and at the Adelaide Oval that day Dad encouraged me: 'Look at Miller, Ian, look at what he does,' Martin said. Keith Miller was born 15 days after Dad, he served in the air force, the same as Martin did and, as in our family, Keith sired only boys. I think deep down he was Martin's idol as well.

The most dashing of cricket's swashbucklers, Miller was one of those larger-than-life characters, the embodiment of an ancient god, here on earth not just for a short time, but for a good time too. He was a carefree soul with a cavalier touch which made him an instant hero. During World War II, Miller flew night-time missions over Germany and occupied France in a de Havilland Mosquito fighter-bomber. A lover of classical music, on one mission he took a slight detour to fly over the city of Bonn, Beethoven's birthplace, surviving flak from German gun crews and from his squadron leader when he got back to base.

There were other Miller antics during his war years—he once flew up the straight at Royal Ascot and another day he buzzed the Goodwood track. But war respects neither friend nor foe . . . Every Friday night Miller used to meet up with mates at the Central Hotel in Bournemouth, not far from where the squadron was based. Miller said, 'Cricket saved my life. I was invited to play in a match at Dulwich College, a fund-raising event. When I got back to Bournemouth there were barricades surrounding the area of the pub. A Focke-Wulf had bombed and strafed the town, causing the church spire next to the Central Hotel to collapse onto the pub, killing eight of my mates.' Every year for more than 50 years after the tragedy Keith returned to the United Kingdom and visited the wives and girlfriends of the men killed that fateful night. The pub was rebuilt, but the clock is stopped at the precise time the bomb struck, a silent reminder of the futility and tragedy of war.

On my first tour of England as captain of Australia, we were at the British Sportsman's Club in Tottenham Court Road, when Keith came rushing up to me, shook hands and said, 'I'm glad they made you captain. Good luck, and by the way, Chappelli, don't take any notice of anything I write about you.' With that Keith disappeared into the crowd almost as quickly as he had materialised. Years later Dennis Lillee was angry with Keith over something he'd written. I told Dennis Keith's philosophy on writing and suggested he make a point of having a chat with him some time. Dennis sought out Miller and afterwards he told me it was an enjoyable experience, as well as a profitable one—Dennis had picked up a couple of tips on bowling.

On a hot, steamy day in Guyana in 1973, opening bowlers Max Walker and Jeff Hammond had put in a mammoth stint at the Bourda Ground to put us in a winning position. As we left the ground for lunch, the team stood back and applauded Walker and Hammond from the field. As I walked up the stairs of the old wooden pavilion, a hand suddenly reached through the crowd and grabbed my arm. 'Tell Walker and Hammond I'm bloody proud of them,' said a voice, and then he was gone. As a kid I had Keith Miller on a pedestal and I am delighted to say that he is still up there.

Miller liked to speak of men such as Guy Gibson and Leonard Cheshire, whose fame lies with their extraordinary courage and deeds with the RAF's famed 617 Squadron—the Dambusters. Another mate of Keith's was Hughie Edwards, who after the war became governor of Western Australia and who, like Guy Gibson and Leonard Cheshire, won a VC, DSO and DFC. Douglas Bader was another man Keith greatly admired. Only two days before Bader died, Miller and ex-England captain Gubby Allen played golf with the famous wartime pilot. Miller kept the ball that Bader used that day.

As a guest on the Michael Parkinson Show, Miller was asked about the intense pressure of Test cricket. 'Pressure?' he said, looking the famous TV host in the eye. 'What bloody pressure? I'll tell you what pressure is . . . pressure is flying a Mosquito with a Messerschmitt up your arse.' To Miller, cricket was a game to be enjoyed.

In 1946 Miller married a Boston-born beauty named Peg. They lived mostly at Newport, on Sydney's northern beaches, and they had four sons, Bill, Denis, Bob and Peter. A few years back Keith and Denis were watching the Test cricket, and a voice-over referred to Don Bradman as the world's best cricketer. Denis said Keith rose to his feet and said, 'Bradman, best batsman? Yes. Best cricketer? Garry Sobers!'

In the last years of his life Miller suffered cancer and a stroke and was confined to a wheelchair. His hearing was going and his voice was unsteady, but he remained a hero to the likes of Richie Benaud and Alan Davidson—themselves heroes to others who became heroes, like Ian Chappell.

One of the saddest episodes of Miller's life was his divorce from Peg in 1999. They had been married some 53 years when Miller went to live with Marie, a long-term friend, who was by his side when he died at a nursing home on Victoria's Mornington Peninsula in October 2004.

As a young woman, Peg Miller was a stunning beauty and she and Keith made a handsome couple. After Keith went to

Melbourne, Ian and Barbara-Ann took Peg under their wing; a kindness the Miller boys will not forget, and something Keith himself admired.

A few weeks before he died, Miller offered this opinion of Ian Chappell, as a bloke, a batsman and a captain. 'I give Ian ten out of ten for all three things,' Miller said. 'He is a man I admire. He was tops as both a batsman and a captain. He is a terrific bloke— a hero to me.'

Miller played 55 Tests, scoring 2958 runs at 36.97 with seven centuries, and he took 170 wickets at an average of 22.97, with best figures of 7/60. But statistics don't tell the Miller story, not by a long way.

Another of Ian's heroes was Bill O'Reilly, regarded by Don Bradman as the best bowler he played with or against. O'Reilly took 144 wickets at 22.59 in just 27 Test matches and he formed, with Clarrie Grimmett, the most famous spin-bowling partnership in history. O'Reilly, the man they called the Tiger, was the sort of bloke who enriched all those who came into contact with him. From the time his father introduced him to Henry Lawson at a pub in Milson's Point, Sydney in about 1915, the English language and the Tiger became lifelong friends.

After retiring from cricket, Chappell's cricket writing and his media commitments as a commentator with Channel Nine gave him the opportunity to mix with O'Reilly. It was, for him, very much a getting of greater wisdom. Ian found the Tiger the most engaging of people. They were on common ground, for there was a passion and a fire about the way they both looked at the game.

The Tiger loved a drink. In fact, he introduced his spinning mate Clarrie Grimmett to the 'delights of the amber fluid' on a trip to South Africa under the leadership of Victor Richardson in 1935/36. It didn't affect their performance, for Grimmett took 44 wickets and O'Reilly 27 wickets in the Test series. Chappell loved to hear the old stories from a man such as O'Reilly. Tiger helped him to learn more about Vic Richardson the cricketer and the captain, and the men who played with and against his grandfather.

I remember Sheffield [Alan Shiell, cricket writer for *The News* in Adelaide] trying to get Tiger to talk about the moderns and I said, 'No Sheff, don't ask him about Lillee or Thomson or Walters. Have him talk about his era—Bradman, Grimmett, Larwood, Voce, Hammond and company.

Once the Tiger told of how he came home whingeing to his father about a sore back after bowling a lot of overs during a hot day in the bush. His dad heard him out for a few seconds and then said: 'Son, would you like to know how not to get a bad back, so you don't have to walk around with a bit of a stoop? And would you like to know how not to get arthritis, so your fingers and knees don't give you hell on cold days?'

The Tiger indicated that he wanted the remedy.

'Die before you're 35.'

The Tiger was nearing 80 when he happened to find himself in the bar at the Sheraton Hotel in Perth with Ian Chappell and Dick Tucker, a cricket reporter for News Limited. A fellow outside the pub had just loaded a tirade of abuse upon Chappell, and he found refuge in the bar.

We were halfway through our first beer when this bloke who was causing the fuss outside turned up and continued his tirade. He suggested we go outside and settle things. Then the Tiger stood up, removed his coat and said, 'If you want a fight, mate, I'll accommodate you.' Dick Tucker convinced Tiger that there was no need to fight the bloke as the security guards would sort him out. But it revealed the fire in the belly of the Tiger still burned brightly.

For more than 30 years Bill O'Reilly covered the Test matches in Australia, writing a column for the Fairfax Group, his work appearing in *The Sydney Morning Herald* and *The Age*. He wrote his copy in beautiful copperplate hand in an old blue-lined exercise book. O'Reilly was well into his 80s when he sat to watch his last Test match at the Sydney Cricket Ground; Ian Chappell asked his producer if he could interview O'Reilly in his favourite seat, where he had composed his columns. When the interview was finished, Chappell said: 'What we'll miss most of all, Tiger, is your company in the press box.'

'From the look in your eyes son,' said Bill, 'I can tell you mean that, and I thank you.'

The last few years of his life were tough for O'Reilly and his family. He had a number of operations and eventually, at the age of 85, had to have a leg amputated.

'They can't no-ball me any more,' he said.

Richie Benaud has been both friend and mentor to Ian Chappell. 'Richie's advice has always been to the point and full of common-sense,' Chappell says. 'Whether it is business or cricket or life in general, he is the person I turn to.'

In 1963, soon after Chappell had scored his maiden first-class century—149 versus Benaud's New South Wales at the Adelaide Oval—he went to England to play a season of Lancashire League. When he arrived at the Ramsbottom Club, there awaiting him was a new Gray-Nicholls cricket bat, courtesy of Richie Benaud.

Just before the start of the 1972/73 Test series against Pakistan in Australia, Ian called members of the Australian team together. He said he would not tolerate the use of the word 'black' in any comments to an opposition player.

Apart from the common decency involved, I pointed out that they didn't, for example, say to an English player, 'You lucky white bastard.' After that meeting and just before the Adelaide Test, selector Sam Loxton dragged me aside at the nets and said he didn't want to see any trouble between the sides, especially on the score of racist remarks. I assured him that there would be no trouble, and there wasn't any.

Jack Roosevelt Robinson, the first black man to play major league baseball in the United States, was a man Ian Chappell greatly admired. In 1987, almost 40 years to the day after Robinson made baseball history, Chappell introduced a story on Jackie Robinson on Channel Nine's *Wide World of Sports* program, which he co-hosted with Mike Gibson.

Forty years ago this season, Jack Roosevelt Robinson became the first black man to play baseball in the major leagues. What Jackie Robinson did in his ten seasons with the Brooklyn Dodgers is one of the great sporting achievements. As a pioneer for his race, Jackie not only had to succeed as a player, which he did admirably, but he had to put up with racist comments and vicious attempts to injure him from the bigots who at that time were as common in the game of baseball as safe hits. Off the field, Jackie Robinson had to endure the threats of some teams not to play against the Dodgers if he was included in the line-up and the indignity of being housed in different hotels to his white team-mates. The Jackie Robinson story is one of skill, bravery and the special intelligence required to overcome ignorant but powerful people. The 1987 American Baseball season has been dedicated to the memory of Jackie Robinson, a great man who died in 1972 . . . In Roger Kahn's book, *The Boys of Summer*, Leo 'The Lip' Durocher, a player/manager with the

Dodgers who had a spiky relationship with Robinson, said:
'Ya want a guy that comes to play. This guy didn't just come
to play. He come to beat ya. He come to stuff the goddam bat
right up your arse.'

Chappell's research had been extensive. His delivery was
passionate and professional. Gibson was blown away. Wherever
racism was involved, or he believed it so, Robinson was prepared
to speak out and fight for justice. As a baseballer he played the
game with all his heart. He had an unquenchable spirit and a
sense of fair play. He also had an inherent dedication to others.

There is a lot of Jackie Robinson in Ian Chappell.

According to Chappell, the consummate competitor was master
golfer Jack Nicklaus. Only Tiger Woods has come close to Nicklaus
in ability and endurance. Nicklaus won the British Open three
times, the US Open four times, the PGA Championship five times
and the US Masters on a record six occasions; 18 majors in all. He
was the world's 'Mr Golf' for many years and was voted the Golfer
of the Century by American Sports Writers in 1986. His introduction to the game of golf came from his father, a chemist. Nicklaus
senior was advised to walk a few miles a day as part of therapy for
an ankle injury, so he took up golf and Jack, then aged ten,
became his caddy. Nicklaus became a chemist before he became a
golf professional, but eventually the bug and the ability took over.

On his first overseas Test tour, South Africa in 1966/67,
Chappell had just begun to play the game of golf seriously and as
his interest in the game coincided with Nicklaus's rise to fame, he
began to follow Nicklaus's fortunes.

I started to follow him because I was impressed by how far he could hit the ball.
I got my first look at Nicklaus [then known as 'Ohio Fats' for the excess weight

he carried] playing at Adelaide's Kooyonga Golf Club in the 1965 Australian Open. Jack had won the Open for the first of six times in 1964 and I set out with a big gallery to follow him for the first round. However, news came through that Gary Player was running hot, and my sense of history took over from my sense of loyalty. I deserted Jack in time to catch 'the man in black' [Player] hit an iron to the ninth green and then make a long eagle putt to send him out in 29. Sensing the chance to see a sub-60 round I stuck with Player, but he blew out to 33 on the back nine and shot a 62. I never 'deserted' Jack again, but in 1979 on a visit to the Mony tournament at the La Costa course in Carlsbad, California, I did follow Jack Newton instead of Jack Nicklaus. I followed 'Newt the Beaut' for four holes and Nicklaus for 14. Newt and I were always a jinx on one another's sporting endeavours. Whenever he came to the cricket ground I invariably got out straight away and when I followed him on the golf course he made bogeys. However, at La Costa I decided this jinx business was too stupid for words.

While I watched, Newton bogeyed the first and the second. If it wasn't a jinx, Jack was playing some mighty uncharacteristic golf, so I headed for the Golden Bear's group. When I got to the last with Nicklaus, I looked at the leader board and saw that Newt was two under after 16—four under since I left him. I dashed off and reached Newton's group in time to see him bogey 17 and 18, to finish at even par. To show me there were no hard feelings, Jack took me into the players' lounge and introduced me to Jack Nicklaus, Tom Watson and Lee Trevino. At that very time we had just finished playing World Series Cricket and Nicklaus was making substantial changes to Sydney's Australian Golf Club. We talked about Kerry Packer's influence on both projects.

'It was through Kerry's television interests and my job with *Wide World of Sports* that I was able to link Jack Nicklaus and Jack Newton a few years later. Jack Newton was badly injured in a horrific accident when he walked into the path of an aeroplane propeller on his way home from a football match. I wanted to get Jack Nicklaus to send Newt a morale-boosting message. When I got through to Barbara Nicklaus, she told me Jack was in Canada for the Open. She asked after Jack Newton and then told me that if I rang her husband's hotel at nine o'clock, their time, I would catch him. When I got through to Nicklaus I told him that I wanted Jack's mates from the US tour to send him a message via television in Australia. Nicklaus was most concerned about Newton's health and he said, 'I know what you want, just tell the local television crew to be by the first tee at eight o'clock tomorrow morning and I'll organise the rest.' True to his word, the Golden Bear had everyone lined up and the messages came through. His wife also sent flowers and a message to Jack's wife, Jacquie Newton . . . I have followed Nicklaus's golf career closely and I believe he's the best competitor I've seen, and I can't think of anyone from any sport who can match him for success over such a long period. He has always been helpful and generous with his time. Jack Nicklaus is a champion in every sense of the word.

Chappell has cricket heroes other than Miller, O'Reilly and Benaud, and is interested in present and future players as well as those from the past. He has a high regard for Ricky Ponting's batting—his fearlessness in pulling and hooking the quicks—and for the mental strength of Matthew Hayden, Michael Clarke and Simon Katich. He marvels at the clean hitting of Adam Gilchrist. Bowlers Shane Warne, Glenn McGrath and Jason Gillespie are high on the list of players who impress him. He also has a healthy respect for a host of batsmen around the world including Brian Lara, Sachin Tendulkar, V.V.S. Laxman, Michael Vaughan and Jayasuriya. Mark Taylor is a recently retired player he enjoyed watching play. He also reckoned Taylor was a terrific captain.

Mark Taylor did what a captain is supposed to do, he improved his team. He took that Australian team and even though it was a good team by the time Allan Border left it, Taylor took it to another level. He beat the West Indies in the Caribbean, which would never have happened under Border. He beat South Africa, which Australia had not been able to do under Border, and he took the side to Pakistan and won over there, something Australia had not done for yonks; three pretty good scalps. He looked at his team and said, 'Now, what are my assets here?' He gave freedom to his stroke-makers, blokes like Mark Waugh, fully aware that the quicker we score runs the more time we have to get the opposition out twice . . . I thought Mark Taylor had a lot of good qualities as a captain. Having spent time with him now in commentary, I can see he's a good bloke. He's easy going, he's a man's man, he likes a drink and there's no bullshit with him—'Here I am, this is Mark Taylor. If you like me that's fine, if you don't, too bad.'

Chappell regards Garry Sobers was the greatest batsman of his time, with Graeme Pollock a near second. He also admired Doug Walters's unique abilities, but he says Viv Richards is the man he would call for to tear an attack apart: 'His 153 not out in just 130 balls at the MCG in 1979/80 was a masterpiece. In that World Series Cup game the Australian attack included Dennis Lillee, Jeff Thomson and Rodney Hogg.' Another batsman to have impressed Ian over the years is his brother Greg: 'Near the end of his career, Greg complained that he wasn't able to dredge up all his concentration as often as he would like,' Ian Chappell says, 'but, typically, he announced his retirement before the last Test against Pakistan in 1983/84, while still needing 69 to pass Sir Donald Bradman's Australian record. Having set himself a task, he summoned all his powers of concentration for one last supreme effort. He finished with 182 and ended his glittering Test career as he'd started it— with a century.' Chappell says that of all the batsmen he has seen, Greg has 'the most organised mind'.

Among the bowlers he played against, Ian had high regard for the fast men such as England's John Snow and West Indian Andy Roberts, and spinners Erapally Prasanna and Derek Underwood.

The best opposition quick I faced was Snow. He was fast, accurate and always learning. He was not in the top bracket in terms of pace, but in a Test match he didn't drop his pace much and he always had a little room under the accelerator pedal for important moments. When I first faced Snow in 1968, he was mainly a cutter of the ball. He had an exceptionally good leg cutter. By the time I last faced him in 1975 he'd added swing to his armoury and also bowled a good slower ball. He had a damned good bouncer, especially in Australia, where he didn't have to pitch the ball in short as in England. Snow gave you no warning signs when he bowled a short one, as he retained his well-balanced jog to the wicket and used just a little bit more shoulder to gain extra pace and bounce. His short deliveries were inevitably well directed and often they rose sharply off quite a reasonable length.

There were a lot of similarities between Snow and Roberts. Both used to cut the ball more than swing it, they were about the same speed, with Roberts a touch quicker, and they were both very accurate for bowlers of their pace. Andy was a shrewd bowler. I credit him with playing a large part in the West Indian renaissance in the mid-70s. It was his hard-nosed attitude, along with Viv Richards and keeper Deryck Murray during World Series Cricket, that helped to catapult the West Indies to the top.

Andy was a mean bowler in the best sense of the word. He had been troubling me with short lifting deliveries into the rib cage area in the first Test of 1975/76. I was sweating on something to hook or pull so that I could do a bit of terrorising of my own and whistle one past the ear of the short-leg fieldsman. I finally got one in the perfect spot, aimed at the right shoulder. Delighted, I smashed it away to the square-leg boundary and looked forward to a few more of those. I played against Andy on a fairly regular basis until I retired in early 1980, but I never got another bouncer aimed at my right shoulder. When I was in the Caribbean in 1991 as a commentator, I was having a drink with Andy one night after play. I asked him if he remembered the delivery at the Gabba.

'Sure I do, Ian.'

'Why didn't you bowl any more at my right shoulder?'

'Do you think I'm a bloody idiot? I could tell you liked them there.' Good fast bowlers have the memory of an elephant.

The fastest bowlers I ever faced were Jeff Thomson and Michael Holding. There may have been a slight difference in speed between the two, but it didn't allow you time to change your mind. If your first choice was wrong, you had to hope your luck was in. Apparently, the best recorded reflexes react in 0.42 of a second. According to the mathematicians, you had 0.47 of a second from the time the ball left Thommo's hand until it reached the batsman. It's no wonder many a batsman was late on the shot and many more felt the sensation of the ball hitting the bat, rather than vice versa.

Thommo was one bloke I reckon was unhookable. His bouncer usually passed by a few feet overhead and the 'climber' was never short enough to hook. Thommo was unique. He was a genuine fast man who liked nothing better than bowling fast. In Trinidad in 1979 he took five wickets in the first innings, but in the second dig on a wicket that had flattened right out it was virtually impossible to bowl him after his opening spell. After we'd won the game by about 20 runs, I had a quiet chat with Jeff.

'Why,' I suggested, 'don't you have a yarn with Dennis [Lillee] about how to cut the ball and bowl on slower tracks?'

'I know what you are saying,' said Thommo, 'but if you don't mind, I'd like to do it my way.'

Chappell understood; the fast man, who for a couple of hot summers was arguably the fastest bowler to draw breath, would live or die by speed. Describing his own bowling, Thomson said, 'I just shuffle up and go "wang".' When Ian related that to ex-New South Wales batsman Warren Saunders, who'd been hit on the head by Thommo when batting for St George, Saunders said, 'Yeah, but he went "wang" pretty bloody quick.'

'The best fast bowler I batted against was Dennis Lillee,' Chappell says. 'He had all the tools of the trade, which he kept finely tuned by training extremely hard, and he was a fast learner. On top of that, he was the most determined cricketer I've ever come across. If anyone ever mastered his bowling, which was rare, they still had to overcome his iron will. Lillee was fast, fiery and fearsome.'

Allan Border, who was handed the Australian Test captaincy when Kim Hughes resigned in tears after the second Test against the West Indies in 1984/85, says: 'I don't think I was influenced by Chappelli's batting so much as his grit and determination. I remember being very influenced by the whole Chappell era, from the time Ian took over the captaincy right up to World Series Cricket and to actually playing a season with him in 1979/80. Ian and I have had many discussions on cricket over the years, most of them ending in massive arguments, but I have always enjoyed those jousts and would say that on the majority of occasions I have taken something out of them. I regret not seeking Ian's counsel more when I first took over as Test captain. I'm positive that I would have approached those early days in a better frame of mind. One major stumbling block in later years was the drama between Ian and Bob Simpson who, as coach, I found myself forever defending. I've never got to the bottom of what the story is there.'

In one of those 'massive arguments' Border suggested to Chappell that his captaincy was bolstered by having Thommo and Lillee most of the time. Ian wouldn't let that delivery pass through to the keeper; 'I told AB he needed a history lesson,' Chappell says. 'Go back and research how often I had Thommo and Lillee together in my team. Actually, Thommo and Lillee played in ten Tests together under my leadership: ten out of the 30 Test matches I captained for Australia.' In those ten Tests Australia won six matches and drew four.

I found England's Derek 'Deadly' Underwood the most difficult spinner to score off. Deadly was difficult for a right-hander because he was too quick through the air to regularly use your feet and because he didn't try to spin them all, rather angle the ball in at you from around the wicket. His line and length was impeccable and you didn't get much to cut. On a dampish pitch he was a nightmare. He'd give you absolutely nothing to score off and then the odd one would take off like Superman—up, up and away. I remember one he bowled to Doug Walters on the 'Fusarium pitch' at Headingly in 1972. It climbed straight over the shoulder of Doug's bat and Alan Knott took it beside his right ear.

What a combination they were—Underwood and Knott. Knotty was the best keeper I saw, just a smidgeon ahead of Rod Marsh, purely for his ability to stand up to Underwood. On that score Marsh was handicapped a little, because the English combination also played together for Kent. Marsh, on the other hand, played a lot on the bouncy WACA pitch and didn't have the luxury of seeing much spin. Both Knott and Marsh were brilliant standing back—where I would give a slight edge to Rodney—agile and never afraid to throw themselves for a wide edge.

Australia made better use of Marsh's agility, with a bigger gap between keeper and first slip than the Englishmen. This has the advantage of giving the slips a wider arc. So often in Ashes Tests, Knott and Marsh used to cancel each other out with their batting. Both players had the happy knack of making runs when their team needed them most.

Today's champion spinner Shane Warne has always been a favourite with Ian Chappell, who admires not only Warne's extraordinary skill as a leg spinner, but also his fielding, his hard hitting with the bat in the lower order, and the glint in his eye; he is a man prepared to take a risk. Ian got to know Shane Warne better when they got together at the US Masters golf tournament in Augusta. He was there commentating for Channel Nine and Warne was there to learn, as part of his work with the Nine Network. They chatted over a few beers most nights and Ian learnt from Shane that he was unhappy with his batting against the short-pitched ball, so they agreed that when they returned to Australia Ian would help him out. Warne visited Chappell while he was conducting his annual 'batting week' at the Australian Cricket Academy in Adelaide.

During the Augusta trip the pair discussed field placement and Chappell said he reckoned Warne would not be able to bowl to him without a deep mid wicket—Warne likes to leave that spot open, to encourage batsmen to hit against his considerable spin. 'Shane was just recovering from his finger injury and he said part of his recovery was to bowl for half an hour each day,' Chappell says, 'so I suggested that perhaps I could have a hit.' As both men are great students of the game this gave Ian a golden opportunity to bat against the great bowler. Warne too had the chance to see at close hand the batting prowess of Ian Chappell, albeit long retired.

Brad Hogg was there too. Hogg gave me a few outside off and I hit him through the covers. Warne was smart. He only tossed the ball up when he bowled a middle and leg line. When he got to off stump they were flatter and quicker. After I finished batting I said to Warney, 'You're allowed to toss them up on off stump as well you know.'

He replied, 'No way. Not after I saw you cover drive Hoggy.'

I reckon he saw Hogg give me room outside off and decided that I wouldn't get any there. That gave me a great insight into his thinking. A very smart cricketer, Shane Warne.

At the end of a highly competitive session, where Ian was able to convince Warne of how good he must have been in his prime against spin bowling, Warne too had a little win as Ian conceded, 'He was more difficult to hit to mid wicket than I thought.' With his shrewd cricket brain, Shane Warne could well have made a great Test captain. Chappell lauds the captaincy of men such as Benaud, Mark Taylor, England's Ray Illingworth and Mike Gatting, but he doesn't rate quite so highly the leadership or the character of Steve Waugh.

Thirteen

Steve Waugh

I didn't like selfish cricketers when I played, so why would I like them
now that I am a commentator? As far as I was concerned
Steve Waugh was a selfish cricketer.

Ian Chappell labels Steve Waugh—the man who played a record
168 Tests for Australia and led the national team to a record streak
of Test wins—a fine batsman, but asserts that he was also a conservative captain and a selfish cricketer.

I had to put up with the Bradman myth for about 30 years, now in recent times
I'm putting up with the Steve Waugh myth. He is trying to be something that he
isn't. One of the most important things you've got to learn in life is who you are:
'This is what I am. If you like me that's fine and if you don't like me there's a few
other people for me to chat to anyhow.' Just being yourself is a very important
thing in life.

Waugh has a quiet nature, he is naturally an introvert, but his batting, when he came into first-class cricket, was striking and imaginative. He played his shots with a flair which belied his seemingly conservative nature. Then he lost form and was axed in favour of his twin brother, Mark, and while Mark celebrated a century in his first Test innings against England on the Adelaide Oval, Steve stewed. He promised himself that he would come back a more determined cricketer. His technique was to change; no more the flamboyant stroke-maker, the risk taker, Steve Waugh would come back as the ultimate survivor, a man to save a match rather than win it. Chappell noted the change in Steve Waugh's technique and attitude in the wake of his axing from the Test side, but in addition to Waugh's new found negativity, he also noted an air of selfishness.

Steve Waugh was a damned good player. I put him in the category of an Allan Border, although I don't think he was as good a player as Border—AB was a much better player of spin bowling than Steve Waugh—but he was like Border in that he was a match saver, rather than a match-winning batsman. Allan should have been more of a match-winning batsman, but I think his personality counted against him; Allan's a bit of a pessimist, so every time a wicket fell he saw a disaster around the corner. The side he had early on could have led to that thought process, but it is also in his nature.

Steve Waugh is not a pessimist like AB, but he's very much, to me, a batsman who batted to survive. He didn't start out that way, he was a very aggressive player at first, but he was a totally changed batsman after he got dropped from the Australian side. It's interesting to hear the blokes who were playing with him talk about it and they say that he was one of the most critical guys of anyone who was selfish—that was before he got dropped—and then when he came back into the side he became a totally different player.

One thing I can say about Steve Waugh the batsman: if you've seen one Steve Waugh innings, you've seen the lot, because they were always alike.

I was only being a little tongue-in-cheek when somebody said to me, 'I'm going out to see Steve Waugh's last Test,' and I said, 'Have you seen him bat before?' The bloke said 'Yeah,' and I said, 'Why are you bothering? If you've seen one, you've seen 'em all.'

I remember being critical of Steve Waugh. It wasn't on air, it was in the commentary box, and Ian Healy said: 'You're being a bit tough, Chappelli.'

'Heals, I didn't like selfish cricketers when I played, so why would I like them now that I am a commentator?' As far as I am concerned Steve Waugh was a selfish cricketer . . .

I much preferred watching Mark Waugh as a cricketer. I much preferred watching his batting and—there's very few blokes I could say this about, Viv Richards was another—Mark Waugh is someone I could have sat there and watched him field. I used to love watching Mark Waugh field.

Greg [Chappell] was in the same category as far as fielding was concerned. The three best all-round fielders I've seen are Viv Richards, Greg Chappell, Mark Waugh, with Azharuddin and Ricky Ponting not far behind. And whenever I say that, Richie [Benaud] says, 'And you'd better include Neil Harvey in that group.'

Back when Steve Waugh was a pretty good bowler I was on air with Tony Greig one day and Greigy said, 'This bloke has to be the best all-rounder in the world.'

I picked up my microphone. 'Tony, he's not even the best all-rounder in his own family.'

In my opinion, Mark was more a match-winning batsman and the way you judge cricketers is to go for the cricketers who play the type of cricket you like. I am always going to place an aggressive, stroke-making style of batsman high on my list. I admired Steve Waugh's batting, but I don't believe he got the best out of his ability. I think he sacrificed a lot of his flair to be the type of batsman he became. Similarly, AB didn't get the best out of himself. There was a period where AB—one of the best pullers and cutters in the game—didn't play those shots.

What I admired most about Steve Waugh's ability as a batsman was the mental application. Greg Chappell was the best mentally organised batsman of my time . . . but he did it without eradicating shots, he still had his full range of shots. Whereas Steve was very good at organising his mind, but he eradicated shots from his repertoire. I've done a little bit of coaching at the Australian and England cricket academies since I retired. There I'd say to the guys, 'If you want to reach the top as a batsman, you simply have to have a full array of shots.' If a bowler knew I didn't cut, I've given away too much information. I don't want to be giving that information away. He must think I can cut you. Same if I go out to bat and the bowler knows I am not going to hook. He knows too much. I want him to think that I might hook. He might be pleased about thinking that I might hook; that's okay, that's a contest between him and me.

Steve Waugh saved his career in the last Test of the 2002/03 series against England. The Ashes were safe and Waugh went into the Sydney match with a big, black cloud over his head. The selectors had doubts about his ability to retain his place in the side as a batsman; he had seemed to back away from the fast bowlers in the MCG Test; there were signs that the end was nigh. England won that Sydney Test, but it will be forever remembered for Waugh's splendid century. He walked to the crease and immediately set about playing his shots; it was as if we were watching the reincarnation of the young Steve Waugh, the risk taker. All caution was thrown to the wind as he carved up the English attack. He dined lavishly on poor Richard Dawson, the Yorkshire off spinner who had so many problems with his technique that he seemed scared to let the ball out of his hand, lest it end up exactly where he feared it would. It was the quick hands of Waugh which dispatched Dawson's ball in the last over of the day to give him his century: a most emphatic response to all the murmurings for the captain's head. What a way to end a Test career!

But Waugh decided to bat on; he wanted to hang around long enough to take Australia to a series win in India in October 2004, so he set about preparing for his last Australian summer—the

Indian summer of 2003/04. Some, including Chappell, thought that announcing it as his last summer was a selfish act. Peter Roebuck said that it should remind us that no individual can be bigger than the game of cricket. Chappell was more forthright:

If you want an example of his selfishness, it was his decision to announce that he was going to retire before the season started, so he could have a grand tour the last season. I thought it was a decision that was ill-judged. It wasn't going to do his team any good and it led to what I thought was a disgraceful perform-ance in the first Test, when Damian Martyn got run out. If Damian Martyn had done what his instincts would have told him to do, he would have stayed put and let the other bloke run himself out. Probably Damian's instincts were telling him just that, but he also realised that because Steve Waugh had made this announcement, if he did what instinctively he should have done, the Gabba crowd were going to lynch him. So Martyn sacrificed himself, and to me he was put in that position by Steve Waugh's decision. I could give you a lot more examples, but this one typifies his selfishness.

Waugh's form had been patchy leading up to the Brisbane Test in November 2003 and when, a week before the Test, Waugh called a press conference and announced that this series against India would be his last, many thought a deal had been done between Cricket Australia and Waugh, assuring him that he would be selected for all the Tests if he agreed to retire after the series.

There was also a belief that Waugh was putting himself above the game. He certainly did not endear himself to those who know the game by walking onto the Gabba to a thunderous ovation before the out-going batsman, Justin Langer, who had just com-pleted a century, had left the arena. To be fair, the Australians always like to 'cross' on the field of play and Chappell himself was ever mindful of the need to send a message to the fielding team that the incoming batsman was eager to get out there and get stuck in, but Waugh's entry did appear premature and could have been construed as an attempt to steal the limelight, which at that moment rightfully belonged to Langer.

Only a few balls later came the run out. Damian Martyn, on 42, drove a ball from Zaheer Khan through the covers and both batsmen had completed two. Martyn moved a couple of paces down the track on a third run, but stopped when he saw Harbhajan Singh gather the ball near the boundary and get set to throw. He indicated the danger with a deafening call of 'No' and lots of waving of the arms, but Waugh put his head down and charged up the track. Martyn could see that Waugh was going to be run out and, even though Harbhajan's throw was wide of the mark, Martyn had to trot towards the non-striker's end knowing that his fate was sealed.

Chappell believes Steve Waugh, as Test captain, allowed coach John Buchanan far too much say in the running of the Australian Cricket Team. Buchanan came into the coaching game overseeing Queensland. He was coach when they began their run of success in the Sheffield Shield competition, now labelled the Pura Cup. Ian Healy always considered the sides coached by Buchanan were the 'best prepared' of his time, but there were question marks; while acknowledging Buchanan's coordination and management skills, Chappell says it is in the area of cricket strategy and technique that Buchanan should be questioned.

I wouldn't want him having anything to do with the cricket side of things, the tactics. If I had a son, the last bloke in the world I would take him to for cricket coaching would be John Buchanan.

Look at Waugh's final season as Test captain, that's the most damning testimony to his captaincy. As far as I was concerned I never saw him [Waugh] bowl to a seven–two field, yet he set such a field for his fast bowlers a lot. In my opinion, in Sydney, when the Indians made 700-plus, much of that score you could put down to Steve Waugh's seven–two field. While Brett Lee bowled to a field placing where he could bowl at the stumps, he had a nice outswinger going and he had a catch dropped and a catch taken off a no-ball. Then back came Waugh's seven–two field.

Lee faced a dilemma. Bowling to the negative seven–two field meant he had to bowl wide outside the line of off stump. It was not only a negative line, but it reduced his effectiveness, because Lee has a good outswinger and when he bowls it on a straighter line he has the chance of getting batsmen out bowled and lbw, and he has a greater chance of getting the edge to the keeper and slips cordon. Bowling such a line with only two men protecting the on side makes it tough work, because it's easy for batsmen to score on the leg side. Ian believes few bowlers in world cricket could bowl to such a negative line.

If there is such a bowler, it would be someone like Glenn McGrath, but only for a short time. I can't think of any others in the Australian team. Jason Gillespie needs to attack the stumps and, really, McGrath is far more effective when he bowls that straighter line . . .

I always thought of Steve Waugh's captaincy that he ran out of ideas very quickly. He displayed lots of energy, lots of ideas when they were steamrolling the opposition. Not so when things got tight. I saw him in India in 2001 . . .

The match in question was the second Test at Eden Gardens. Australia hit 445, India 171, having to follow on 274 runs in arrears. Then India slammed on 7/657 with V.V.S. Laxman belting 281 and Rahul Dravid 180 in an extraordinary fifth wicket stand of 376—a stand which people saw as a symbol of the new and exciting, modern India.

Steve Waugh's tactics soon went to the seven–two field. He either employed that sort of field placing when things got tight, or had a ring of fieldsmen on both sides of the wicket and looked to stop the scoring as his main source of taking wickets. It was very poor captaincy by Steve Waugh at Eden Gardens.

Off spinner Harbhajan Singh spun India to a famous victory by taking 6/73 off 30.3 overs to bowl Steve Waugh's Australians out for 212 in their second innings.

Chappell cites other instances of Steve Waugh's negative tactics as captain:

I recall a match where Marlon Samuels was on 46. The West Indies were nine down and Australia was on the verge of an easy innings victory. And there was Steve Waugh putting the field back to stop Samuels getting 50. Had I, as a captain, come to you as the bowler and said, 'We are going to have a crack at number eleven,' any top-line bowler would say to me, 'Mate, I want the challenge of trying to get this bloke out. If he gets 50, good luck to him.'

If the bloke is good enough to hit a four and get 50, so be it. But if he tries to score that boundary it also increases the bowler's chance of getting him out.

Another example was the Barbados Test match in 1998/99, where Brian Lara steered the Windies to a one-wicket victory, hitting an unconquered 153.

I wasn't at the Test, but I awoke in the early hours of the morning, went downstairs, put the earplug in and turned on the radio. It promised to be an exciting finish. That's when I heard that Shane Warne was bowling to Brian Lara and he had nine men on the boundary. I fumed. The Windies at one stage were 8/248. Lara was in, batting well, but who did they have to come? Courtney Walsh and Curtly Ambrose. And here was Warne bowling with nine men on the boundary. That's the equivalent of having nine on the fence for Dennis Lillee. I wouldn't have done it for two reasons: one because I value my health and Dennis would have punched me in the head—what's more he would have been entitled to punch me in the head—and two, it is an insult to set such a field, nine on the fence, to blokes of the calibre of Shane Warne and Dennis Lillee.

I'm not just talking about their class here, I am talking about their style. They are attacking bowlers. Just before you run in to bowl, a bowler needs to see field placings that have some catching positions, giving the bowler hope that there are ways of getting the batsman out. To set such a negative field immediately diminishes your effectiveness as a bowler by 50 per cent. If he's got nine men on the fence, Shane Warne shouldn't be bowling. If he wants to bore Lara out he should be bowling himself or someone like that, but to have used Shane Warne in such a way was a total waste of his talent.

To be fair, that was very early in his captaincy career, yet against the Indians in that Eden Gardens match in 2001, as soon as the game got tight, Waugh went defensive.

The loss at Eden Gardens ended a record run between October 1999 and March 2001, when the Australian team under Steve Waugh won 16 Test matches in a row. Win number 16 had been in the previous Test, in Mumbai. On the final day of that match, Rahul Dravid whipped a ball to Michael Slater at square leg. Slater claimed the catch while Dravid stood his ground, thinking the ball had bounced before Slater held it. Umpire Venkat agreed with Dravid and ruled not out. Slater remonstrated with the umpire and became very heated. In his diary of the tour, Steve Waugh wrote: 'Unfortunately for Slats, the combination of the heat of the moment and a green light sparked his uncharacteristic display, which caught me off guard. By the time he had confronted Venkat and Dravid, all I could do was yell out from a distance, "Get out of there, Slats." Unfortunately, Slats either didn't hear me or it didn't sink in.' That Slater was not penalised for his outburst, Chappell considered was a disgrace. He adds:

Slater was fielding at square leg when he said he had caught the ball—I didn't actually think he caught it anyhow—and Steve Waugh was fielding at mid wicket, so my question is how did Michael Slater ever get to the umpire at the bowler's end?

Some players might catch you by surprise, but at that stage Michael Slater was going through some problems and was in a very tense state, which everybody knew about, and when you know that, as a captain you sort of keep a bit of a wary eye, and particularly on someone like Slater, who can be a bit emotional anyhow. So if someone says, 'Oh, he caught Steve Waugh by surprise,' I don't accept that he did.

Having remonstrated with Umpire Venkat, he then managed to get to Dravid. I don't recall him [Steve Waugh] trying to drag Slater away from the umpire, so how did he get to Rahul Dravid?

I've read where Steve Waugh says, 'We discuss it in the dressing-room, but when you are out in the field it's up to the players.' That attitude completely ignores the laws of cricket, which state that the captain is responsible for his players.

Chappell is also critical of Waugh's leadership of New South Wales in Pura Cup matches during his last summer. With all his Test players available, New South Wales lost matches when Victoria scored 452 on the last day to win and Tasmania scored 359 on the last day for victory. 'When you have a good attack and the opposition are scoring those sorts of numbers on the last day,' Chappell says, 'there has to be a question mark against your leadership.'

As Australian captain, Steve Waugh had the luxury of two magnificent bowlers in Shane Warne and Glenn McGrath, to call upon when Australia was in any trouble in the field. But he had also inherited a good batting side and a group of young men who were highly skilled and had the mental capacity to finish any job they started, efficiently and with attention to detail. In addition, most of the opposition was palpably weak. A half-decent Australian first-class team could have beaten Zimbabwe, and Bangladesh was hardly up to first-class standard, let alone Test match status.

There wasn't much opposition around, let's be brutally frank. England were useless and the West Indies were regressing quickly. The only time this

Australian team was challenged was overseas. In Australia they were steam-rolling teams. The only team which challenged Australia and took them on was New Zealand under Stephen Fleming.

Chappell was unimpressed to read in the 2004–05 edition of *Wisden Australia* that Steve Waugh was the most 'influential Australian cricketer since Don Bradman'.

That is a nonsense. There are a list of players with far more influence. Richie Benaud turned cricket around in the late 1950s and early 1960s. His leadership style changed the way players approached the game. In the 1950s attendances at Test matches were falling. The Australia–West Indies series injected new life into the game. It also brought back the people to watch—in droves. A lot of the credit for that great series has to go to Richie Benaud and to West Indian captain Frank Worrell.

Chappell cites Dennis Lillee's greatness: his skill, his comeback from injury and the very sight of the great fast bowler charging in to bowl won the hearts of Australian sports people. The people flocked to see Lillee in action. His influence as a cricketer was immense.

His return from injury for the Ashes series in 1974/75 and the way he bowled brought back huge crowds to Test cricket. Lillee also played a vital role in World Series Cricket. So Benaud and Lillee had more influence than Waugh. Allan Border also had a huge influence. Had his batting fallen away in the mid-1980s and beyond, Australian cricket would have taken ten years to recover instead of five. He began his captaincy with a poor side, unlike Steve Waugh who inherited a winning combination from Mark Taylor.

Chappell says that Shane Warne is another cricketer whose influence has been quite remarkable. When everyone thought leg spin bowling had gone the way of the dinosaurs, along came Warne. People sit transfixed watching Warne weave his magic over the batsman. Don Bradman said Warne was 'the greatest thing to happen to Australian cricket in 30 years'.

What has Steve Waugh done to change Australian cricket? There are claims that fast scoring has been a huge factor. Well, Victor Trumper got a hundred before lunch at Old Trafford in 1902, Charlie McCartney scored a century before lunch at Headingly in 1926 and Don Bradman hit a ton before lunch on the same ground in 1930. So fast scoring has been with Australian cricket for over a hundred years.

Steve Waugh's record of 16 Test wins on the trot is his big achievement as a captain, but we must remember it's difficult to fully assess that feat because a lot of the opposition was ordinary. And if a team scores 400 or more runs in a day, mostly that means you are up against a very poor attack.

Steve Waugh was no doubt a great player. And he was a good, if not great, captain. His influence came from commitment, persistence and longevity in the game. Waugh played a record 168 Test matches, 116 more than Bradman and 93 more than Ian Chappell. Had he begun in an era where there were a host of top-notch players, Waugh may not have played nearly so many games at the highest level; he persisted and he improved, and created a career that has to be admired. But Ian Chappell likes to tell it as it is: 'Steve Waugh didn't have the sort of influence people say. He didn't change the way Australian teams play cricket, either. Writers who say this sort of stuff about Steve Waugh really need to take a history lesson in cricket.'

Another name should be added to the list of people who have had great influence on Australian cricket ahead of Steve Waugh, that of Ian Michael Chappell. When Chappell took over the captaincy from Bill Lawry, Australia had not won a match for ten Tests. A number of retirements were imminent, including such players as Alan Connolly and Graham McKenzie. Chappell led with great skill and verve, he took on board the comments of his players, he empowered them and he built a team which ranks as one of the really great combinations in Test history.

But it was not merely his influence as a leader and a batsman for which he will be remembered: Chappell took on the board where he saw injustice to his men over pay and conditions, a revolt that became known as World Series Cricket. The instigators of that revolution—Lillee, Chappell, Kerry Packer—created the beginning of the new order. Not just a better deal for the players, but a deal where they could play the game they loved without having to worry about where the next dollar was coming from.

Fourteen

The mellowing

I think in any human being there is always a softer side. Why do you
have wives and children and animals? You have them because
you love them. I'm surprised that other people are surprised that
I have a softer side.

The most competitive among us always seem to find a way to
unsettle the opposition. Dennis Lillee did it with a barrage of
bouncers. Ian Chappell found a different strategy one night in
Derbyshire in 1975. He and Rodney Marsh had had a few days off
from cricket and jumped at an invitation to play golf with Garth
Pettit, an Australian dentist domiciled in England.

To avoid getting up at some ungodly hour—and a lot of travelling—in order
to be at the course for a 9 am hit-off, it was agreed that we stay at Garth's
home that night. We sat there that night sipping beer with our host and a few
of his friends, talking about things in general. We'd been on the subject of gay

sportsmen for about an hour when someone pointed out that it was 5 am and we weren't going to get much sleep.

Rodney [Chappell's golfing opponent next day] and I were shown to our room and were somewhat aghast to find that it contained only one bed—a double bed. Still, we had to get some sleep. We gingerly climbed into our respective sides of the bed, each of us hugging the edges to avoid physical contact, and Rodney turned out the light.

As he lay there, Chappell thought about the upcoming match and how he might get a competitive edge on his mate. He came up with an idea that was sure to get Rodney's attention and, hopefully, to cause his golf opponent more than momentary concern.

We must have looked like a couple of bodies in the mortuary with rigor mortis setting in. I lay there thinking about our recent conversation [about gay sportsmen] and it seemed like a good idea to grab, there and then, a certain advantage. So I casually reached across the bed and firmly squeezed his penis. Rod's reaction was far better than I expected. He rose vertically from the bed and screamed, 'Jesus, what's going on here?'

Rod didn't sleep a wink that night. I slept soundly, secure in the knowledge that he was huddled on the edge of the bed watching me with deep apprehension and suspicion.

And who won the game? Rodney Marsh. He is a fierce competitor.

Ian's daughter, Amanda, is head trainer of cabin crew for Virgin Airlines, overseeing the training of more than 1500 staff. Based in Brisbane, Amanda is very close to both her mother and father. 'I spend every second Christmas with Dad,' she says, 'and we meet up when he comes to Brisbane for work or when I go to Sydney.' She is also patently aware of Ian's competitiveness.

'Years ago when Dad used to play a bit of tennis with me, Mum would say, "Ian, why don't you let Amanda win occasionally?" And

Dad would reply, "Amanda will win when she's good enough to beat me."'

'Amanda and I still joke about it now,' Chappell says. 'When we have a hit of tennis, I say, "The biggest mistake I made was not sending you to dancing lessons to get your bloody feet moving." She has quite a bit of skill as a tennis player, but she has horrible footwork.'

Amanda is not surprised her father has taken on the cause for refugees. 'He has always had concern for people less fortunate,' she says. 'I think these days he has more time for family and friends. Dad has developed a wider range of interests and has increased his awareness.'

With such a competitive attitude on the tennis court, how can people say Ian has mellowed? Is there a soft side to Ian Chappell? His mother, Jeanne Chappell, thinks so: 'Boy, is there ever a soft side to him. There always has been, really.'

His brother Trevor says Ian is a hard man by 'most people's understanding of the term', but says he has a good sense of fair play, of what is right and wrong, and he knows the importance of being loyal to your mates, within or outside a team environment.

Ian rationalises his mellowing: 'I think in any human being there is always a softer side,' he says. 'Why do you have wives and children and animals? You have them because you love them. I'm surprised that other people are surprised that I have a softer side.'

The stress and tension of playing competitive sport never really dawned on him until about two years after his retirement.

You don't realise how much you are bubbling when you are playing. You're bubbling inside, just below boiling point. I guess that is part of being competitive. I didn't realise it until I'd retired and I said to Barbara-Ann: 'Gee, I was just below boiling point all the time.' Obviously now that the cricket is over, I'm more relaxed. My mates give me a hard time about it. If someone walks up to me in

the bar these days I sign for them, and my mates say, 'Oh, you're signing autographs in bars now, are you?'

So I guess I've always tried to separate the two—the private me and the
public me. I am a pretty private person and I live with a very private person, and
that suits me fine. But having lived the sort of life where you are in the public eye
a bit, you do have a slightly louder voice at times, and I have learnt that at times
you do need to use that voice.

Tennis is still one of his sporting loves. John Newcombe and
Tony Roche are mates. Ross Edwards, who still plays competitive
cricket, golf, hockey and tennis, watched the rise and rise of Ian's
tennis from close quarters. 'Chappelli and I started playing tennis
against each other while away on cricket tours. He was a gritty
opponent. To begin with I could beat him reasonably comfortably,
but Ian being Ian, this wasn't good enough for him. As our
competition continued he improved dramatically by taking
lessons from an ex-Australian player [Phil Dent] and practising
for hours. Eventually Ian was my superior by some margin—a fact
that continues to frustrate me.'

However, Ross Edwards has seen Ian's soft side as well: 'The
Oval Test of 1975 was Ian's last as captain and my final match for
Australia. Midway through the game I got a telegram which told
of the death of a close friend. Ian had seen the telegram. He
quietly came over to me and said in a private moment, "Rosco, if
you prefer not to go back on the field next session, it's okay with
me." A very human thing for him to do.'

In recent times Chappell has played tennis for Roseville in the
Sydney Badge competition. In 2003 he won the Bayview Tennis
Club championship doubles and was runner-up in singles.

When I learnt that my opponent in singles was an eleven-year-old kid, I spoke
to my doubles partner Ken Grey and said, 'I'm not comfortable playing against

an eleven year old. If I serve hard and hit him everyone will say I'm a prick. Grey said, 'If you don't serve hard he'll run you all over the court, Chappelli. You'd better be on top of your game or the kid will demolish you.'

I served hard and the kid—Michael Clisby— beat me in straight sets.

Sport will always play an important part in Ian Chappell's life. For a while he played off a seven handicap at Glenelg Golf Club, although now that tennis has taken over his handicap has gone out to 15. He played Masters baseball and, with his mate Kevin 'Crazy' Cantwell, in 1999 he played for the Australian over-50s baseball team that reached the play-offs in the World Series, played in Phoenix, Arizona. Cantwell, a former champion Australian baseballer and manager of the seniors team, says of Ian: 'We played great, but the greatest performance was Chappelli behind the mask. He caught an incredible eleven days in a row. He's still the iron man he was all those years ago.'

Time stood still for Ian Chappell when he heard the sad news of the death of former team-mate David Hookes, who was assaulted and fatally injured in a Melbourne street in January 2004. His death shocked the cricket world and hit Chappell particularly hard. Hookes was the new kid on the block in 1975/76 when Chappell's South Australian team shrugged off two seasons in a row as wooden spooners to win the Sheffield Shield. It was on his beloved Adelaide Oval that Hookes scored the bulk of his 12 671 runs in first-class cricket. After his career on the field ended in 1992, Hookes became a radio celebrity, doing his apprenticeship on an afternoon talk show in Adelaide before heading for Melbourne, where he worked for 3AW and won the hearts of the Victorian people. He also won fame as a cricket commentator with Fox and covered many a tour of the sub-continent, working alongside his cricketing hero, Ian Chappell.

Former West Torrens and South Australian team-mate of
Hookes, Barry Curtin, said, 'Hookesy idolised Ian Chappell. He did
everything like Chappelli. The cross-legged stance at the non-
striker's end, the flamboyance, the aggression. He even developed
an Ian Chappell moustache. People would say to Hookesy, "You've
copied Ian Chappell," and he would reply, "Yes, I have. I make no
apology for that. I have copied him; why wouldn't you copy him?"'

People kept telling me that Hookesy emulated me, but I can't say that I ever
really saw it myself. Hookesy and I always got on pretty well together. In that
period when I was doing a lot of commentary, Hookesy was commentating a
fair bit as well. We had quite a few overseas trips together. We used to play a
lot of tennis against each other.

Once in India we played on clay—we used to play pretty close, I always felt
on the faster surfaces I'd probably be just ahead of him—but on the clay, Jesus,
he bloody beat me every game we had on that Indian tour. He had a better all-
round game than I did; I had a serve–volley game, not suited to clay. He just
worked me over and there was nothing worse than losing all the time to
Hookesy, because you'd never stop hearing about it.

Actually, it was a good thing for me. Because of the twelve-year age difference I was really struggling with the heat. I'd come to the net and Hookesy
would lob me, and by the time we had finished one set I was absolutely knack-
ered. So if I was to continue playing my serve–volley game, I knew I had to do
something about my fitness. I didn't want to run any more and I was not keen
on the gymnasium, but everywhere we went, there was a bloody swimming
pool. There was an upside to losing every game to Hookesy because it got me
into swimming, and I wish I had started swimming a long time ago.

Ten thousand people gathered at the Adelaide Oval on
27 January 2004 for Hookes's funeral. The Australian and South
Australian teams were there and people came from all walks of
life. Ian Chappell paid tribute to Hookes:

Hookesy, I knew I'd get a rocket if I turned up in a tie, so relax pal, I didn't let you down.

It is appropriate that we should be paying tribute to David here at the Adelaide Oval, because it was up there and out there [in the dressing-room and on the field] that I got to know Hookesy as a cricketer and as a man. It is always exciting to be around at the start of somebody's career and I have very fond memories of the start of his career, that first season with South Australia. I was obviously impressed with his ability and I was also impressed with the fact that he was a confident young man. But he was, fortunately for me, respectful of age. He loved to sit around and have a chat about the game of cricket, and it wasn't always a one-sided conversation with David. He would always have his two-pence worth, but he showed great respect to the senior players of that South Australian side . . . He loved nothing better than to talk about the game. That was the thing that came through when I first met him. This kid who loved the game, loved to talk about it, loved to sit down and learn about the game.

Hookes's passion for the game and boots-and-all approach reminded Ian Chappell of his own early days in cricket, but Chappell is thankful that his commentary and media work enabled him to make a good living and continue his involvement with the game. Meeting Barbara-Ann (they wed in 1982) added new dimension and meaning to his life. She has encouraged him to use his public voice to go in to bat for the refugees and to get involved with A Just Australia.

I don't think I would ever get so comfortable that all I would think about is my own comfort and my family's comfort. You have to be aware of other people's problems. If I ever get too comfortable I will get jolted out of it by Barbara-Ann. She worries about all the bad things going on in the world. Sometimes she does so to her own detriment. I think it gets her down at times, so I suggest she not watch the TV news or read newspapers for a while.

I like to be comfortable, but money has never been a driving force with me.

I feel that you shouldn't make money by doing things that are detrimental to other people. So I would like to think that with my upbringing and then Barbara-Ann's niggling and needling from time to time, I would never get too comfortable.

Chappell doesn't travel as much as he used to, preferring instead to enjoy life in their idyllic home overlooking the water north of Sydney. Ian and Barb have a golden cocker spaniel and two cats. They enjoy live music—Ian likes the blues and live bands—and they flew to England last year especially to catch a series of Eric Clapton concerts at The Royal Albert Hall. Chappell is also an avid reader, he enjoys a game of backgammon, and on three occasions has been to Pamplona, Spain, for the running of the bulls. He has business interests and directorships in the hotel, land development and information technology industries.

'People seem staggered that I haven't got any cricket gear from my playing days and particularly miffed that I haven't kept a baggy green cap,' Chappell says. If you want to see an Ian Chappell baggy green cap you have to go along to the Glenelg Cricket Club, where there is one in the display cabinet.

Chappell loved Glenelg and it was one of his few regrets that he didn't play in a grand final with them. Glenelg won the SACA Premiership in 1973/74, but Chappell was in New Zealand with the Test side and the team was captained by Brian Illman. 'I know that Chappelli would have loved to have led us in that game,' Illman says. 'He was very interested to hear results and before the game I received a short letter from him. I still have the letter, which I dearly cherish. I read it to the team before we took the field and I am sure we all felt his presence during the game . . . I have never known anyone who played in the same side as Ian in cricket or baseball who would not go in to bat for him and his team. Chappelli has never forgotten his grass roots. He has touched our lives at Glenelg in many ways. He has left his mark on all of us. He has been an inspiration.'

Former South Australia and Test leg spinner Rex Sellers was a member of the state team when Chappell first began playing with South Australia. Sellers was a state selector when Chappell returned to South Australia to lead the team in 1979/80 after his World Series Cricket involvement, and has carefully watched his development, both as a cricketer and a man. Sellers says, 'Ian Chappell has a foundation of a firm and committed self-belief, the ability to quickly appraise any situation on or off the field and to respond swiftly and incisively. These attributes made him a natural leader, which permeated through to his team-mates and developed the team spirit during his tenure. Today that continues with his media work, his coaching and his philosophy on world events. He is all Australian.'

Everyone you meet who knows Ian Chappell reckons he has mellowed. 'Like all of us,' said Greg Chappell, 'Ian has mellowed as he has gotten older. Experience has done that, but Barbara has had a big influence too. I think Barbara has been able to make Ian see that sometimes there is a grey, that it is not all black and white. That's an area where he got into trouble in the early days—there weren't too many shades of grey with him.'

Bill Lawry agrees, adding: 'Ian and I are like chalk and cheese, but we have always got along. We don't always agree, but we respect each other . . . I am not surprised that Chappelli has taken up worthwhile causes, because he is a lot deeper than he makes out. Ian Chappell is a good citizen.'

Chappell himself says:

Hopefully you get a bit wiser as you get older. I'm not really a confrontational person, but when you are in a sporting environment and you are trying to win and you're in charge of the team, you are going to find yourself in confrontational situations. I had been brought up, particularly through the influence of Martin, to learn to stand up for myself. And it was bloody important that Martin did that because guys would run roughshod over you if you didn't stand up for yourself, especially in the two sports I played. In cricket the fast bowlers would try and intimidate you and in baseball everyone was out to intimidate you

There were times when I needed to stand up and say my piece and I'm quite happy to do that, if I believe strongly enough in what it is I am standing up for. I have found as I get older, that if I come across somebody who annoys me, or someone I don't like or respect, I don't particularly want to have anything to do with them. I'd rather be in a situation where I don't have to mix with them. As you get a bit older you think, 'Shit, I've got less and less time here, I'm not going to waste it mixing with people who bore the shit out of me.'

Dennis Lillee apparently wrote in his book, and Paul Allott said to me, 'You and Botham are stupid bastards, you should get together because you have so much in common.' I can't think of a person I have less in common with than Ian Botham. As I said to Paul Allott, and I would say to Dennis if he said it to my face, I find Botham extremely boring . . .

If you don't get a bit smarter as you go along in life, what the hell are you doing? I think one of the most interesting things in life is to learn new things. A lot of things have been important in my relationship with Barbara, but because of her I've learned a lot of different things.

I am glad that I played when I did. We had a rest day, which was usually a Sunday, and when we played golf we played with and against a host of people who were also having a day off. These days the guys play cricket on Sundays and play golf during the week between matches, so they play among themselves. We would play on Sunday, network with people, and often get invited to their homes for barbecues. Being a commentator is different, you have more time to get out and about. The old story of hotel to the ground is pretty true when you are playing.

I think all of those things have hopefully made me a better person and I guess have given Jeanne and others the impression that I have mellowed.

Australian Players' Association president, ex-champion Test wicket-keeper and fellow Channel Nine cricket commentator Ian Healy worked closely with Chappell and Cricket Australia to help the drive to have the 1868 Aboriginal team recognised. Healy says: 'If Chappelli is the antagonist he is a very thoughtful one who never shoots off without calculated opinions, which makes him difficult to topple, if that is the aim. He has a memory ten times better than an elephant. He will take you back to the origins of cricket and trace the history, through to the present day . . . There is a softness in parts, especially where family is concerned and, of course, with Barb and their pets [but] I cannot believe how tough and unwavering he must have been, if what we see today is the mellow Chappelli.'

What now for Ian Chappell? Certainly he will continue to agitate for changes which he thinks necessary in the laws of cricket. He believes the law regarding illegal actions must be changed. Some describe the brilliant Sri Lankan off spinner Muttiah Muralitharan to be either a genius or a cheat. Bishan Bedi, the great Indian left-arm spinner of the 1970s, calls Murali a 'javelin thrower', while legendary West Indian off spinner Lance Gibbs says Murali chucks all of his deliveries. Chappell blames the law.

According to the law as it stands, I have no doubt that Muralitharan's action is illegal, but in this case the law really is an ass. It is confusing enough to have one type of bowler, the fast man, allowed to bend the arm more than another bowler, the slow man. How can an umpire be asked to adjudicate on degrees of crookedness with the naked eye? The law on throwing needs to be over-hauled and the whole process surrounding the legality or otherwise of a bowler's action must be kept simple. Yet before the administrators work upon the simpli-fying of the law, they must first decide what they are trying to achieve with the legislation.

Were the law-makers to decide that there was to be a zero-tolerance for flex in the bowler's arm, we would be in for some very boring cricket. Matches would surely become batting exhibitions. If you are critical of Muralitharan for an arm that goes 'bent to straight', then you have to apply the same principle throughout and that means virtually every bowler is in some doubt. If that's what the administrators want then fine, but please don't ask me to watch the resulting debacle when Australia amass 1350 runs to draw with India who made 1246.

However, if the law-makers opt for a sensible law, it might be framed in such a way: 'If, in the umpire's opinion, the bowler is not gaining an unfair advantage from his action, then the delivery is legal.' Such a simple law would make life a whole lot easier for umpires; the simplicity of the law would allow umpires on the field to make judgments. This is critical because a bowler who pelts only the odd delivery is the most difficult for batsmen to handle. It also allows for a bit of flexibility in the bowling action, which is vital if bowlers of all types are to remain competitive in their battle with batsmen.

Lastly, but importantly, such a law would keep to the absolute minimum the influence of the legal battles, ensuring that cricket matches, unlike the America's Cup, will not be decided in the courtroom. Certainly umpires need to watch very carefully; a throw needs to be discernible to the naked eye and has to be blatantly gaining a real advantage. The umpires might need to work out among themselves which bowlers' actions have the potential to provide such players with an unfair advantage.

There are enough tell-tale signs with a chucker—bent and splayed front-leg and open-chested action. Umpires could utilise video footage to check up on the bowlers whom they think need to be watched closely. However, I believe the use of video to decide whether a bowler's arm action is legal or not is fraught with danger; all bowlers who use a 'cocked wrist' style look dubious when the action is seen in slow motion. Most of the doubt in Murali's action is created by an extremely flexible wrist; it's wrong to penalise Muralitharan, or any other player, because he's physically able to do things others aren't capable of achieving . . .

I think the administrators and law-makers must have a moratorium of the current crop of Test and first-class bowlers. The way to clean up actions and ensure that there is not a wave of chuckers on the horizon is to address the actions of the emerging cricketers, the youngsters in the various countries' under-age squads. That is where the big effort must be made to ensure that chuckers do not get through to big cricket.

Chappell says it is difficult to have a game running smoothly with high-class, competitive cricket when the administration is sub-standard. He has suggested ten changes which he would like to see implemented to improve the game. These measures would reduce the power broking and politicking among officials which, in turn, would lead to an improved standard of play and more respect between players, umpires and administrators.

1. A revamp of the ICC
The constitution of the ICC should be rewritten with priority to 'all decisions being taken in the best interests of the game'. It must be run by an impartial board, a global body empowered to run all aspects of international cricket. An ICC president should be appointed—importantly, a person with world-wide credibility in cricket. The president would need to have such standing in the game that he is listened to and universally respected by the players. A short list for that vital role would include Richie Benaud, Sir Garfield Sobers, Sunil Gavaskar and Imran Khan.

2. Speeding up the game
Extending a day's play into overtime is a sure way to annoy TV magnates and fans and should be avoided at all costs. The president would offer compromises to speed up playing time. For instance, sightboards carrying advertising (which often break down and need to be moved every time a bowler changes from over to around the wicket) could be replaced with large advertising-free boards that cover both sides of the wicket. Simplified

boundary laws would do away with the need for replays to determine how many runs were actually scored. Penalties could be introduced to ensure overs are bowled in the scheduled time. Depending on the type of match where the infringement occurs, the captain could be suspended for either two Tests or five one-day internationals.

3. Back-foot no-ball law

A return to the back-foot law would virtually eradicate no-balls and help with over rates. It would also act as a real punishment to bowlers and the odd no-ball delivered would create genuine excitement (unlike the nonsensical free-hit ploy). Taped footage could be used to decide where a bowler's back foot needed to land, indicated by a white disc. This law would give umpires more time to view the action at the striker's end and would improve the standard of decision-making.

This is one area where Ian Chappell and Sir Donald Bradman are in agreement; Bradman consistently opposed the introduction of the front-foot no-ball rule and felt he was something of a lone voice in trying to persuade the MCC law-makers to return to the old back-foot rule.

4. Simplify the law on illegal bowling actions

As outlined in this chapter above.

5. Ease restrictions on bowlers in the one-day game

Putting more onus on captains by allowing them discretion in field placement and bowler use could make the one-day game more of a tactical battle. For example, two catching men have to be in place for 15 overs and at least five bowlers must complete a minimum of five overs in a 50-over innings. This would allow the captain flexibility in using his catching men and manipulating his attack. Legislation won't make captains aggressive, but sensitive laws can encourage a bit more enterprise.

6. Introduce a two-tiered system for Test cricket

A top division of eight teams would play Test cricket with a World Championship every four years to decide the best team on the field, not on a computer. The second-tier teams would play against each other in four-day matches (not deemed Test matches), with occasional matches against the stronger 'A' teams. Once the standard of the second-tier teams was considered good enough, a promotion/relegation system would apply between the two levels.

7. A Super-six ODI competition

Allocate points for all ODI series, with the top six teams qualifying to play in an elite tournament every two years. This way each ODI series has meaning and a highly saleable tournament is played every two years that won't detract from the World Cup, which would remain an expanded competition.

8. Overhaul the laws of the game

Simplify them and don't involve replays in the decision-making process unless the evidence is inconclusive. On-field umpires need to be given more responsibility with decision-making, not less. Ideas like having the umpire wired to enable him to connect to the television coverage to detect edges are more likely to disturb concentration rather than be of any benefit. Revert to previous laws on run-outs at the non-striker's end and eradicate penalty runs.

9. Clamp down on excessive and intimidatory appealing

Ask the players this question, 'Would you like to be cheated out of your wicket?' If the answer is anything other than 'No,' then they are either a liar or a fool. If the answer is 'No', ask, 'Then why try to cheat someone else?' Excessive appealing contributes to a lower standard of umpiring. The penalty would involve suspension of the captain, as he has control of his players.

10. Ensure batsmen have some peace and quiet while at the crease

Mindless chatter on the field is a problem; it can lead to insulting comments and the likelihood of an on-field altercation. The motto should be to encourage gamesmanship and eradicate inane chatter.

It has been a long and colorful life-journey for Ian Chappell. He has achieved much in his life as a cricketer and as a man. No doubt he will continue writing thought-provoking articles for a variety of publications in Australia, England and India. He will also keep on with his TV cricket commentary and will continue using his public profile to lobby for justice for asylum seekers, Australia for UNHCR and A Just Australia.

On Friday, 12 December 2003, Jeanne, Ian, Greg and Trevor Chappell stood on Adelaide Oval as SACA president Ian McLachlan announced the naming of the Chappell Stands, located on the eastern side of the oval, a short distance from the Victor Richardson Gates. As McLachlan spoke in tribute to the Chappells, no doubt Martin, who died aged 64 in 1984, and Vic had a heavenly view of proceedings, the pair of them as proud as Punch. What would Ian's grandfather think?

If ever I get the chance to meet up with Vic, wherever that might be, I would like to think that we could sit down over a cold beer and he would say to me, 'Well then Ian, there were three or four things you did that I didn't agree with, but on the whole I thought you did a pretty good job.'

Bibliography

A note on the interviews

This book is based on extensive interviews with Ian Chappell.
Many others—family, friends and colleagues of Ian Chappell—
have spoken to me over the years. Their recollections are used
throughout the book.

Books consulted

Philip Bailey, Philip Thorn and Peter Wynn-Thomas, *Who's Who of
Cricketers*, Newnes Books, 1984

Jack Bannister, *Innings of My Life*, Headline, London, 1994

Denzil Batchelor, *The Book of Cricket*, Collins, 1952

Ian Botham with Peter Hayter, *Botham: My autobiography*, Harper-
CollinsWillow, 2000

Bradman: The Don declares, ABC Radio biography of Sir Donald
Bradman with Norman May

Bradman's First Tour: Articles and cartoons from Australia's 1930 tour of England,
introduced by Sir Donald Bradman, Rigby, Adelaide, 1981

Ian Brayshaw, *The Chappell Era*, ABC Enterprises, Sydney, 1984

John Bright-Holmes, *The Joy of Cricket*, Secker & Warburg, London,
1984

Ian Chappell, *Chappelli: Ian Chappell's life story*, Hutchinson, Richmond,
Victoria, 1976

Ian Chappell, My World of Cricket, Jack Pollard Publishing, Sydney, 1973

Ian Chappell, Tiger Among the Lions, Investigator Press, South Australia, 1972

Ian Chappell, Austin Robertson and Paul Rigby, The Best of Chappelli, Swan Publishing, Byron Bay, 1982

Mike Coward, The Chappell Years: Cricket in the seventies, ABC Books, Sydney, 2002

Bill Frindall, The Wisden Book of Test Cricket: 1876–1978, Macdonald & Jane, London, 1979

David Frith, The Golden Age of Cricket: 1890–1914, Omega Books, United Kingdom, 1978

David Frith, The Slow Men, Horwitz Grahame, Sydney, 1984

Tony Greig with David Lord, Tony Greig: Cricket, the men and the game, Ure Smith, Sydney, 1976

Chris Harte, The History of the Sheffield Shield, Allen & Unwin, Sydney, 1987

Chris Harte, The History of the South Australian Cricket Association, Sports Marketing, Adelaide, 1990

David Hookes with Allan Shiell, Hookesy, ABC Books, Sydney, 1993

Dennis Lillee, Lillee: An autobiography, Hodder Headline, 2003

Adrian McGregor, Greg Chappell, Collins, Sydney, 1985

Ashley Mallett, Bradman's Band, University of Queensland Press, St Lucia, 2000

Ashley Mallett, Lord's Dreaming, Souvenir Press, London, 2002

Johnny Moyes, A Century of Cricketers, Angus & Robertson, 1949

M.A. Noble, The Game's the Thing, Cassell & Company, 1926

Bill O'Reilly, Tiger, Collins, 1985

Michael Page, Bradman: The illustrated biography, Macmillan, 1983

Jack Pollard, Six and Out, Jack Pollard Publishing, Sydney, 1971

Jack Pollard, Australian Cricket: The game and the players, Hodder and Stoughton, Sydney, 1982

V.Y. Richardson with R.S. Whitington, *The Vic Richardson Story*, Rigby Limited, Adelaide, 1967

Ray Robinson, *On Top Down Under*, Cassell Australia, 1975

Shane Warne with Mark Ray, *My Own Story*, Swan Publishing, Perth, 1997

Pelham Warner, *Book of Cricket*, Sporting Handbooks Ltd, 1947

Roy Webber, *The Phoenix History of Cricket*, Phoenix Sports Books, 1960

Bernard Whimpress and Nigel Hart, *Adelaide Oval: Test cricket 1884–1984*, Wakefield Press, Adelaide, 1984

R.S. Whitington, *An Illustrated History of Australian Cricket*, Lansdowne Press, 1972

Wisden Cricketers' Almanacks (various) including the years 1949, 1973 and 1976

Ian Wooldridge, *Travelling Reserve*, Collins, London, 1982

Acknowledgements

My thanks to the following: John Arlott*, Dennis Amiss, Jack Bannister, Ali Bacher, Robin Bailhache, Stephanie Beltra, Richie Benaud, Chester Bennett*, Fred Bennett*, Alan Barnes*, Eddie Barlow, Big Sid*, Henry Blofeld, Michael Bollen, Allan Border, Don Bradman*, Sir Ron Brierley, Tom Brooks, Bill Brown, Ian Brayshaw, Dr Donald Beard, Jack 'the Flea' Butler, Bill Brown, Kevin 'Crazy' Cantwell, Cos Cardone, Amanda Chappell, Greg Chappell, Barbara-Ann Chappell, Jeanne Chappell, Ian Chappell, Martin Chappell*, Trevor Chappell, Ben Cheshire, David Colley, Colin Cowdrey*, Jack Clarke, Dr Brian Corrigan, Mike Coward, Jeff Crowe, Martin Crowe, Roden Cutler*, Barry Curtin, Alan Davidson, Cec Davies*, Ed Devereaux*, Jack Dunning*, Ross Duncan, Tony Dell, Geoff Dymock, Ross Edwards, Stephen Fry, Jack Fingleton*, Geoff 'Goomfer' Forsaith, Brian 'Banger' Flaherty, Les Favell*, Lance Gibbs, Trevor Gill, Clarrie Grimmett*, Arthur Gilligan*, Frank Gardiner, Neil Harvey, Neil Hawke*, Ian Healy, Jonathan Herreen, David Hookes*, Rodney Hogg, Ray Illing-worth, Brian Illman, John Inverarity, Annie Jenner, Graham Koos, Bill Lawry, Arthur Lance*, Dennis Lillee, Clive Lloyd, David Lloyd, Sam Loxton, Stephanie Luke, Benjamin Mallett, Christine Mallett, Dennis Miller, Keith Miller*, Rodney Marsh, Bob Merriman, Kevin McCarthy, Alan McGilvray*, Dave 'the Doc' McErlane, Ian McLachlan, Tom Moody, Pastor Dr Douglas Nicholls*, Max O'Connell, Bill 'Tiger' O'Reilly*, Len Pascoe, Bob Parish, Wayne

Phillips, Wayne Prior, Erapally Prasanna, Kerry Packer, Viv Richards, Phil Ridings*, Albert 'Dusty' Rhodes, Ray Robinson*, Austin Robertson, Barry Richards, Peter Roebuck, Vic Richardson*, Des Selby, Rex Sellers, Garry Sobers, David Sincock, Keith Stackpole, Naomi Steer, Ray Steele*, Paul Sheahan, Faith Thomas (nee Coulthard), Garry 'Darky' Thompson, Jeff Thomson, Mark Waugh, Doug Walters, Graeme 'Beatle' Watson, Shane Warne, Robyn Windshuttle, Phil Wilkins.

Thanks also to Ian Bowring, Patrick Gallagher and Rebecca Kaiser of Allen & Unwin for their encouragement, suggestions and professional expertise with this project.

---

* deceased

Peter Roebuck
IT TAKES ALL SORTS
Celebrating cricket's colourful characters

In *It Takes All Sorts*, Peter Roebuck revisits his 25-year career in reporting cricket to reveal the people and the personalities who have touched his life and contributed to his life-long passion for the game.

Roebuck provides warts-and-all insights into the greats and not-so-greats, their debuts and retirements, the controversies of recent professional cricket and some impressive innings in between. Roebuck has seen it all and isn't afraid to comment: he's interviewed Sir (or is it Saint?) Garfield Sobers' mum, was on the scene (and on the front page) when Gilchrist 'walked', poked gentle fun at Inzamam's fielding, and touched many with his account of young Sri Lankan boys playing on the beach in Galle.

Roebuck pulls no punches—whether friend or foe, all his subjects are linked by the great and noble game of cricket and he is not afraid to tell it how he sees it.

ISBN 1 74114 542 2

Peter Roebuck
IT TAKES ALL SORTS
Celebrating cricket's colourful characters

In *It Takes All Sorts*, Peter Roebuck revisits his 25-year career in reporting cricket to reveal the people and the personalities who have touched his life and contributed to his life-long passion for the game.

Roebuck provides warts-and-all insights into the greats and not-so-greats, their debuts and retirements, the controversies of recent professional cricket and some impressive innings in between. Roebuck has seen it all and isn't afraid to comment: he's interviewed Sir (or is it Saint?) Garfield Sobers' mum, was on the scene (and on the front page) when Gilchrist 'walked', poked gentle fun at Inzamam's fielding, and touched many with his account of young Sri Lankan boys playing on the beach in Galle.

Roebuck pulls no punches—whether friend or foe, all his subjects are linked by the great and noble game of cricket and he is not afraid to tell it how he sees it.

ISBN 1 74114 542 2

Alexander Buzo
LEGENDS OF THE BAGGY GREEN
Dubious behaviour and achievements from
cricket's chequered history

Full of brigands and bogans, legends and sledgends, *Legends of
the Baggy Green* is an acerbic commentary on the codes and
manners of cricket behaviour. Part sociology, part blooper tape,
this book takes sports comedy back to where it all began.

The sins of modern cricket—sledging, chucking, match-fixing, plus
the heinous practice of putting the ball in the freezer to make it
bounce higher—are all here, along with a rogues' gallery that
includes everyone from 'Horseshoe' Herby Collins to Salim 'The
Rat' Malik.

From the watermelon presented to Syd Gregory to the brown
paper bag full of cash that was given the late Hansie Cronje, there
is full disclosure in *Legends of the Baggy Green*, as well as
comment on the commentators who have observed cricket's
transit from Lord's to Hollywood, and from the Gabbatoir to the
Elysian, desalinated fields of Sharjah.

There is ample scope for both humour and criticism here, and
playwright, satirist and genuine cricket 'tragic' Alexander Buzo has
sharpened his pen to provide plenty of both.

ISBN 1 74114 385 3